The Brahms Notebooks
The Little Treasure Chest of the Young Kreisler

Des jungen Kreislers Schatzkästlein.

Aussprüche von Dichtern,
Philosophen und Künstlern.

Zusammengetragen
durch
Johannes Brahms.

Herausgegeben von Carl Krebs.

Berlin.
Verlag der Deutschen Brahmsgesellschaft m. b. H.
1909.

The Brahms Notebooks

The Little Treasure Chest of the Young Kreisler

Quotations from poets, philosophers, and artists
gathered by Johannes Brahms
Edited by Carl Krebs

Translated by Agnes Eisenberger
Annotations by Siegmund Levarie

PENDRAGON PRESS
Hillsdale, New York

The drawing of Brahms on the cover of this book is the work of
Jean-Joseph Bonaventure Laurens and is used with the kind
permssion of the Bibliothèque Inguimbertine at Carpentras,
France.

Cover design by Stewart Ross

Library of Congress Cataloging-in-Publication Data

Jungen Kreislers Schatzkèastlein. English & German
  The Brahms notebooks : the little treasure chest of the young Kreisler
: quotations from poets, philosophers, and artists / gathered by Johannes Brahms ;
edited by Carl Krebs ; translated by Agnes Eisenberger ; annotations by Siegmund
Levarie.
       p. cm.
German ed. published: Berlin, 1909.
Original German text and English translation on opposite pages.
  ISBN 1-57647-082-2 (alk. paper)
  1. Quotations, German. 2. Quotations, English. I. Krebs, Carl, 1857-1937. II.
Brahms, Johannes, 1833-1897. III. Title.
  PN6090 .J8613 2003
  083'.1—dc21

iv

CONTENTS

v

INTRODUCTION TO THIS EDITION

In view of the rich literature about Johannes Brahms, a brief sketch of the significant events in his life will here suffice. He was born in Hamburg in 1833. His father, a town musician, had taken up the musical profession in protest against his parents, who descended from a long line of tradesmen and innkeepers. Johannes showed a strong inclination toward his father's profession and was therefore summoned, even as a boy, to supplement the family income by playing dance music at local taverns. He was allowed to take piano lessons in which he made such fabulous progress that, upon the death of Felix Mendelssohn in 1847, his teacher declared that although a great master was gone, an even greater one was arising in Brahms. About that time, Brahms made his first public appearance in his native town and soon after gave his first solo concert.

His meeting Joseph Joachim, the widely respected violinist, marked his formal entrance into the musical world. Brahms later wrote his only violin concerto for Joachim. He met the Schumanns—Robert the composer and Clara his wife, an accomplished pianist. An intimate friendship developed, which survived Robert's death in 1856 and lasted until Clara's death in 1896. Robert Schumann published an enthusiastic article entitled "New Paths" in the *Neue Zeitschrift für Musik,* an influential journal he had founded, in which he pronounced that the twenty-year old Brahms was the promise of the future in music. Brahms's sucessful career fulfilled this promise.

After occupying various positions in various German towns, composing all the while, in 1867 he finally took up permanent residence in Vienna, the capital of the Habsburg empire and a center of lively musical activity. At that time, a contemporary describes Brahms as having a short, square figure with broad shoulders so that he gave the impression of great strength, physical as well as moral. He had sandy-colored hair, fiery blue eyes, and a protruding underlip, which almost lent a cynical expression to his face. His mouth was sensitive, yet virile, his forehead high above an aristocratically modelled nose. Later, when he had grown a beard, his head was reproduced in a geography textbook as a typical example of the Caucasian race, and it is said that Brahms was very flattered.

When he died in 1897, the Viennese paid a suitable last tribute by burying him next to Schubert and Beethoven, as it is said he always secretly wished.

Always an avid reader, Brahms began, in his early youth, to copy passages from books he wished to remember into notebooks he kept for this purpose. This practice belongs to an old tradition. In the sixteenth century, Erasmus published an essay *De Copia* with instructions on how to proceed, and many writers followed suit (e.g., Ben Jonson, John Milton). Four such Brahms notebooks have been preserved and are the basis of this publication. Three are of the kind children carry to school. One is leatherbound and probably was given to him as a present.

In 1909, twelve years after Brahms's death, the German music critic, author, scholar, and professor Carl Krebs (1857-1937) collected and published these notebooks in

a handsome small volume (5 by 7 inches). The limited edition was soon exhausted; the collection has never been reprinted, let alone translated.

The copy leading to the this publication belonged to my father, the Viennese pianist and piano teacher Severin Eisenberger, who as a boy once heard Brahms play at a private chamber music concert. It is now in my possession. I translated it from the original German some years ago for my own amusement, to make it available in English a century after its only publication. It is an intimate reflection of Brahms's thoughts and feelings.

Carl Krebs wrote an informative Preface to his edition, obligatory reading for a full understanding of Brahms's enterprise (*cf* p. xii). In his effort, Krebs received the generous help of the music critic and author Max Kalbeck, the first volume of whose monumental Brahms biography had appeared in 1903. Since he owned three of the four notebooks, Kalbeck was able to assert that they ". . .offer the key to Brahms's innermost being." He lists the names of the most significant authors, but exact citations are rare.

These quotations are of interest to us today, for not only do they show Brahms's extensive knowledge of the literary and philosophical writing at a time when books were not as obtainable as they are today, but they reveal the composer's character and personality. Brahms, unlike many other musicians and composers, such as his contemporaries Berlioz, Schumann, and Wagner, did not express his thoughts and feelings in speech or writing; except for letters, we have no written communication from him. The letters that have come down to us—many were

destroyed by him and Clara Schumann during their life-time—deal mostly with day-to-day events in the life of the composer and his close friends. One often finds a discussion of the technical aspects of one of his compositions, of a specific performance, or of current activities in music. Many of these letters, especially those to his publisher, reveal his wit, humor, charm, and interest in the daily lives of his friends, but they do not reveal his most personal ideas and feelings. The natural medium of expression for him was music into which he poured all that he experienced or thought. But in the Notebook quotations, Brahms adopted the mode of expression of his favorite authors and poets whose thinking was akin to his and through whose writings he could articulate his own ideas.

I once tried to re-arrange the Notebook entries according to topics. Some rubriques were obvious: nature, friendship, love, music, artist, critics, life, etc.—but others defied rigid classification since they pursued more than one idea. Readers of this book are free to group the citations as they wish and read them in any order, but the possible advantages are more than vitiated by the loss of Brahms's chronological flow as he moves from one impression to the next.

A notable number of writers quoted by Brahms participated by word or action in the upheavals of 1848 and suffered the consequences of arrest, jail, dismisssal, or exile. Brahms clearly showed his sympathy with their strivings for reform and liberty. By his quotation choices, he also reveals a deep and abiding moral sense, respect for the artistic creator, and a profound and touching humility.

A prose translation of verse is almost inevitably flat and deprived. An asterisk (*) next to the number of an entry warns the reader that the German original (available on the facing page) is in poetic verse, chosen by Brahms either for meaning or rhythm or sound or any combination of these elements.

The music world, of which I am a part, is deeply indebted to Pendragon Press and its superb editor, Claire Brook, for bringing to life hidden aspects of Brahms's personal and spiritual concerns. I also wish to thank Siegmund Levarie, Professor Emeritus of Music at the City University of New York and good friend, for providing informative footnotes, and enhancing Krebs's rather barren list of authors cited by Brahms with illuminating annotations. Priscilla Robinson has earned my gratitude for typing the entire manuscript with utmost care and devotion.

A..E.

New York, 2002

PREFACE TO THE ORIGINAL EDITION

Johannes Brahms was a passionate reader all his life. Even as a schoolboy in Hamburg, he carried every penny left from his very small and mainly self-earned pocket money to the Bernhard lending library, and when he played dance music in pubs, he kept a volume of Tieck, Eichendorff, Arnim, or Brentano on his music stand. His fingers rattled off automatically the waltzes, polkas, and mazurkas which he had played a hundred times, while the spirit of the young artist wandered through the wonderland of romantic fantasies. When he went for strolls in the country, he carried a volume in his pocket in order to browse in his beloved books while resting, lying on his stomach with his head supported by his hands. Later, when his name became better known and his income increased, he turned into a zealous collector of valuable old books and music, of first editions of German poets, woodcuts, and engravings.[1] And he also rummaged in the libraries of good friends for unknown works and absorbed what he found. This is what J.V. Widmann wrote about Brahms's stay in Thun in the summer of 1886[2]:

> When he traveled every Saturday to Bern to spend the Sunday and usually to stay with me until Tuesday or Wednesday, he had a leather travel bag flung over his shoulder, similar to a wandering

[1] Cf. Max Kalbeck, *Johannes Brahms,* 2nd ed. (Berlin, 1908), vol. I, pp. 20, 36, 47.
[2] *Johannes Brahms in Erinnerungen* (Berlin, 1898), 56.

mineralogist's bag full of stones, but which contained
mainly books which I lent him the last time and
which he returned to exchange for others!

From Widmann we also learn what kind of reading material Brahms preferred. While fairly curious about all new
publications, he chose to read older books for a second or
third time before finding dubious entertainment in new
ones. "On top of Nietzsche I promptly put an Italian book
of short stories so that I can think twice whether I want to
wander under a blue or a gray sky," he once wrote one of
his friends who had sent him a volume of Nietzsche. He
greatly valued the work of Hermann Kurz, dipped deeply
into Herder, into the dramas and poetry of Grillparzer,
stories by Gottfried Keller, and often read much in *Des
Knaben Wunderhorn*. He was particularly interested in
philological works such as Grimm's dictionaries which he
always had on hand in Vienna; also in travel books, expe-
ditions to the North Pole, and so on.

In Hamburg, Brahms started to copy out quotations
which he especially liked. He acquired a sturdy octavo
notebook with a linen backing and boldly wrote on it
"Schatzkästlein des jungen Kreisler"[3] (Treasure Chest of
the Young Kreisler). In it he notated all sorts of sentences
from his extensive reading that had made a deep impression on him. We do not know exactly when this notebook
was started; we only read "in Hamburg" without a more
precise date. It was finished "in Düsseldorf, March 1854."

Among the quoted poets, Novalis and Jean Paul oc-

---

[3] As is well known, Brahms, in remembrance of E.T.A. Hoffmann's
ingenious-fantastic kapellmeister (*Kater Murr, Kreisleriana*), called himself
in his early compositions "Johannes Kreisler, Junior" or "Joh. Kreisler II."

Goethe, Shakespeare, Lichtenberg, Moses Mendelssohn, B. Auerbach, Waiblinger, Grillparzer, Dante, Tasso, Andersen, Blumauer, Seume, Bürger, Tieck, Swift, Pestalozzi, Kinkel, Heinse, Schiller, Eichendorff, J. Kerner, Chamisso, Th. von Hippel, Gryphius, Lessing, Richard Wagner (the last sentence from *Oper and Drama*), Herder, Elisabeth Kulmann whose poems Robert Schumann had probably called to his attention, Macaulay, Hebbel, Tiedge, Raupach, Rückert, Voss, Fr. von Sallert, A.v. Humboldt. A specialty are the entries by Josef Joachim signed f.a.e. in musical notes or in letters.[4] These show a lively spirit practiced in philosophical thinking and well acquainted with Jean Paul. They must have increased Brahms's respect for his highly revered artistic colleague.

In March 1854 when the first volume ended, a second one similar to *Des jungen Kreislers Schatzkästlein* was begun. It started with long selections from Jean Paul's *Flegeljahre* (Teenage Years). In between, Brahms had read Scherenberg, some Shakespeare, then Grabbe whose dramas he ran through one after the other (*Kaiser Friedrich, Kaiser Heinrich VI., Don Juan und Faust*). After Uhland, there follow long quotations from Sallets' *Kontraste und Paradoxen*, Jean Paul (*Titan*), E.T.A. Hoffmann from whom surprisingly little is selected notwithstanding that his writings are a veritable treasure chest of musical and general artistic wisdom, and at the end there is a lot from G. Büchner's dramas and letters as well as quotations from Immermann's *Münchhausen*.

The date he concluded notebook II is not known, but by September 1853 Brahms started a new collection

---

[4] f.a.e.: "Frei, aber einsam" was at that time Joachim's motto. Cf. A Moser, *Joseph Joachim*, 2nd ed. (Berlin, 1908), pp.. 180, 189.

in Düsseldorf entitled *Schöne Gedanken über Musik* (Beautiful Thoughts about Music). Here he gathered quotations about music that had been scattered throughout the earlier books, the *Treasure Chests*. Jean Paul is again the most prominent, followed by Shakespeare, E.T.A. Hoffmann, and other previously cited authors. New additions are Wolfgang Menzel whose *Literatur-Blatt*, a supplement of the *Morgenblatt für gebildete Stände* (Morning Paper for Educated People) since 1836, which Brahms eagerly read and excerpts (he always calls them "Kunstblatt"), Rollet, C.M.von Weber, Gluck, Byron, F. Schlegel, Beethoven, A. Grün, Thibaut, Klopstock, von Zedlitz, von Collin, Stifter, H. Grimm, Eckermann, Laube, Thiersch. This first little volume of *Beautiful Thoughts about Music* was finished in July 1854 and immediately a new one was begun that carries the subtitle *Schatzkästlein des jungen Kreisler* below the title *Schöne Gedanken über Musik, Heft II* . Max Kalbeck may be right[5] when he assumes that Brahms, by diligently continuing his collection of quotations about music, wanted to give pleasure to his beloved master Schumann who at that time was ill in Endenich and in whose recovery his devoted friends still believed. In fact, Schumann had in earlier years planned to gather together what important people, poets, and philosophers had thought about music as much as possible . At the beginning of 1854, he returned to this plan and excerpted for his collection, which he called *Dichtergarten*, Shakespeare and Jean Paul, also including the Bible as well as Roman and Greek classics [6]. Probably at Schumann's suggestion, Brahms had begun a

[5] In handwritten notes on this collection, kindly made available to me.
[6] Cf. Robert Schumann, *Gesammelte Schriften über Musik und Musiker*, ed. F. Gustav Jansen (Leipzig, 1891), vol. I, pp. 22.

systematic arrangement of the quotations in his third notebook and at the end defined the following categories:
"Beautiful Images," "About Study and Form," "About
Criticism," "Audiences," listing the numbers under each
of the corresponding quotations. But he did not continue
nor restrict himself to music in both notebooks of *Beauti-*
ful Thoughts about Music but entered sayings on poetry,
sculpture, and everything else that attracted him. New
authors appeared rarely; one may perhaps name Th. Körner,
J. Feski, A.Kahlert, von Sonnenberg, von Stolberg, Bulwer,
Zelter, Wackenroder, Platen, von Rotteck.

It seems as if Brahms did not long continue the con-
templative activity of gathering quotations, for the struggle
with life and the struggle for his art occupied him totally.
But shortly before his death, when sick and brokenhearted
he could no longer spend his evenings at the usually happy
roundtable in the restaurant, he reached again for the old
Notebooks.[7] Leafing through them carried him back to
his youth, which had been so difficult and yet so happy.
With a shaky hand, he made new entries: Hebbel's Letters, Goethe's *Farbenlehre* (Theory of Color) and *Wilhelm*
Meister, Schiller's poems, Jean Paul's *Quintus Fixlein* and
Die Unsichtbare Loge (The Invisible Club), Luther, Horace's
Satires, and the *Kladderadatsch,* then Bismarck's speeches,
Jesus Sirach, and at the end *Ecclesiastes*—these are the works
and authors that brought relief to the tired wanderer.

Of the four booklets here described, which Dr. Josef
Reitzes saved from being burned, the first three are in the
possession of Mr. Max Kalbeck, and the last one belongs
to the Gesellschaft der Musikfreunde in Vienna. Both own-

---

[7] From Kalbeck's notes.

ers were so kind as to give the books to the German Brahms Society for publication, for which our gratitude should here be expressed.

Now just a few words about the printing. The publication of Brahms's excerpts needs no defense. It is of high interest to see what a great artist read in the years of his development and what he found especially meaningful and worthy of copying. By itself, the collection also has intrinsic value because it contains citations from authors rarely read widely today, and unjustly so as can be conceded after consulting them. Of those authors, one may name the following: Novalis, von Sallet, Büchner, Menzel, Wackenroder, Seume. Thus a perusal of the *Treasure Chest* will inspire not only artists but all kinds of thinking people to continue on their own in pursuit of thoughts here quoted.

Opinions will differ on whether in an edition of such a collection of quotations, the sources not designated by Brahms should be identified. People whose opinions I highly respect emphasized that such documentation was absolutely not necessary. I agree, for various reasons. First of all, any philological effort toward a collection so loosely arranged by Brahms is inappropriate; for Brahms, who according to Kalbeck did not know the name of the tree in whose shadow he rested nor the name of the flower whose fragrance and color enchanted him, would have laughed at such a degree of anxious precision. Furthermore, some of the quotations are indeed easy to identify, but others would be more difficult, and the incredible effort of research would be disproportionate to whatever might be gained by it. This edition is not directed to philologists, but to the wide public interested in Brahms. And would

a beautiful quotation be felt more profoundly if the source states that it comes from *Titan* or *Flegeljahre* and exactly at what spot? The next step would lead to a critique of the edition and of variants—and where would all this end?

I would have liked to render the quotations in exactly the irregular manner devised by Brahms's unsystematic artistic spirit, for he sometimes writes Goethe, sometimes Göthe; sometimes, J. Paul, sometimes Jean Paul; sometimes he puts the author's names before, sometimes after the quoted lines, and so forth. Concerned people definitely dissuaded me from this course.

When I thought of how we are brought up, I began to feel uneasy myself and to ignore how few people would recognize in the research a desire to mirror the personal touch of the collector Brahms; how many, on the other hand, would tend to accuse the editor of sloppiness and of being a bad scholar. Hence I put the greatest discrepancies in order, silently corrected mistakes as far as they could be determined by comparison, and added a few words in brackets which Brahms omitted and probably overlooked. The separate notebooks are not sorted, but the quotations, after elimination of duplications and of a few insignificant notations, are reprinted and numbered one after the other. I gave to the whole the title Brahms chose for his first notebook, *The Young Kreisler's Treasure Chest*. Thus may it go forth into the world.

Berlin-Friedenau, June 1908

Carl Krebs

Des jungen Kreislers Schatzkästlein

The Little Treasure Chest of the Young Kreisler

1.

Hypothesen sind Netze, nur der wird fangen,
der auswirft;
Ist nicht Amerika selbst durch Hypothese gefunden?
Hoch und vor allen lebe die Hypothese, nur sie
bleibt
Ewig neu, so oft sie auch schon sich selber besiegte.

Novalis.

2.
Sinn und Tat.

Viele Blumen tun sich der Sonne auf; doch
nur eine folget ihr immerfort. Herz, sei die
Sonnenblume; nicht bloß offen sei dem Gott,
sondern gehorche ihm auch.   Jean Paul.

3.

Fern von Menschen wachsen Grundsätze;
unter ihnen Handlungen.   Jean Paul.

4.

Lorenzo (zu Stephano): .... Bringt die Musi=
kanten hin ins Freie.
Wie süß das Mondlicht auf dem Hügel schläft!
Hier sitzen wir und lassen die Musik
Zum Ohre schlüpfen; [sanfte Still' und Nacht]
Sie werden Tasten süßer Harmonie.

1.[1]

Hypotheses are nets, only he will catch who fishes;
Was not America discovered by hypothesis?
Long live hypothesis, it alone remains
Eternally new, no matter how often it defeats itself.

Novalis

2.

Sense and Deed

Many flowers open themselves to the sun; but only
one follows it always. Heart, be the sunflower; be not
only open to God, but obey him as well.

Jean Paul

3.

Principles materialize away from people, *actions* with
them.

Jean Paul

4.

Lorenzo: And bring your music forth into the air.

How sweet the moonlight sleeps upon this bank!
Here will we sit, and let the sounds of music
Creep in our ears; soft stillness and the night
Become the touches of sweet harmony.

---

[1]It says a lot about Brahms's intellectual acumen that he begins his
Notebooks with quotations from Novalis and Jean Paul—both superior but
not easy authors. Consult the Annotated List of Cited Authors (pp. 349 ff.)
for information about them.

Komm, Jeſſika! Sieh, wie die Himmelsflur
Iſt eingelegt mit Scheiben lichten Goldes!
Auch nicht der kleinſte Kreis, den du da ſiehſt,
Der nicht im Schwunge wie ein Engel ſingt,
Zum Chor der hellgeaugten Cherubim.
So voller Harmonien ſind ew'ge Geiſter,
Nur wir, weil dies hinfäll'ge Kleid von Staub
Ihn grob umhüllt, wir können ſie nicht hören.
                          (Muſikanten kommen.)
Ha, kommt und weckt Dianen auf mit Hymnen,
Rührt eurer Herrin Ohr mit zartem Spiel,
Zieht mit Muſik ſie heim.   (Muſik.)

    Jeſſika. Nie macht die liebliche Muſik
                     mich luſtig.

    Lorenzo. Der Grund iſt, eure Geiſter ſind
                     geſpannt.
Bemerkt nur eine wilde, flücht'ge Herde,
Der ungezähmten jungen Füllen Schar;
Sie machen Sprünge, blöken, wiehern laut,
Wie ihres Blutes heiße Art ſie treibt:
Doch ſchallt nun die Trompete, oder trifft
Sonſt eine Weiſe der Muſik ihr Ohr,
So ſeht ihr, wie ſie miteinander ſtehn,
Ihr wildes Auge ſchaut mit Sittſamkeit,
Durch ſüße Macht der Töne. Drum lehrt der
                     Dichter,
Gelenkt hab' Orpheus Bäume, Felſen, Fluten,
Weil nichts ſo ſtöckiſch, hart und voll von Wut,
Das nicht Muſik auf eine Zeit verwandelt.
Der Mann, der nicht Muſik hat in ihm ſelbſt,
Den nicht die Eintracht ſüßer Töne rührt,
Taugt zu Verrat, zu Räuberei und Tücken;

Sit, Jessica. Look how the floor of heaven
Is thick inlaid with patines of bright gold;
There's not the smallest orb which thou behold'st
But in his motion like an angel sings,
Still quiring to the young ey'd cherubims:
Such harmony is in immortal souls;
But, whilst this muddy vesture of decay
Both grossly close it in, we cannot hear it.

(Enter Musicians)

Come, ho, and make Diana with a hymn;
With sweetest touches pierce your mistress' ear,
And draw her home with music.   (Music)

Jessica: I am never merry when I hear sweet music.

Lorenzo:The reason is, your spirits are attentive:
   For do but note a wild and wanton herd,
   Or race of youthful and unhandled colts,
   Fetching mad bounds, bellowing, and neighboring
        loud,
    Which is the hot condition of their blood —
   If they but hear perchance a trumpet sound,
   Or any air of music touch their ears,
   You shall perceive them make a mutual stand,
    Their savage eyes turn'd to a modest gaze
   By the sweet power of music: therefore the poet
   Did feign that Orpheus drew trees, stones, and floods;
   Since naught so stockish, hard, and full of rage
   But music for the time doth change his nature.
   The man that hath no music in himself,
   Nor is not mov'd with concord of sweet sounds,
   is fit for treasons, stratagems, and spoils;

Die Regung seines Sinns ist dumpf wie Nacht,
Sein Trachten düster wie der Erebus.
Trau keinem solchen! — Horch auf die Musik!

Shakespeare (Kaufmann v. Venedig).

5.

Nur keine Musik, diese Spötterin unserer
Wünsche sollt' es geben: fließen nicht auf ihren
Ruf alle Fibern meines Herzens auseinander und
strecken sich als so viele saugende Polypenarme
aus und zittern vor Sehnsucht und wollen um=
schlingen — wen? was?... Ein ungesehenes,
in andern Welten stehendes Etwas.

Jean Paul.

6.

O Musik! Nachklang aus einer entlegnen
harmonischen Welt! Seufzer des Engels in uns!
Wenn das Wort sprachlos ist, und die Um=
armung, und das Auge, das weinende, und
wenn unsre stummen Herzen hinter dem Brust=
gitter einsam liegen: O, so bist nur du es,
durch welche sie sich einander zurufen in ihren
Kerkern und ihre entfernten Seufzer vereinigen
in ihrer Wüste!

Jean Paul.

7.

Großer Unfug mit mittelmäßigem Treiben
der Kunst entsteht daher, daß viele eine leb=
hafte äußere Anregung für einen wahren Beruf
zur Kunst hielten.   E. T. A. Hoffmann (Der Artushof).

The motions of his spirit are dull as night,
And his affections dark as Erebus:
Let no such man be trusted. — Mark the music. [2]
          Shakespeare (*Merchant of Venice*, Act V, Scene 1)

5.

There should be no music, this mocker of our wishes: when music calls, do not all the fibers of my heart dissolve and extend like so many polyp arms, trembling with desire, wanting to embrace — whom? what? ... An unseen something, existing in other worlds.

          Jean Paul

6.

Oh Music! Resonance from a faraway, harmonious world! Sigh of the angel within us! When the word is speechless, and the embrace, and the eye, weeping, and when our mute hearts lie lonely behind the breast's grate: Oh, then it is only you through which they call to each other in their prisons and their distant sighs join their emptiness in their desert!

          Jean Paul

7.

Great mischief with mediocre artistic doings derives because many mistake a strong external stimulus for their true artistic vocation.

          E.T.A. Hoffmann (Der Artushof)

---

[2] Brahms cites Shakespeare in German.

8.
Trommel und Laute.

Rühre die Laute nicht, wenn ringsum
Trommeln erschallen!
Führen Narren das Wort, schweiget der Weisere
still.

Herder (Bramanen=Gedanken [1]).

9.
Das Gold.

Gold, du Vater der Schmeichler, du Sohn der
Schmerzen und Sorgen,
Wer dich entbehret, hat Müh'; wer dich besitzet,
hat Leid. Herder.

10.
Gebet.

Allvater, Gutes gib mir, und wenn ich auch
nicht darum bäte;
Böses wende von mir, fleht' ich auch sehnlich
darum. Herder.

11.
Höhere Natur.

Wird im quälenden Hunger der Löw' am
Grase sich laben?
So auch ein hohes Gemüt sinke nie unter sich selbst.

Herder.

---

[1] Dies Epigramm befindet sich nicht in den „Gedanken einiger
Bramanen", sondern in „Blumen aus morgenländischen Dichtern".

8.*3
Drama and Lute
Do not play the lute when drums are beating all
around!
When fools are spokesmen, the wise man remains
silent.

Herder (Brahmanen-Gedanken)

9.*
Gold
Gold, you father of flatterers, you son of pain
and sorrow,
Those who lack you have trouble; those who
possess you, have grief.

Herder

10.*
Prayer
Almighty, give me virtue, even if I do not pray for it;
Avert evil, even if I passionately asked for it.

Herder

11.*
Higher Nature
Will a lion, tortured by ravenous hunger, turn to
eat grass?
Thus, too, a noble soul must never descend below
itself.

Herder

---

[3] A note by Krebs informs us that the "epigram is not in the *Brahman Thoughts* but in *Flowers from Oriental Poets.*" The citation is in metric verse.

12.

Das Licht.

So wie die Flamme des Lichts auch um=
gewendet hinaufstrahlt;
So, vom Schicksal gebeugt, strebet der Gute empor.

Herder.

13.

Die höheren Wolken scheinen langsamer zu
gehen; so geht für unsere Augen alles Höhere.

Jean Paul.

14.

Der Merkur ist durch die Nähe der Sonne
uns unbekannt, so stellt der Sonnenschein uns
manches ins Unsichtbare.   Jean Paul.

15.

Alle Höhlen scheinen der Leere, der Dunkel=
heit wegen um die Hälfte größer; so das Grab.

Jean Paul.

16.

Die Blume schläft, das Herz schläft, aber
um voller wieder zu erwachen.   Jean Paul.

17.

Die Freundschaft duldet Mißhelligkeiten
weniger als die Liebe; diese kitzelt damit das
Herz, jene spaltet es damit.   Jean Paul.

18.

Viele Menschen leben in der Erdnähe,
einige in der Erdferne, wenige in der Sonnen=
nähe.   Jean Paul.

12.*
The Light
Just as the flame radiates upward, even if the
candle is inverted,
So, bent by fate, the good man strives toward height.

Herder

13.
The higher clouds seem to move more slowly; so, in
our eyes, do all exalted things.

Jean Paul

14.
Mercury is unknown to us because of the proximity
of the sun, thus the sunshine makes some things for us
invisible.

Jean Paul

15.
All caves appear to be larger by half because of their
emptiness, their darkness: so does the grave.

Jean Paul

16.
The flower sleeps, the heart sleeps, but only to awake
again more fully.

Jean Paul

17.
Friendship endures misunderstandings less readily
than love; love tickles with the heart, friendship is split by
it.

Jean Paul

18.
Many people live close to the earth, some far from it,
very few close to the sun.   *Jean Paul*

19.

Im Wort Gelehrter steckt, nur der Be=
griff, daß einem vieles gelehrt ist, aber nicht,
daß man auch etwas gelernt hat; daher sagen
die Franzosen sinnreich, wie alles, was von
diesem Volke kommt, nicht les enseignés, sondern
les savans, und die Engländer nicht the taught
ones, sondern the learned.   Lichtenberg.

20.

Einen Roman zu schreiben ist deswegen vor=
züglich angenehm, weil man zu allen Meinungen,
die man gern einmal in die Welt laufen lassen
will, allemal einen Mann finden kann, der sie
als die seinigen vorträgt.

                 Bernardin de Saint Pierre.

.21.

Ein Herz voll Liebe kann alles vergeben,
sogar Härte gegen sich, aber nicht Härte gegen
andere; denn jene zu verzeihen, ist Verdienst,
diese aber Mitschuld.   Jean Paul.

22.

Das Traurigste, was die französische
Revolution für uns bewirkt hat, ist unstreitig
das, daß man jede vernünftige und von Gott
und Rechts wegen zu verlangende Fortsetzung als
einen Keim von Empörung ansehen wird.

                 Bernardin de Saint Pierre.

19.

In the term "man of learning" [Gelehrter] there hides only the concept that one has been taught many things but not that one also has learned something; therefore the French say, sensibly, like everything that comes from these people, not *les enseignés* but *les savans,* and the English say not the *taught ones,* but the *learned.*

Lichtenberg

20.

To be able to write a novel is especially pleasant, for one can always find a man who proclaims as his own all the ideas which one would like to toss out into the world.

Bernardin de Saint Pierre

21.

A heart full of love can forgive everything, even rigor against itself, but not rigor against others; for to forgive the former is merit, but the latter means sharing the guilt.

Jean Paul

22.

The saddest effect of the French revolution is indisputably that every reasonable continuation, justly demanded by God and law, will be perceived as a seed of rebellion.

Bernardin de Saint Pierre

23.

Das Unglück gleicht dem schwarzen Berge Komber, am äußersten Ende des glühenden Reiches Lahor. Solange ihr hinaufsteigt, sehet ihr nichts als unfruchtbare Felsen vor euch; aber seid ihr einmal auf dem Gipfel angelangt, dann erblicket ihr über eurem Haupte den Himmel und zu euren Füßen das Königreich Kaschmir.

Bernardin de Saint Pierre. (Worte des Paria.)

24.

Die Einsamkeit erscheint dem Unglücklichen als ein ruhiger Hafen, von wo aus er die Leidenschaften der anderen Menschen dahinstürmen sieht, ohne selbst dadurch erschüttert zu werden.

Nach dem Englischen des Poung.

25.

Der Verstand ist ein Diamant, der durch Witz geschliffen unstreitig heller strahlt, aber auch ohne Schleiferei Diamant bleibt.

Nach dem Englischen des Poung.

26.

O Freiheit!
Silberton dem Ohr!
Licht dem Verstand und hoher Flug zu denken!
Dem Herzen groß Gefühl!
O Freiheit! Freiheit! Nicht nur der Demokrat
Weiß, wer du bist, des guten Königs glücklicher
Sohn, der weiß es auch!   Klopstock.

23.

Misfortune resembles the black mountain Komber at the extreme end of the scorching country Lahor. While ascending, you see nothing but barren rocks before you, but when you reach the summit then you discover above your head the sky and beneath your feet the kingdom of Kashmir.

Bernardin de Saint Pierre (Words of the Pariah)

24.

Loneliness appears to the unhappy person as a quiet harbor where he sees the stormy passions of other people without being himself shaken by it.

After the English by *Young*

25.

Intelligence is a diamond which polished by wit indisputably shines more brightly but which remains a diamond even wihtout being polished.

After the English by *Young*

26.*

Oh Freedom!
A silvery sound to the ear!
A light for the intellect and soaring flight for thoughts!
A great feeling for the heart!
Oh freedom! Freedom! Not only the democrat
Knows what you are, but the good King's happy
son also knows it!

Klopstock

27.

Trennung ist die Gattin des Todes, beides
häßliche Eltern,
Aber sie zeugten der Kinder schönstes, das
Wiedersehn.

G. A. Waldemar Dohl.

28.

Der Staat hat aufgehört zu sein, sobald er
Eigentum Eines ist.   Sophokles.

29.

Wir sind dem Aufwachen nah', wenn wir
träumen, daß wir träumen.   Novalis.

30.

Unser Leben ist kein Traum, aber es soll
und wird vielleicht einer werden.   Novalis.

31.

Der Traum belehrt uns auf eine merk=
würdige Weise von der Leichtigkeit unserer
Seele, in jedes Objekt einzudringen, sich in
jedes sogleich zu verwandeln.   Novalis.

32.

Ein Kind ist eine sichtbar gewordene Liebe. —
Wir selbst sind ein sichtbar gewordener Keim
der Liebe zwischen Natur und Geist oder Kunst.

Novalis.

27.*

Separation is the wife of death, both ugly parents,
But they begot the most beautiful child, reunion.

G.A. Waldemar Dohl

28.

A state has ceased to exist when it becomes the property of *one* individual.

Sophocles

29.

We are about to wake up if we dream that we are dreaming.

Novalis

30.

Our life is not a dream, but it should and perhaps will become one.

Novalis

31.

Our dreams teach us in a strange manner about the facility with which our soul penetrates and immediately transforms itself into every object.

Novalis

32.

A child is love made visible.—We are a seed of love made visible between nature and spirit or art.

Novalis

33.

Sprechen und hören ist befruchten und emp=
fangen.   Novalis.

34.

Die Menschheit ist der höhere Sinn unseres
Planeten, der Stern, der dieses Glied mit der
oberen Welt verknüpft, das Auge, das er gen
Himmel hebt.   Novalis.

35.

Wenn alles Anschließen, Festwerden und
Verdichten mit Wärme verbunden und jede Ver=
flüchtigung, Zerrinnung und Verdünnung von
Kälte begleitet ist, so macht das Lernen und
Lieben im eigentlichen Sinne warm, und das
Müßiggehn und die Absonderung kalt, und es
lassen sich überhaupt manche Phänomene der
Seele hieraus erklären.   Novalis.

36.

Klarer Verstand mit warmer Phantasie ver=
schwistert, ist die echte, Gesundheit bringende
Seelenkost.   Novalis.

37.

Das Ideal einer vollkommenen Gesundheit
ist bloß wissenschaftlich interessant. Krankheit
gehört zur Individualisierung.   Novalis.

38.

Je mehr man lernt, nicht mehr in Augen=
blicken, sondern in Jahren usw. zu leben, desto
edler wird man. Die hastige Unruhe, das klein=

9

33.

Speaking and hearing are impregnating and conceiving.

Novalis

34.

Mankind is the higher sense of our planet, the star which binds this link to the upper world, the eye which lifts toward heaven.

Novalis

35.

If all joining, solidifying, and condensing is connected with warmth, and if every dissolution, liquification, and dilution is accompanied by cold, so learning and loving actually makes warm, and idleness and seclusion makes cold, and altogether some phenomena of the soul can thereby be explained.

Novalis

36.

Sound intelligence allied with warm fantasy is the true, healthy food for the soul.

Novalis

37.

The ideal of perfect health is only of scientific interest. Illness is part of individualization.

Novalis

38.

The more a person learns to live not in moments but in years, etc. the nobler he becomes. Anxious restless-

liche Treiben des Geistes, geht in große, ruhige, einfache und vielumfassende Tätigkeit über und die herrliche Geduld findet sich ein. Immer triumphierender werden Religion und Sittlichkeit diese Grundfesten unseres Daseins.   Novalis.

39.

Jede Krankheit ist ein musikalisches Problem, die Heilung eine musikalische Auflösung. Je kürzer und dennoch vollständiger die Auflösung, desto größer das musikalische Talent des Arztes. Sollte man nicht Krankheiten durch Krankheiten kurrieren können?   Novalis.

40.

Es gibt nur einen Tempel in der Welt, und das ist der menschliche Körper. Nichts ist heiliger als diese hohe Gestalt. Das Bücken vor Menschen ist eine Huldigung dieser Offenbarung im Fleisch. — Man berührt den Himmel, wenn man einen Menschenleib betastet.   Novalis.

41.

Die Skulptur und die Musik stehen sich als entgegengesetzte Härten gegenüber. Die Malerei macht schon den Übergang. Die Skulptur ist das gebildete Starre. Die Musik das gebildete Flüssige.   Novalis.

42.

Die Jungfrau ist ein ewiges weibliches Kind. Ein Mädchen, das nicht mehr Kind ist, ist nicht mehr Jungfrau. (Nicht alle Kinder sind Kinder.)   Novalis.

ness, petty impulses of the spirit turn into great, quiet, simple, steady comprehensive activity, and glorious patience is found at last. Religion and ethics become the ever more triumphant foundation of our existence.

Novalis.

39.

Every illness is a musical problem, the cure a musical resolution. The shorter and yet more complete solution, the greater the musical talent of the physician.

Should it not be possible to cure illness with illness?

Novalis

40.

There is only one temple in the world, and that is the human body. Nothing is holier than this high form. Bowing before people is rending homage to this manifestation in the flesh. — One touches heaven when feeling a human body.

Novalis

41.

Sculpture and music stand at opposite poles of hardness. Painting makes the transition. Sculpture is formed rigidity. Music is formed fluidity.

Novalis

42.

A virgin is an *eternally feminine* child.
A girl who is no longer a child is no longer a virgin.
(Not all children are children).

Novalis

43.

Die Muſik redet eine allgemeine Sprache, durch welche der Geiſt frei, unbeſtimmt an= geregt wird; dies tut ihm ſo wohl, ſo bekannt und vaterländiſch; er iſt auf dieſe kurzen Augen= blicke in ſeiner Heimat. Alles Liebe und Gute, Zukunft und Vergangenheit regt ſich in ihm, Hoffnung und Sehnſucht. Unſere Sprache war zu Anfang viel muſikaliſcher, ſie hat ſich nur nach und nach ſo proſaiert, ſo enttönt; ſie iſt jetzt mehr S ch a l l geworden, L a u t, wenn man dieſes ſchöne Wort ſo erniedrigen will; ſie muß wieder G e ſ a n g werden. Die Konſonanten verwandeln den Ton in Schall.   Novalis.

44.

Der Ton ſcheint nichts als eine gebrochene Bewegung zu ſein, in dem Sinn, wie die Farbe gebrochenes Licht iſt.   Novalis.

45.

Ein Lichtſtrahl bricht ſich noch in etwas ganz anderes als Farben. Wenigſtens iſt der Licht= ſtrahl einer Beſeelung fähig, wo ſich dann die Seele in Seelenfarben bricht. Wem fällt nicht der Blick der Geliebten ein?   Novalis.

46.

Alle geiſtige Berührung gleicht der Berührung eines Zauberſtabes. Alles kann zum Zauber= werkzeug werden. Wem aber die Wirkung einer ſolchen Berührung ſo fabelhaft, wem die Wirkungen eines Zauberſpruches ſo wunderbar vorkommen,

43.

Music speaks a universal language which stimulates the spirit in a free, *indefinite* manner; this is so soothing to it, so familiar and patriotic; in these brief moments it is at home. All that is lovely and good, past and future, stirs in it hope and desire. In the beginning our language was much more musical, and gradually it became prosaic and lost the quality of song. Little by little it has become *sound*, *Laut*, if one must so debase this beautiful word. It must become *song* again. The consonants transform tone into sound.

Novalis

44.

Tone seems to be nothing else but a broken movement, in the sense in which color is broken light.

Novalis

45.

A ray of light breaks also into something else than colors. The ray of light is at least capable of animation so that the soul breaks into soulful colors. Who does not think of the beloved's glance?

Novalis

46.

All spiritual contact resembles the contact with a magic wand. Everything can become a tool of magic. But if someone considers the effect of such contact fabulous, and the magic verses miraculous, let him remember the

der erinnere sich doch an die erste Berührung
der Hand seiner Geliebten, an ihren ersten be=
deutenden Blick, wo der Zauberstab der ab=
gebrochene Lichtstrahl ist, an den ersten Kuß,
an das erste Wort der Liebe, und frage sich,
ob der Bann und Zauber dieser Momente nicht
auch fabelhaft und wundersam, unauflöslich und
ewig ist.   Novalis.

47.

Bücher sind eine moderne Gattung historischer
Wesen, aber eine höchst bedeutende. Sie sind
vielleicht an die Stelle der Traditionen getreten.
                                            Novalis.

48.

Es ist kein Merkmal größerer Bildung und
größerer Kräfte, wenn man ein Buch richtig
tadelt; durch die Neuheit des Eindrucks ist die
größere Schärfe des Sinnes ganz natürlich.
                                            Novalis.

49.

Klopstocks Werke scheinen größtenteils freie
Übersetzungen und Bearbeitungen eines un=
bekannten Dichters, durch einen sehr talentvollen
aber unpoetischen Philologen zu sein.
                                            Novalis.

50.

Journale sind eigentlich schon gemeinschaftliche
Bücher; das Schreiben in Gemeinschaft ist ein
interessantes Symptom, das noch eine große
Ausbildung der Schriftstellerei ahnen läßt. Man
wird vielleicht einmal in Masse schreiben, denken
und handeln; ganze Gemeinden, selbst Nationen
werden ein Werk unternehmen.   Novalis.

first touch of his beloved's hand, the first meaningful glance, where the magic wand is the refracted way of light, the first kiss, the first words of love, and ask him if these charmed and magic moments are not also fabulous, miraculous, indissoluble, and eternal.

Novalis

47.

Books are a modern species of historic beings, but a highly significant one. Perhaps they are taking the place of tradition.

Novalis

48.

To criticize a book justly is not indicative of better education and greater powers. The novelty of the impression renders quite natural the increased keenness of the senses.

Novalis

49.

Klopstock's works seem to be chiefly free translations and adaptations of an unknown poet by a very talented and unpoetic philologist.

Novalis

50.

Journals are actually books written jointly; joint writing is an interesting symptom which anticipates a great development for the writing profession. Perhaps one day one will write, think, and act en masse; whole communities, even nations will undertake a work.

Novalis

51.

Die Schriftsteller sind so einseitig wie alle Künstler e i n e r Art und nur noch hartnäckiger. Unter den Schriftstellern von Profession gibt es gerade wenig liberale Menschen, besonders, wenn sie gar keine andere Subsistenz als ihre Schriftstellerei haben.   Novalis.

52.

In heitern Seelen gibt es keinen Witz. Witz zeigt ein zerstörtes Gleichgewicht an, er ist die Folge der Störung und zugleich das Mittel der Herstellung. Den stärksten Witz hat die Leiden=schaft. Es gibt eine Art des geselligen Witzes, die nur magisches Farbenspiel in höheren Sphären ist. Der Zustand der Auflösung aller Verhältnisse, die Verzweiflung und das geistige Sterben ist am fürchterlichsten witzig.

Novalis.

53.

Je verworrener ein Mensch ist (man nennt die Verworrenen oft Dummköpfe), desto mehr kann durch fleißiges Selbststudium aus ihm werden; dahingegen die geordneten Köpfe trachten müssen, wahre Gelehrte, gründliche Enzyklopädisten zu werden. Die Verworrenen haben im Anfang mit mächtigen Hindernissen zu kämpfen, sie dringen nur langsam ein, sie lernen mit Mühe arbeiten, dann aber sind sie auch Herren und Meister auf immer. Der Ge=ordnete kommt geschwind hinein, aber auch geschwind heraus. Er erreicht bald die zweite Stufe, aber da bleibt er gewöhnlich stehen. —

51.

Writers are just as one-sided as all artists who practice one art, only more obstinate.

Among professional writers one finds very few liberal people, especially if they have no other subsistence than their writing.

Novalis

52.

Wit is not found in serene souls. Wit indicates a disturbed equilibrium, it is the result of the disturbance and at the same time the means of restoration. Passion has the most powerful wit. There is a kind of social wit which is merely a magical play of colors in higher spheres. The state of dissolution of all relations, despair, and spiritual death is the most frightfully witty.

Novalis

53.

The more confused a man is (often the confused are called dumb), the more he may achieve something by diligently studying himself, whereas orderly heads must try to become true scholars and thorough encyclopedists. But the confused ones have to fight mighty obstacles at the onset, they penetrate only slowly, they learn with difficulty how to work, but then they are forever lords and masters. The orderly man gets into the matter quickly but just as quickly out of it. He soon reaches the second step, but there he usually remains. The last steps become

Ihm werden die letzten Schritte beschwerlich, und selten kann er es über sich gewinnen, bei einem gewissen Grade von Meisterschaft sich wieder in den Zustand eines Anfängers zu ver= setzen. — Verworrenheit deutet auf Überfluß an Kraft und Vermögen bei mangelhaften Ver= hältnissen; Bestimmtheit auf richtige Verhältnisse, aber sparsames Vermögen und Kraft. Daher ist der Verworrene so progressiv, so perfektibel; dahingegen der Ordentliche so früh als Philister aufhört. Ordnung und Bestimmtheit allein ist nicht Deutlichkeit. Durch Selbstbearbeitung kommt der Verworrene zu jener himmlischen Durchsichtigkeit, zu jener Selbsterleuchtung, die der Geordnete so selten erreicht. Das wahre Genie verbindet diese Extreme. — Es teilt die Geschwindigkeit mit dem letzten und die Fülle mit dem ersten.   Novalis.

54.

Es ist eine falsche Idee, daß man Lange= weile haben würde, wenn man alles wüßte. Jede überwundene Last befördert die Leichtigkeit der Lebensfunktionen und läßt eine Kunst übrig, die nachher zu etwas anderm bleibt. Es ist mit dem Wissen wie mit dem Sehen; je mehr man sieht, desto besser und angenehmer ist es.   Novalis.

55.

Fürsten sind Nullen, sie gelten an sich nichts, aber mit Zahlen,
Die sie beliebig erhöh'n, neben sich, gelten sie viel.   Novalis.

progressively more difficult for him, and seldom can he bring himself at a certain grade of mastery to see himself as a beginner.

Confusion points to abundant power and ability in deficient conditions; certainty, to right conditions but little ability and power. Therefore one who is confused is so perfectible, so progressive, whereas the orderly ends early as a philistine. Order and certainty alone do not make for clarity. Through working on himself, the confused man arrives at that heavenly transparence and self-illumination which the orderly man seldom reaches. The real genius combines those two extremes. He shares the speed with the latter and the fullness with the former.

Novalis

54.

It is wrong to think that one would be bored if one knew everything. Every burden overcome furthers the ease of life's functions and leaves a skill which afterwards is available to something else. It is with knowledge as it is with sight; the more one sees, the better and the more pleasing it is.

Novalis

55.*

Princes are zeros, by themselves they amount to little,
　　but with numbers at their side,
Which they increase at will, they amount to a great deal.

Novalis

56.

Der Geist der Poesie ist das Morgenlicht, das die Statue des Memnon tönen macht.

Novalis.

57.

Echte poetische Charaktere sind schwierig genug zu erfinden und auszuführen. Es sind gleichsam verschiedene Stimmen und Instrumente; sie müssen allgemein und doch eigentümlich, bestimmt und doch frei, klar und doch geheimnisvoll sein. — In der wirklichen Welt gibt es äußerst selten Charaktere; sie sind so selten wie gute Schauspieler. Viele Menschen haben gar nicht einmal die Anlage zu Charakteren. Man muß die Gewohnheitsmenschen, die Alltäglichen, von den Charakteren wohl unterscheiden. Der Charakter ist durchaus selbsttätig.

Novalis.

58.

Die Kunst, auf eine angenehme Art zu befremden, einen Gegenstand fremd zu machen und doch bekannt und anziehend, das ist die romantische Poetik.

Novalis.

59.

Die Gegenstände des Romantischen müssen wie die Töne der Äolsharfe da sein, auf einmal, ohne Veranlassung, ohne ihr Instrument zu verraten.

Novalis. (III. Moralische Ansichten.)[1]

---

[1] Dieser, wie die vorhergehenden Aphorismen, stehen in der II. Abteilung der „Fragmente vermischten Inhalts" („Ästhetik und Literatur"); erst die folgenden sind der III. Abteilung („Moralische Ansichten") entnommen.

56.

The spirit of poetry is the morning light which makes
the statue of Memnon sing.

Novalis

57.

Genuine poetic characters are difficult enough to invent and develop. They are, as it were, divers voices and
instruments; they must be general and yet individual, defined yet free, lucid yet mysterious. In the real world, characters are rare; they are as scarce as good actors. Many people
do not even have the capacity for character. One must dis-
tinguish ordinary people of habit, common place, from
people of character. Character is throughout autonomous.

Novalis

58.

The art to astonish in a pleasant manner, to make a
subject strange and yet familiar and attractive, this is romantic poetry.

Novalis

59.[4]

The objects of the romantic have to be like tones of
the Aeolian harp, all at once, without cause, without re-
vealing their instrument.

Novalis (III. Moralische Ansichten)

---

[4] Krebs comments that all preceding quotations by Novalis including this
one are from "Mixed Fragments" in *Aesthetics and Literature*. The source
indicated by Brahms applies only to the following aphorisms.

60.

Der Staat ist immer instinktmäßig nach der relativen Einsicht und Kenntnis der menschlichen Natur eingeteilt worden; der Staat ist immer ein Makroanthropos gewesen: die Zünfte die Glieder und einzelnen Kräfte, die Stände das Vermögen. Der Adel war das sittliche Vermögen, die Gelehrten die Intelligenz, der König der Wille. So daß jeder Staat immer ein allegorischer Mensch gewesen ist.   Novalis.

61.

Liebe ohne Eifersucht ist nicht persönliche Liebe, sondern indirekte Liebe — man kann Vernunftliebe sagen; denn man liebt hier nicht als Person, sondern als Glied der Menschheit: man liebt die Rivale mehr als den Gegenstand.   Novalis.

62.

Die Ehe bezeichnet eine neue, höhere Epoche der Liebe — die gesellige, die lebendige Liebe. Die Philosophie entsteht mit der Ehe.   Novalis.

63.

Jeder Tugend entspricht eine spezifische Unschuld. Unschuld ist moralischer Instinkt. Tugend ist die Prosa, Unschuld die Poesie. Es gibt rohe und gebildete Unschuld; die Tugend soll wieder verschwinden und Unschuld werden.   Novalis.

64.

Scham ist wohl ein Gefühl der Profanation. Freundschaft, Liebe und Pietät sollten geheimnis=

60.

The state has always been instinctively arranged according to the relative judgment and knowledge of human nature; the state has always been a makro-anthropos: the guilds the limbs and individual forces, the estates the capacity. The aristocracy was the ethical capacity, scholars the intelligence, and the king the will. So that every state has always been an allegorical human being.

Novalis

61.

Love without jealousy is not personal love but indirect love—one can call it reasonable love; for here one does not love as a person but as a member of humanity; one loves the rival more than the object.

Novalis

62.

Marriage marks a new, higher epoch of love—the sociable, lively love. Philosophy originates with marriage.

Novalis

63.

To every virtue corresponds a specific innocence. Innocence is moral instinct. Virtue is prose, innocence is poetry. There exists coarse or refined innocence. Virtue shall again vanish and become innocence.

Novalis

64.

Shame is likely a feeling of profanation. Friendship, love, and piety should be treated mysteriously. One should

voll behandelt werden. Man sollte nur in seltenen, vertrauten Momenten davon reden, sich stillschweigend darüber einverstehen. Vieles ist zu zart, um gedacht, noch mehreres, um besprochen zu werden.   Novalis.

65.

Die Geistlichen und Herrnhuter haben das Vorzügliche und Bemerkenswerte, daß sie Idealisten von Profession sind und Religion ex professo treiben, sie zu ihrem Hauptgeschäfte machen und eigentlich auf dieser Welt in einer andern und für eine andere leben.   Novalis.

66.

Es gibt manche Blumen auf dieser Welt, die überirdischen Ursprungs sind, die in diesem Klima nicht gedeihen und eigentliche Herolde, rufende Boten eines besseren Daseins sind. Unter diese Boten gehören vorzüglich Religion und Liebe. Das höchste Glück ist, seine Geliebte tugendhaft zu wissen, die höchste Sorge ist die Sorge für ihren Edelsinn. Aufmerksamkeit auf Gott, Achtsamkeit auf jene Momente, wo der Strahl einer himmlischen Überzeugung und Beruhigung in unsere Seelen einbricht, ist das Wohltätigste, was man für sich und seine Lieben haben kann.   Novalis.

67.

Man sollte sich schämen, wenn man es nicht mit den Gedanken dahin bringen könnte, zu denken, was man wollte. Bitte Gott um seinen Beistand, daß er die ängstlichen Gedanken ver-

talk of them only in rare, intimate moments and agree about them silently. Much is too delicate to be thought, still more too delicate to be discussed.

Novalis

65.

Clergymen and Herrnhuter[5] have the excellent and remarkable quality of being professional idealists, practicing religion *ex professo*, making it their principal business, and while in this world, actually living in and for another world.

Novalis

66.

There are some flowers in this world which are of supernatural origin; they do not thrive in this climate and are actually heralds, beckoning messengers of a better existence. Foremost among these messengers are religion and love. The greatest happiness comes from knowing one's beloved to be virtuous, the anxiety from concern about her noble sense. Attention to God, attention to those moments when the ray of a heavenly conviction and reassurance enters our souls, is the greatest benefaction we can obtain for ourselves and our loved ones.

Novalis

67.

One should be ashamed if one could not guide one's thoughts to think as one wills. Pray to God for his assistance to help disperse anxious thoughts. Learn to recog-

---

[5] Member of a Moravian or Bohemian brotherhood very active in the 18th century.

jagen helfe. Lerne nur erſt einen ängſtlichen
Gedanken auch gleich als ſolchen kennen. Mit
innigem Gebet und feſtem Vorſatz iſt vieles
möglich. Sobald du ängſtlich wirſt und traurige
bängliche Vorſtellungen ſich dir aufdringen, ſo
fange an, recht herzlich zu beten. Gelingt es
dir die erſten Male nicht, ſo gelingt es gewiß
mit der Zeit. Hat man Gott im Herzen, ſo
grübelt man nicht: dann iſt nur eine große er=
habene Empfindung in der Seele. Jean Paul.

68.

Die Bibel fängt herrlich mit dem Paradieſe,
dem Symbol der Jugend, an und ſchließt mit
dem ewigen Reiche, mit der heiligen Stadt.
Auch ihre zwei Hauptbeſtandteile ſind echt groß=
hiſtoriſch. (In jedem großhiſtoriſchen Gliede
muß gleichſam die große Geſchichte ſymboliſch
verjüngt liegen.) Der Anfang des Neuen Teſta=
ments iſt der zweite höhere Sündenfall (Sünde:
was geſühnt werden muß) und der Anfang
der neuen Periode. Die Geſchichte eines jeden
Menſchen ſoll eine Bibel ſein. Chriſtus iſt der
neue Adam. Eine Bibel iſt die höchſte Aufgabe
der Schriftſtellerei.   Jean Paul.

69.

Jedes erſte Gefühl iſt ein Morgenſtern, der,
ohne unterzugehen, bald ſeinen Zauberſchimmer
verliert und, durch das Blau des Tages verhüllt,
weiterzieht . . . .   Jean Paul.

nize promptly an anxious thought. Fervent prayer and firm resolution make many things possible. As soon as you become anxious and sad, uneasy images force themselves upon you, begin to pray with all your heart. If you do not succeed the first time, surely you will succeed with time. With God in one's heart, one does not brood; for only then a great, exalted feeling pervades the soul.

Jean Paul

68.

The Bible begins magnificently with paradise, the symbol of youth, and ends with the eternal kingdom, with the holy city. Also, its two main parts are truly great history. (Every great historical portion must also contain the great story, symbolically rejuvenated.) The beginning of the New Testament marks the second, the higher fall of man (sin: that which has to be expiated) and the beginning of a new era. The history of every man should be a Bible. Christ is the new Adam. A Bible is the highest task of writing.

Jean Paul

69.

Every first sensation is a morning star which, without setting, soon loses its magical gleam and, veiled by the blue of the day, moves on....

Jean Paul

70.

Über den Plan eines Romans (aber nicht
über die Charaktere) muß man schon aus dem
ersten Bande zu urteilen Befugnis haben; alle
Schönheit und Ründe, mit der die folgenden
Bände den Plan aufwickeln, nimmt ja die Fehler
und Sprünge nicht weg, die er im ersten hatte.

Jean Paul.

71.

Der Wunder höchstes ist,
Daß uns die wahren, echten Wunder so
Alltäglich werden können, werden sollen.
Ohn dieses allgemeine Wunder hätte
Ein Denkender wohl schwerlich Wunder je
Genannt, was Kindern bloß so heißen müßte,
Die gaffend, nur das Ungewöhnlichste,
Das Neuste nur verfolgen.   Lessing (Nathan).

72.

Begreifst du aber, wieviel a n d ä c h t i g
s c h w ä r m e n leichter a l s   g u t   h a n d e l n ist?
wie gern der schlaffste Mensch andächtig schwärmt,
um nur — ist er zuzeiten sich schon der Ab=
sicht deutlich nicht bewußt — um nur gut handeln
nicht zu dürfen?   M. Mendelsjohn (Phaedon).

73.

Wir können die ganze Kette von Wesen, vom
Unendlichen an bis an das kleinste Stäubchen,
in drei Glieder einteilen. Das erste Glied be=
greift, kann aber von andern nicht begriffen
werden: dieses ist der einzige, dessen Vollkommen=

70.

One is entitled to judge the plot, but not the characters, in the first volume of a novel; all the beauty and polish with which the succeeding volumes may develop the plot do not remove the defects and cracks which the first one contained.

Jean Paul

71.[6]

The highest miracle is that true genuine miracles may become, should become, so commonplace. Without this universal miracle a thinking man would hardly have called a miracle what only children would thus designate, who gaping pursue only what is strangest and newest.

Lessing (Nathan)

72.

Do you realize how much easier it is to be *devoutly enthusiastic* than to *act wisely*? How the slackest person likes to go into devout ecstasies—even if it at the time he is not clearly conscious of the intent—to be relieved from actually having to act wisely?

Mendelssohn (Phaedon)

73.

We can arrange the whole chain of beings, from the infinite down to the smallest particle, in three ranks. The first rank comprehends what cannot be comprehended by others, this is the only one where perfection surpasses all finite concepts. The created spirits and souls from the

---

[6] From a famous monologue in Lessing's most famous play on tolerance (*Nathan, the Sage*).

heit alle endlichen Begriffe übersteigt. Die er=
schaffenen Geister und Seelen machen das zweite
Glied: sie begreifen und können von andern
begriffen werden. Die Körperwelt ist das letzte
Glied, die nur von andern begriffen werden,
aber nicht begreifen kann.

M. Mendelsjohn (Sokrates in Phaedon).

74.

Es liegt eine tiefe Erfrischung in dem drängen=
den Treiben, das die Künstlerseele tagtäglich zu
neuen Gebilden erweckt, die wahre nachhaltige
Erquickung liegt aber nur in der Treue, in der
unabläjsigen sorgsamen Vollendung dessen, was
man in der Stunde der Weihe empfangen hat;
in dieser Treue entsteht die Schaffensfreude,
wiedergeboren durch den Willen, erhöht und ver=
klärt.   Berthold Auerbach (Die Frau Professorin).

75.

Das Korn am Halme, das zur Erde nieder=
geworfen ist, geht in Verwesung über und setzt
nur zu seinem eigenen fruchtlosen Untergange
neue Keime an. Der Mensch aber gleicht nicht
dem Halme, er kann sich aufrichten durch die
Kraft seines Willens.   Berthold Auerbach.

76.

Ein alter Volksglaube sagt: Wiegt man eine
Wiege, in der kein Kind ist, so nimmt man dem
Kinde, das man später hineinlegt, die gesunde
Ruhe. Ja, unnützes Wiegen ist schädlich, und

second rank; they comprehend and can be be comprehended by others. The material world forms the last rank which can only be comprehended by others but is itself not capable of comprehension.

M. Mendelssohn (Sophocles in Phaedon)

74.

There is a deep re-creation in the pressing activity which daily awakens the soul of the artist to new creation, but the true, lasting refinement lies only in the sincerity,in the incessant, careful perfection of that which has been perceived in the hour of inspiration; the joy of creation arises from this sincerity, regeneration through the will, exalted and transfigured.

Berthold Auerbach (Die Frau Professorin)

75.

The grain on the stalk beaten down to earth rots and produces new seeds only for its own futile ruin. But man does not resemble the grain, he can rise again by his own willpower.

Berthold Auerbach

76.

An old popular belief asserts: if one rocks an empty cradle, one robs the child, whom one later puts in it, of healthy repose. Yes, unnecessary rocking is harmful, and

das gilt noch mehr von dem Schaukeln und
Hin= und Herbewegen der Gedanken, in denen
kein Leben ruht.   Berthold Auerbach (Luzifer).

77.

Die gelehrten Frauen brauchen ihre Bücher
etwa wie ihre Uhr, nämlich sie zu tragen, damit
gesehen zu werden, daß sie eine haben, wenn
sie auch gleich gemeiniglich stillesteht oder n i c h t
n a c h   d e r   S o n n e   g e r i c h t e t   i s t.
                    Wilh. Waiblinger (Aus dessen Tagebuch).

78.

Unsere Leidenschaften sind Phönixe; wie der
alte verbrennt, steigt der neue gleich wieder
hervor.   Wilh. Waiblinger.

79.

Pedanterie ist ein Insektenauge, welches
nur das Nächste und Kleinste unendlich vergrößert
sieht und nie viel, geschweige ein Ganzes über=
sehen kann.   Wilh. Waiblinger.

80.

Die W i s s e n s c h a f t ist ein Meer, auf dem
Tausende nebeneinander, friedlich und feindlich,
der eine auf einem Nachen, der andere auf einem
stolzen Schiffe, der dritte gar auf dem vom
Schiffbruch eines andern geretteten Balken umher=
schwimmen. Tausende können sich freundlich
begegnen, wenn sie nicht unklugerweise gegen=
einander steuern und sich selbst und ihrem Fahr=

this applies even more to the rocking and see-sawing of thoughts in which new life rests.

Berthold Auerbach (Luzifer)

77.

Educated women use their books somewhat like their watch, namely, to carry it so that everybody can see that they have one, even if it may have stopped or does not agree with the sun.

Wilhelm Waiblinger (From his Diary)

78.

Our passions are phoenixes; when the old one burns up, a new one promptly rises again.

Wilhelm Waiblinger

79.

Pedantry is the eye of an insect which sees only the nearest and smallest things infinitely enlarged, but which can never survey much, let alone a totality.

Wilhelm Waiblinger

80.

Science is an ocean in which thousands are swimming around, peaceful or hostile, some in a boat, others in a proud ship, the third perhaps on a beam, rescued from the shipwreck of another. Thousands can meet in a friendly encounter, if they do not unwisely steer against

zeuge schaden wollen. Aber wenn sie auch alle ihre Kräfte vereinigen wollten, **das Meer können sie nimmer ausschöpfen.**

Wilh. Waiblinger.

81.

Es gibt viele Dichterlinge und Poeten, Roman= schreiber und Novellisten, aber sie verschwinden im Meer der Vergessenheit; es sind die Arabesken die in dem Zimmer eines Reichen ein wertvolles Gemälde umgeben, an denen sich das vorüber= gleitende Auge ergötzt, um immer zu dem Bild selbst zurückzukehren. Das Gemälde, der wahre Dichter bleibt ewig, die Arabesken verschwinden, und der Zimmermaler fertigt **neue, selten bessere.**

Wilh. Waiblinger.

82.

Umsonst nicht hat der Musen Chor
Den unfruchtbaren Lorbeer sich erwählt,
Kalt, frucht= und duftlos drücket er das Haupt,
Dem er Ersatz versprach für manches Opfer;
Gar ängstlich steht sich's auf der Menschheit Höhn
Und ewig ist die arme Kunst gezwungen,
Zu betteln von des Lebens Überfluß.

F. Grillparzer (Sappho, Akt I, Szene 3).

83.

Das eben ist der Liebe Zaubermacht,
Daß sie veredelt, was ihr Hauch berührt,
Der Sonne ähnlich, deren goldner Strahl
Gewitterwolken selbst in Gold verwandelt.

F. Grillparzer (Sappho, Akt I, Szene 5.)

each other, wishing to damage themselves and their crafts. But even if they wanted to unite all their forces, they will never be able to drain the ocean.

Wilhelm Waiblinger

81.

There are many versifiers and poetasters, novelists and short-story writers, but they disappear in the ocean of oblivion; they are the arabesques framing a valuable painting in the room of a rich man, in which the passing eye delights but always returns to the picture itself. The painting, the true poet remain eternal, the arabesques disappear, and the housepainter fashions new, but rarely better, ones.

Wilhelm Waiblinger

82.*

Not in vain has the choir of the Muses chosen for themselves the barren laurel. Cold without fruit or fragrance, it oppresses the noble head to which it promised recompense for past privations. Uneasy it is to stand on mankind's heights, and always the poor art is forced to beg of life's abundance.

F. Grillparzer (Sappho, Act I, Scene 3)

83.

Such is the magic force of love that it ennobles all it breathes upon, like the sun whose golden rays can change the tempestuous clouds into gold.

F. Grillparzer (Sappho, Act I, Scene 5)

84.

Sonett.

(An Beatrice.)

So edel sittig ist mein teures Leben,
Die Herrin, andern sich zum Gruße neigend,
Daß jede Zunge bebt, in Ehrfurcht schweigend,
Und nicht ein Auge wagt, sich zu erheben.

Sie hört ihr Lob von jedem Munde schweben
Und geht, so sanft sich und bescheiden zeigend,
Daß sie ein Wunder scheint, vom Himmel steigend,
Um ihn auf dieser Erde kundzugeben.

Sie scheint so hold, wer immer sie betrachte,
Und gießt durchs Aug' ins Herz so süße Triebe,
Daß die nur, die sie fühlten, sie verstehen;

Und von den Lippen scheint ein Geist zu wehen,
So voll von Huld und Innigkeit und Liebe,
Daß er zu jeder Seele flüstert: schmachte!

Dante Alighieri aus „Vita nuova“, 1295 verfaßt.

85.

Sonett I.

Weißt du von Phaëton, von Icarus?
Der erste wollt' im goldnen Sonnenwagen
Das Licht heran vom fernsten Morgen tragen,
Die Stirn umstrahlt, und fiel in diesen Fluß;

Der zweit' ins Meer, im törichten Entschluß,
Mit Wachs beschwingt, durch hohe Luft zu jagen.
Hier sieh, was solchen, die sich kecklich wagen,
Auf hoher Himmelsbahn begegnen muß.

84[7]

Sonnet *(To Beatrice)*

So gentle and honest
Appears my lady when she greets somebody
That every voice must tremble and be mute,
And eyes do not dare to look at her.

Hearing herself praised by every mouth
She walks showing herself so mild and humble
That she seems to be a miracle, come from heaven
To reveal it on this earth.

Appearing so pleasant to every beholder,
She pours through the eyes a sweetness to the heart
Which nobody can understand who does not experi-
        ence it.

And from her lips seem to move
A gentle spirit full of love
Which says to the soul: Sigh!
        Dante Alighieri (Vita nuova) [1295]

85.*

Sonnet I

Do you know of Phaëton, of Icarus?
The former wanted to bring the sun's golden cart,
The light to us from the farthest East.
His head radiated, and he fell into the river.

The latter fell into the sea after foolishly deciding
To chase, wax in his wings, through the high air.
Here see what they encounter who brazenly dare
To travel in high heaven.

[7] Brahms quoted numbers 84-86 in German. The original poems are in
Italian. These translations are by A.E.

Doch wer wird Furcht vor hehrem Flug be=
weisen,
Wenn Amor Mut gebeut, er, dessen Macht
Den Himmel oft der Erde gleich gemacht?

Dianen rief er aus des Himmels Kreisen,
Wie er von Idas Höhn im leichten Flug
Zum Himmel hin den schönen Jüngling trug.

Torquato Tasso.

(Es ergibt sich von selbst, daß dieses Sonett
die Liebe zu einer sehr hochgestellten Dame und
die Hoffnung, die äußere Ungleichheit durch
Gegenliebe ausgeglichen zu sehen, ausspricht.)

Deutsch von C. Streckfuß.

86.

Sonett II.

Ein Höllenschlund voll Angst ist mir das Leben,
Und meine Seufzer — Furien sind's voll Wut,
Und meine Wünsche — böser Schlangen Brut,
Die gegen dieses Herz den Giftzahn heben.

Die Hoffnung sah ich treulos mir entschweben,
Wie jenen Armen in der ew'gen Glut;
Und meine Tränen brennen, gleich der Flut
Des Phlegethon, bei Jammerton und Leben.

Und meine Stimm' ist Cerberus, der bellt;
Das Höllental, in das kein Lichtstrahl fällt,
Ist meine trübe, nachtgefüllte Seele;

Nur daß noch Huld das Schicksal mir beweist;
Es will, daß jene dort ein Höllengeist,
Mich eine Göttin dieser Erde quäle.

Tasso, um 1575.

But who will be scared away from exalted flight
When Amor commands courage, he whose power
Has often turned earth into heaven?

He called Diana from the circles of heaven
When carrying from Ida's summit in easy flight
The beautiful youth up to heaven.

Torquato Tasso

(It is self-evident that this sonnet expresses love for a high- ranking woman and the author's wish to balance the external inequality by mutual love.)

86.*
Sonnet II

Life is to me a hellish abyss full of fear,
And my sighs—they are furies full of rage,
And my wishes— the brood of ugly snakes
Who raise their poisonous teeth against this heart.

I saw hope faithlessly escape from me
As from those wretches in the eternal fire;
And my tears burn like the flood
Of Phlegeton at the sound of lament and life.

And my voice is Cerberus who barks;
A vale of hell without light
Is my troubled soul, dark as night.

Fate wants to show me a kindness:
It wants that those in hell are tortured by a ghost,
I by a goddess of this earth.

Torquato Tasso, around 1575

87.

Freude mit guten frommen Leuten, in Gottes=
furcht, Zucht und Ehren, ob gleich ein Wort oder
Zötlein zu viel, das gefällt Gott wohl.

M. Luther.

88.

Krieg führt der Witz auf ewig mit dem
Schönen,
Er glaubt nicht an den Engel und den Gott —
Den lauten Markt mag Momus unterhalten,
Ein edler Sinn liebt edlere Gestalten!

Schiller (Jungfrau v. Orleans.)

89.

Schüchtern trete der Künstler vor die Kritik
und das Publikum, aber nicht die Kritik
vor den Künstler, wenn er nicht einer ist,
der ihr Gesetzbuch erweitert.

Schiller: „Verteidigung des Rezensenten"[1].

90.

Beim ersten Sakramente (der Taufe) geht
die Bildung des Herzens an, beim zweiten
(Abendmahl) die des Kopfes.   Jean Paul.

91.

Es gibt einen poetischen Wahnsinn, aber
auch einen humoristischen, den Sterne hatte;
aber nur Leser von vollendetem Geschmack halten
höchste Anspannung nicht für Überspannung.

Jean Paul.

---

[1] Dgl. die Bemerkung im Autorenregister.

87.

Gaiety in the company of good pious people, with awe of God, discipline, and honor, even with a word of bawdiness too much, this gives pleasure to God.

M. Luther

88.*

Wit forever wars against beauty,
Denies belief in angels and in Gods—
The loud market may be entertained by Momus,
A nobler mind prefers nobler beings.

Schiller (Jungfrau von Orleans)

89.[8]

Shyly shall the artist appear before the critics and the public, but not so the critics before the artist, unless he is one who expands their book of rules.

Schiller

90.

At the first sacrament (baptism) the formation of the heart begins, at the second sacrament (holy communion) that of the head.

Jean Paul

91.[9]

There exists a poetical madness, but there is also a humoristic one which Laurence Sterne possessed; but only readers with the most perfected taste do not take the highest intensity for excess.

Jean Paul

[8] A footnote by Krebs informs that Schiller defends a critique he had written about a poem by Bürger.
[9] The reference is to Laurence Sterne, whom Jean Paul read in English and greatly admired.

92.

Die einzigen Arzneien, die Weibern mehr nützen als schaden, sind höchstens Kleider. — Nach vielen Naturforschern verlängert das Mausern das Leben der Vögel: aber auch das der Weiber, setz' ich dazu, die allemal so lange siechen, bis sie wieder ein neues Gefieder an= haben. Jean Paul.

93.

Der junge Jüngling bewundert und begehrt zugleich, der ältere Jüngling ist fähig, bloß zu bewundern. Jean Paul.

94.

Die Mädchen wissen nicht, wie sehr sie Ge= schäftigkeit verschönert, wie sehr an ihnen und den Taubenhälsen das Gefieder nur schillert und spielt, wenn sie sich bewegen, und wie sehr wir Männer den Raubtieren gleichen, die keine Beute haben wollen, welche festsitzt.

Jean Paul.

95.

Wahrhaftig, weder der klappernde Mentor noch seine Bücher, d. h. weder die Gartenschere noch die Gießkanne sättigen und färben die Blume, sondern der Himmel und die Erde, zwischen denen sie steht, d. h. die Einsamkeit oder Gesellschaft, in der das Kind seine ersten Knospen=Minuten durchwächst. Jean Paul.

92.

The only medicines which do more good than harm to women are at best the clothes. According to many scientists, molting prolongs life of birds; but I can add, also of women, who pine away until they are again wearing new feathers.

Jean Paul

93.

The young bachelor admires and desires at the same time; the older bachelor is capable only of admiring.

Jean Paul

94.

Young girls do not know to what extent bustling enhances their beauty, how much the plumage, be it on theirs or a dove's throat, glistens and glitters only when they move, and how much we men resemble predatory animals who do not want any prey which is sitting still.

Jean Paul

95.

Truly, neither the chatting mentor nor his books, i.e., neither the garden shears nor the watering pot satisfy and color the flower, but the heaven and the earth between which it stands, i.e., either the solitude or the company in which the child grows in its first budding minutes.

Jean Paul

96.

Das von so vielen Jahren, von so vielen Pfeilen aufgerissene Herz tauchte sich mit allen seinen Wunden in warme Tränenströme unter, um zuzuheilen, wie sich zersprungene Flöten durch das Liegen im Wasser schließen und darin ihre Töne wiederfinden.

Jean Paul (Quintus Fixlein).

97.

Mit der Schriftstellerei ist's wie mit der Liebe: man kann beide Jahrzehnte lang begehren und entraten; ist aber einmal der erste Funke von ihnen in dein Pulverlager gefallen, dann brennt's fort bis ans Ende.

Jean Paul.

98.

Herder und Schiller.

Zu Wundärzten wollten beide in der Jugend sich bilden; aber das Schicksal sagte: „Nein! Es gibt tiefere Wunden als die Wunden des Leibes — heilet die tiefern!" Und beide schrieben.

Jean Paul.

99.

Von der dunkeln Schreibart.

Wer die Gebrechen seiner Gedanken in eine dunkle Sprache einkleidet und verhüllt, ahmet klüglich die Wirte nach, die gerne trübes Bier in einem undurchsichtigen Gefäß auftragen.

Jean Paul.

96.

The heart, torn up by so many years, by so many arrows, submerged itself with all its wounds in warm floods of tears in order to heal, just as cracked flutes close up by lying in water and thereby regain their tones.

Jean Paul

97.

With writing, it is the same as with love: for decades one can desire and abjure both, but once their first spark has fallen into your powderkeg, it burns forth to the end.

Jean Paul

98.[10]

Herder and Schiller

Both in their youth wanted to become surgeons, but fate said: "No! There are deeper wounds than the wounds of the body—heal the deeper ones!" And both became writers.

Jean Paul

99.

Of Dark Writing

Those who clothe and cover the defects of their thoughts in obscure language imitate cleverly the innkeepers who serve clouded beer in opaque mugs.

Jean Paul

---

[10] Consult the Annotated List of Cited Authors on Herder and Schiller.

100.

Die Liebe ſtirbt, wie die Menſchen, öfters
am Übermaß als am Hunger; ſie lebt von
Liebe, aber ſie gleicht den Alpenpflanzen, die
ſich vom Einſaugen der naſſen Wolken er=
nähren, und die zugrunde gehen, wenn man
ſie beſprengt.   Jean Paul ([Quintus] Fixlein).

101.

Man ſollte ſich in allem mäßigen, im Schreiben,
Trinken und Freuen; und wie man den Bienen
Strohhalme in den Honig legt, damit ſie nicht
in ihrem Zucker ertrinken, ſo ſollte man allezeit
einige feſte Grundſätze und Zweige vom Baume
des Erkenntniſſes in ſeinen Lebensſirup ſtatt
jener Strohhalme werfen, damit man ſich darauf
erhielte und nicht darin wie eine Ratte erſöffe.

Jean Paul.

102.

Belehrung.

Bitter erſcheint dir der Tod, hoch preiſe die
ewige Weisheit,
Daß ſie des Bittern ſo viel hat in den Becher
gemiſcht!
Würden der Freiheit Trank nicht alle begierig
ergreifen,
Schreckte das Bittre ſie nicht, froh dem Erretter
zu nahn?

Auguſt Mahlmann.

28

100.

Love dies, like people, more frequently of excess than
of hunger; it lives on love, but it resembles alpine plants
which subsist by absorbing the moisture of clouds but
perish when drenched with water.

Jean Paul ([Quintus] Fixlein)

101.

One should be moderate in everything, in writing,
in drinking and rejoicing; and just as one puts some straw
into the honey to keep the bees from drowning in their
sugar, so one should always throw a few firm principles
and twigs from the tree of knowledge into one's life's syrup
to be supported by them and not to drown in it like a rat.

Jean Paul

102.*
Poetry

Death seems bitter to you, but praise eternal wisdom
For having mixed so much bitterness into the cup!
Would not everyone eagerly reach for freedom's
     draught
If the bitterness had not alarmed them to approach
     the saviour with joy?

August Mahlmann

103.
Das Sprachversehen.

Was! Du nimmst sie jetzt nicht und warst
der Dame versprochen?
Antwort: Lieber! Vergib, man verspricht
sich ja wohl.   Heinrich v. Kleist.

104.
Freundesrat.

Ob du's im Tag'buch anmerkst? Handle!
War es was Böses?
Fühl es, o Freund, und vergiß; Gutes? Vergiß
es noch eh'r!
E. v. Kleist (Frühling[1]).

105.

Wir beginnen mit Gott und vollenden in Gott;
Wir leben in Gott und streben nach Gott;
Wir wandeln vor Gott und handeln für Gott;
Wir sprechen aus Gott und schwören bei Gott;
Wir trauen auf Gott und bauen nächst Gott;
Wir kommen von Gott und gehn zu Gott.

(Nach einem arabischen Philologen von Herrn v. Hammer.)

106.

Soll ich den Himmel noch länger bewundern?
Ist ein Menschen= ein Mädchenauge nicht heller,
nicht schöner? Oder wie hinter der sanft=
gebogenen glatten Fläche ein Geist erscheint, eine
Liebe herausstrahlt, ja heraus und hinüber in

---

[1] Brahms irrt sich hier. Das Epigramm „Freundesrat" ist
nicht von Ewald, sondern von Heinrich von Kleist.

103.[11]
Double Meaning of Words
What! You are not taking her now
      and were engaged to the lady?
Answer: Dear! Forgive, one can have
      a slip of the tongue.

Heinrich von Kleist

104.[12]
Advice from a Friend
Did you note it in your diary? Act!
Was it something wicked?
Feel it, oh friend, and forget. Something good?
Forget it even more quickly.

E. von Kleist (Frühling)

105.*
We begin with God and end in God;
We live in God and strive for God;
We walk before God and act for God;
We speak out of God and swear by God;
We trust in God and build next to God;
We come from God and go unto God.

(After an Arabic philologist by Herr von Hammer*)*

106.
Should I admire the heaven much longer? Is a human or a girl's eye not brighter, more beautiful? Or as a
spirit appears behind the gently bent, smooth surface and
love radiates from it , yes, out and over into mine, so warm

---

[11] Untranslatable pun on the German word "versprechen," which refers to a
promise as well as to a slip of the tongue.
[12] A footnote by Krebs accuses Brahms of having erroneously ascribed this
verse to Ewald von Kleist rather than to Heinrich von Kleist; but Brahms
was correct.

meines, warm lebend lebendig machend, selig
und beseligend; soll ich nicht auch hinter dem
einförmig=blau gefärbten Himmel ebenso, ach noch
einen viel seligeren, liebenderen Geist ahnen als
in dem Mädchenauge, in welchem ich nur mein
kleines Bild erblicke?

Leopold Schefer (Violante Beccaria).

107.

Ein Einziges auf Erden ist nur schöner
und besser als ein Weib ... Das ist die Mutter.

L. Schefer (Der Sklavenhändler).

108.

Urteile sind wie Uhren; es geht keine der
andern gleich, doch recht scheint jedem seine.

Alex. Pope.

109.

Die Verwandlung.

(Aus dem Französischen.)

Es wundert dich, daß ein so garstig Ding,
Als eine Raupe ist, zum schönsten Schmetterling
In wenig Wochen wird; — mich wundert's nicht.
Denn wiss': auch manche Schöne kriecht
Als Raupe morgens aus dem Bette
Und kömmt als Schmetterling von der Toilette.

Aloys Blumauer.

110.

Es ist niemals ein Beweis von dem Flor
eines Landes, wenn es viele, ungewöhnlich reiche
Partikuliers hat — denn sonst müßte Polen seit
einem Jahrhundert das blühendste Land ge=

with life, enlivening, blest and blessing— should I not also surmise behind the uniformly blue heaven a more blest and loving spirit than in the eye of the girl in which I see only my own small image?

Leopold Schefer (Violante Beccaria)

107.

Only one thing on earth is more beautiful and better than a wife... that is the mother.

L. Schefer (Der Sklavenhändler)

108.

Judgments are like watches; no two go alike, but each person believes his own.

Alexander Pope

109.[13]

Metamorphosis
(From the French)
You are surprised that such an ugly thing
As a caterpillar can in several weeks take wing,
Become the prettiest butterfly. I am not at all
    surprised,
For know: that likewise many beauties crawl
As caterpillars early morning out of bed
And reappear as butterflies from their *toilette*.

Aloys Blumauer

110.

Many unusually rich particulars are never proof of the bloom of a country — otherwise Poland since the past century should have been the most flourishing country

---

[13] Brahms cites in German.

wesen sein —, sondern mehr, wenn der Kern
der Nation im Gedeihen seiner Gewerbe den
Reichtum der wenigen entbehren kann.

J. G. Seume (Briefe über Rußland).

111.

Zweimal muß man in seinem Leben einsam
sein: in der Jugend, um vieles zu lernen und
eine Denkart zu erwerben, die Stich hält durchs
Leben, und noch einmal im Alter, um alles zu
überdenken, was uns begegnete, alle Blumen,
die wir pflückten und alle Stürme des Schicksals.

Zimmermann.

112.

Mann mit zugeknöpften Taschen,
Dir tut niemand was zulieb;
Hand wird nur von Hand gewaschen,
Wenn du nehmen willst, so gieb!

Goethe.

113.

Vult: Aber nur der Paradiesesfluß der
Kunst treib' eure Mühlen nicht. Darfst du
Tränen und Stimmungen in die Musik ein=
mengen, so ist sie nur die Dienerin derselben,
nicht die Schöpferin. Eine elende Pfeiferei, die
dich am Todestage eines geliebten Menschen aus
den Angeln höbe, wäre denn eine gute. Und
was wäre das für ein Kunsteindruck, der wie
die Nesselsucht sogleich verschwindet, sobald man
in die kalte Luft wiederkommt? Die Musik
ist unter allen Künsten die rein menschlichste,
die allgemeinste.   Jean Paul.

— but rather when the heart of a nation by the growth of its trade can dispense with the riches of a few.

J..G. Seume (Letters on Russia)

111.

Twice during our lifetime we have to be lonely: in our youth so that we can learn much and acquire a way of thinking which will hold good throughout life, and then again in old age, so that we can think over everything we encountered, all the flowers we gathered and all the storms of fate.

Zimmermann

112.*

You button your pockets and find
No man will ever be kind;
Remember, live and let live,
If you take, you must give.

Goethe

113.

Vult: But do not let the paradise river of art drive your mills. If you mix tears and moods into the music, it remains merely their servant, not their creator. Otherwise a miserable piping lifting you off your hinges on the death day of a beloved person would be good music. And what kind of artistic impression is one that quickly disappears like a nettle rash as soon as one returns into the cold air? Among all the arts, music is the most human and universal.

Jean Paul

114.

Wer nie in schnöder Wollust Schoß
Die Fülle der Gesundheit goß,
Dem steht ein stolzes Wort wohl an,
Das Heldenwort: „Ich bin ein Mann!"
Bürger.

115.

Gebunden führt der Schmerz uns alle durch
das Leben,
Sanft, wenn wir willig gehn, hart, wenn wir
widerstreben.
Haller.

116.

Süße Liebe denkt in Tönen,
Denn Gedanken stehn zu fern.
Nur in Tönen mag sie gern
Alles, was sie will, verschönen.
L. Tieck.

117.

Waldeinsamkeit,
Die mich erfreut
So morgen wie heut
In ewiger Zeit:
O wie mich erfreut
Waldeinsamkeit.
L. Tieck (Der blonde Eckbert).

118.

Aphorismen von Swift.

Parteiwut ist die Tollheit vieler zum
Nutzen weniger.
Swift.

114.*

He who never poured the fullness of health
Into the lap of vile lust,
He deserves a proud word,
A heroic word: "I am a man!"

Bürger

115.*

Grief leads us fettered all through life,
Kindly if we go willingly, cruelly if we resist.

Haller

116.*

Sweet love thinks in tones,
For thoughts are too remote;
Only tones can beautify
Everything it wants.

L. Tieck

117.[14]

Solitude in the forest
Which pleases me
Tomorrow as much as today
In time eternal.
Oh how it pleases me,
Solitude in the forest.

L. Tieck (The Blond Eckbert)

118.[15]

Aphorisms by Swift
Party passion is the madness of many for the gain of a few.

Swift

---

[14] All six lines have the same rhyme.
[15] In numbers 118 to 122, Brahms quotes in German. When there is no other source indication, the English translation is by A.E.

119.

Ein König ist vielleicht ein Werkzeug, ein Strohmann; dient er jedoch dazu, unsre Feinde zu schrecken und unser Eigentum zu sichern, so ist er gut genug; eine Vogelscheuche ist ein Ding von Stroh, beschützt jedoch unser Korn.

Swift.

120.

Blumiger und rhetorischer Stil bei ernstem Stoff gleicht den blauen und roten Blumen im Korne. Sie gefallen denen, welche nur zum Vergnügen spazieren gehen, erweisen jedoch demjenigen Schaden, welcher die Früchte ernten will.

Swift.

121.

Weiber sind wie Rätsel; sowohl wegen ihrer Unverständlichkeit wie auch hauptsächlich deshalb, weil sie uns nicht länger gefallen, sobald wir sie haben kennen lernen.

Swift.

122.

Ein feiner und hochgebildeter Geist ist bei weitem nicht so nützlich wie der gemeine Menschenverstand; vierzig verständige Männer gehen auf ein Genie; wer nichts als Gold im Beutel führt, ist täglichen Verlusten aus Mangel an kleiner Münze ausgesetzt.

Swift.

123.

Daß jemand behauptet, die so schöne und vollkommene Welt könne zufällig aus einzelnen und festen Körpern entstanden sein, wundert mich nicht so sehr; aber das sehe ich schlechter=

119.

A king is perhaps a tool, a strawman; if he serves to chase away our enemies and to secure our property, he is good enough; a scarecrow is a thing of straw, but it protects our corn.

Swift

120.

Flowery and rhetorical style in serious matters is like the blue and red flowers in a cornfield. They please those who take a walk for amusement but cause damage to him who wants to harvest the fruit.

Swift

121.

Women are an enigma: as much because of their incomprehensibility as also because they do not appeal to us any longer after we get to know them.

Swift

122.

A refined and highly cultured spirit is by far not so useful as common sense; forty reasonable men are the equivalent of one genius; he who carries nothing but gold in his purse is exposed to daily losses for want of small change.

Swift

123.

I am not surprised when somebody claims that this beautiful and perfect world could have come into being

dings nicht ein, wie ein solcher nicht ebensogut
glaubt, daß, wenn man eine große Anzahl Buch=
staben untereinander und auf die Erde wirft,
daraus die Annalen des Ennius entstehen könnten.

Cicero (De Nat. Deor. II, 37.)

124.

Ein Kind will ich bleiben bis ans Grab,
stets lieben, glauben, und mich an andre an=
schließen wie ein Kind, noch so oft getäuscht,
will ich immer wieder Vertrauen zu dem Menschen=
herzen fassen und dem Klugen wie dem Toren
verzeihen, wenn sie das Ihrige tun, um mich
irre zu machen.   Pestalozzi.

125.

Von Nektar trunken sein und doch besonnen,
In heitern Lügen ew'ge Wahrheit künden,
Aus Luftgebilden feste Tempel gründen,
So wird des Dichters Lorbeerkranz gewonnen.

Friedr. v. Sallet.

126.

Das Fatum, das uns drückt, ist die Träg=
heit des Geistes. Durch Erweiterung und
Bildung unsrer Tätigkeit werden wir uns selbst
in das Fatum verwandeln. Alles scheint auf
uns hereinzuströmen, weil wir nicht hinaus=
strömen. Wir sind negativ, weil wir wollen;
je positiver wir werden, desto negativer
wird die Welt um uns her.   Novalis.

127.

Kann denn der gebildete und edle Mensch
nicht sein wie die Sonnenstrahlen, die unverletzt

accidentally from simple and solid bodies; but I cannot understand that this same person does not likewise believe that the Annals of Ennius could have come into being by throwing a huge number of the letters of the alphabet casually on the earth.

Cicero (De natura Deorum II, 37)

124.

I want to remain a child until I die, always loving, believing, and attaching myself to others like a child; even if ever so often deceived, I shall always again have faith in human hearts and forgive the sage as well as the fool when they do what they do in order to lead me astray.

Pestalozzi

125.*

To be drunk with nectar yet clear of mind,
To proclaim in serene lies eternal truth,
To found from phantasms firm temples,
Thus is earned the poet's laurel wreath.

Friedrich von Sallet

126.

The fate which oppresses us is the indolence of spirit. By widening and shaping our activity we transform ourselves into our fate. Everything seems to rush upon us because we do not rush out. We are negative because we want it so; the more positive we become, the more negative the world becomes around us.

Novalis

127.

Could not the educated and noble person be like

und ohne den Glanz einzubüßen, über die feuchte
Erde mit all ihren Sümpfen hinübergehn? —
Er kann es und tut es!   Franz Horn.

128.

Das höchste Opfer, was die Liebe und die
Freundschaft bringen kann, ist nicht das Leben,
sondern die Überzeugung.   Fr. Hoffmann.

129.

Wer sein Leben höher achtet als seine Kunst,
wird nimmermehr ein Künstler.

1832.   Neukomm (Aus R. Schumanns Album).

130.
Die Fuge.

Festigkeit bezeichnet meinen Gang,
Unabänderlich ist der Gesang.
Gegensatz verbindet sich mit mir,
Eins in [dem] Einen bilden wir.
                              C. M. v. Weber.

131.

Gern erwählen die Götter der Einfalt kind=
liche Seelen,
In das bescheidne Gefäß schließen sie Gött=
liches ein.
                              Schiller.

132.

Es kann ein Mensch lange Zeit in den besten
Grundsätzen wie ein Schneemann eingefroren
sitzen, aber die lustigen Frühlingsbäche unter=
waschen schon heimlich plaudernd und neckend

rays of the sun, which unharmed and without losing any lustre pass over the earth with all its swamps? He can and does it!

Franz Horn

128.

The highest sacrifice which love and friendship can offer is not one's life but one's conviction.

Franz Hoffmann

129.

A man who values his life more than his art will never become an artist.

1832.   *Neukomm* (from R. Schumann's *Album)*

130.*
The Fugue

Steadfastness determines my step,
Unchangeable is the song.
Contrast connects with me,
One into one we form.

Carl Maria v. Weber

131.*

The gods choose gladly the childlike souls of simplicity,
Into this modest vessel they enclose divinity.

Schiller

132.

A man, like a snowman, may sit for a long time frozen in his best principles, but the merry brooklets of spring,

den Sitz unter ihm — ein Laut, der leise Flug
eines Vogels: und er stürzt kopfüber und ver=
schüttet alle guten Vorsätze wieder.

Joseph Freiherr von Eichendorff.

133.

Die Leichtsinnigkeit des Genies ist nicht die=
jenige, welche bei einigen andern, aus leichtem
Leim und flüchtigem Geist gemachten Kindern
des Prometheus auch anzutreffen ist. — Sein
Auge läßt wohl seine Blicke über gewöhnliche
Gegenstände leicht weggleiten; allein es macht
sie bei jedem Gegenstande, bei welchem etwas
zu bemerken ist, stille stehen, ihn genau zu
untersuchen.   Wilhelm Heinse (Laidion).

134.

So lang noch fest die Berge stehn
Und grün der Mai sich wird entfalten,
Müßt es doch wunderlich ergehn,
Wenn man nicht könnt' sich stark erhalten!

Gottfried Kinkel.

135.

Daß wir die geistigsten sind der Bewohner
                der Erde des Sandkorns,
Daß wir, betrachtend das All, fühlen das irdische
                Nichts,
Das ist einzig der Stolz und der Ruhm, der dem
                Menschen gebühret!
Stolz auf Demut nur zeigt den gereiften Verstand.

Gottfried Kinkel.

secretly chatting and teasing, wash away the seat under him—a sound, the gentle flight of a bird: and he topples over and spills again all his good intentions.

Joseph Freiherr von Eichendorff

133.

The frivolity of a genius is not the one that can be found with some other children of Prometheus, made of light glue and fleeting spirit. True, his eyes easily pass over ordinary objects, but if something noteworthy comes along, they pause to examine it.

Wilhelm Heinse (Laidion)

134.*

As long as the mountains stand fast,
As long as May turns green.
It would be strange
If one could not maintain one's strength.

Gottfried Kinkel

135.*

That we are the most spiritual inhabitants of
      earth's grain of sand,
That we, observing the universe, feel the earthly
      nothingness,
This alone is the pride and glory due to mankind!
Pride in humility only shows the mature mind.

Gottfried Kinkel

136.

Ja, man freut sich wohl einmal,
Sieht man den Gießbach schäumen zu Tal;
Aber ewig jungen Genuß,
Gibt nur der tiefe, der stille Fluß.

Gottfried Kinkel.

137.

Wer jetzt noch dichtet fürs Publikum,
Den heißen die klugen Leute dumm —
Mir aber ist das ein Jammerpoet,
Dem nicht immer sein Volk vor Augen steht.

Gottfried Kinkel.

138.

In allen Sprachen verkleinert die Liebe ihr
Geliebtes, gleichsam um es zu verjüngen und
zum Kinde zu machen, das ja der Amor selber
ist. Und das Kleine, gleichsam als das Liebere,
verkleinert man wieder, daher man öfter
Lämmchen, Täubchen, Kindlein, Büchelchen
(letzteres ist nach Voß dreimal verkleinert) sagt,
als Elefantchen, Fürstchen, Tyrannchen, Wal=
fischchen.

Jean Paul.

139.

O Volk, und immer Friede nur in deines
          Schurzfells Falten,
Sag an, birgt es nicht auch den Krieg? den
          Krieg herausgeschüttelt,
Den zweiten Krieg, den letzten Krieg mit allem,
          was dich büttelt,
Laß deinen Ruf: „die Republik!" die Glocken
          überdröhnen,
Die diesen allerneuesten Johannesschwindel tönen!

Freiligrath (Die Toten an die Lebenden).

136.*

Yes, one rejoices once in a while,
Seeing the torrent foaming down to the valley;
But eternally young pleasure
Offers only the deep, the silent river.

Gottfried Kinkel

137.*

He who still writes poetry for the public
Is called stupid by the intelligent people—
But for me the poet is lamentable
Who does not always have his people in full view.

Gottfried Kinkel

138.

In all languages, love uses diminutives for the beloved, to make it, as it were, younger and childlike, because Amor is himself a child. And little being dearer, one dimishes further, in that one more often speaks of little lamb, little dove, little child, little booklet (the latter, according to Voss, is reduced three times) rather than little elephant, little prince, little tyrant, little whale.

Jean Paul

139.*

Oh people, and always peace only in the fold of your leathern apron, tell! does it not also lodge war? Shakeout war, the second war, the last war with all that manhandles you, let your call "the Republic" boom above the bells which sound this newest swindle.

Freiligrath (The Dead to the Living)

140.

Im Glück nicht jubeln und im Sturm nicht
zagen,
Das Unvermeidliche mit Würde tragen,
Das Rechte tun, am Schönen sich erfreun,
Das Leben lieben und den Tod nicht scheun,
Und fest an Gott und andre Zukunft glauben,
Heißt Leben, heißt dem Tod sein Bittres rauben.

Streckfuß.

141.

O Zeit der schweren Not! O Not der schweren
Zeit!
O schwere Zeit der Not! O schwere Not der Zeit!

Chamisso.

142.

Wer von Freuden nie gewußt,
Fern von Leid ist dessen Herz,
Denn nur das ist echter Schmerz,
Der beweint des Glücks Verlust.

Geibel.

143.

Liegt dir Gestern klar und offen,
Wirkst du Heute klar und frei,
Kannst auch auf ein Morgen hoffen,
Das nicht minder glücklich sei.

Goethe.

144.

Zwei sind der Wege, auf welchen der Mensch
zur Tugend emporstrebt;
Schließt sich der eine dir zu, tut sich der andre
dir auf!

140.*

Not to rejoice in good fortune, not to despair in a
      storm,
To bear the unavoidable with dignity,
To be just, to delight in beauty,
To love life and not to shun death,
And to believe firmly in God and the future
Means to live and to rob death of its bitter sting.

Streckfuss

141.*

Oh times of heavy want! Oh want of heavy times!
Oh heavy times of want! Oh heavy want of times!

Chamisso

142.*

One who has never known pleasures,
His heart is far from pain,
For only this is deep sorrow
Which weeps over lost happiness.

Geibel

143.*

If your yesterday is clear and open,
Then today you act clear and free,
You can also hope for a tomorrow
Which be no less happy.

Goethe

144.*

There are two paths on which man climbs toward
      virtue:
If one path is closed to you, the other one will open
      up for you!

handelnd erringt der Glückliche sie, der Leidende
duldend;
Wohl ihm, den sein Geschick liebend auf beiden
geführt. Schiller.

145.

Der süßen Wehmut, dem Mitschmerze öffne
sich das Herz, aber nicht dem kalten Mitschmerze
und dem Niedergeschlagensein, so wie die Blume
zwar vor dem Tau offen bleibt, sich aber vor
dem Regen zuschließt. Jean Paul.

146.

Der Vogel singt nur, wenn er Frühlings=
kraft und Liebestriebe fühlt; Memnons Gestalt
ertönt erst, wenn Sonnenstrahlen sie berühren
und wecken; ebenso erschaffe das beseelte Wort
den Klang und nicht der Klang das Wort.
Jean Paul.

147.

Das wahre Genie richtet sich zwar zuweilen
an fremdem Urteile auf, aber das entwickelte
Gefühl seiner Kräfte macht ihm bald diese
Krücke entbehrlich. Schiller.

148.

Jede Fertigkeit der Vernunft, auch im Irr=
tum, vermengt ihre Fertigkeit zum Empfängnis
der Wahrheit. Goethe.

The fortunate man reaches them by acting, the
    passive one by suffering.
Blessed he whose loving fate has led him on both.

Schiller

145.

Let the heart open up to sweet melancholy, to sympathy, but not to cold compassion and depression, just as
the flower remains open under dew but closes up under
rain.

Jean Paul

146.[16]

A bird sings only when feeling the power of Spring
and the force of love; Memnon's statue gives forth musical
sounds when touched and wakened by the rays of sun.
Just so let inspired word create the sound, and not the
sound the word.

Jean Paul

147.

True genius now and then supports himself on judgments not his own, but the developed consciousness of
his powers soon makes him independent of this crutch.

Schiller

148.

Every proficiency of reason, even in error, mingles
its proficiency for the reception of truth.

Goethe

---

[16] A colossal statue near Thebes, Egypt, connected with the name of
Memnon, King of the Ethiopians, gave forth musical sounds every morning
when touched by the rays of the rising sun.

149.

Die Genügsamkeit des Publikums ist nur
ermunternd für die Mittelmäßigkeit, aber be=
schimpfend und abschreckend für das Genie.

Goethe.

150.

Mache der Schwärmer sich Schüler, wie
Sand am Meere — der Sand ist
Sand, die Perle sei mein, du, o vernünftiger
Freund!   Goethe.

151.

Welchen Leser ich wünsche? den un=
befangensten, der mich,
Sich und die Welt vergißt, und in dem Buche
nur lebt.   Goethe.

152.

So erhaben, so groß ist, so weit entlegen
der Himmel!
Aber der Kleinigkeitsgeist fand auch bis dahin
den Weg.   Goethe.

153.

Es ist gewiß; ein ungemäßigt Leben,
Wie es nur schwere, wilde Träume gibt,
Macht uns zuletzt am hellen Tage träumen.

Goethe.

154.

Die Menschen fürchtet nur, wer sie nicht kennt,
Und wer sie meidet, wird sie bald verkennen.

Goethe.

149.

Easy satisfaction of the public is encouraging only for the mediocrity but insulting and deterring for the genius.

Goethe

150.*

Let the enthusiast find pupils like sand by the ocean— sand is sand, the pearls be mine, you, oh reasonable friend!

Goethe

151.*

What kind of reader do I wish for? The most unembarrassed, who forgets himself, me and the world, and lives only in the book.

Goethe

152.*

So lofty, so great, so far away is the heaven!
But petty minds have also found the way to it.

Goethe

153.*

It is certain, an immoderate life,
like heavy wild dreams,
makes us in the end dream in broad daylight.

Goethe

154.*

Only somebody who does not judge people, fears them, and if he avoids them, he will soon misjudge them.

Goethe

155.

Ein Herre mit zwei Gesind',
Er wird nicht wohl gepflegt;
Ein Haus, worin zwei Weiber sind,
Es wird nicht rein gefegt.   Goethe.

156.

Es ist wohl angenehm, sich mit sich selbst
Beschäft'gen, wenn es nur so nützlich wäre.
                                    Goethe.

157.

Was härter treffe, Kränkung oder Schimpf,
Will ich nicht untersuchen; jene dringt
Ins tiefe Mark, und dieser ritzt die Haut.
Der Pfeil des Schimpfs kehrt auf den Mann
                              zurück,
Der zu verwunden glaubt. Die Meinung Andrer
Befriedigt leicht das wohl geführte Schwert —
Doch ein gekränktes Herz erholt sich schwer.
                                    Goethe.

158.

Es bildet ein Talent sich in der Stille,
Sich ein Charakter in dem Strom der Welt.
                                    Goethe.

159.

Das Wort verwundet leichter, als es heilt.
Und ewig wiederholend strebt vergebens
Verlornes Glück der Kummer herzustellen.
                                    Goethe.

155.*

A man with two servants
Is not well cared for;
A house with two women
Is not swept clean.

Goethe

156.

It is certainly pleasant to be preoccupied with one's self, if it were only useful.

Goethe

157.*

What hits harder, insult or abuse,
I will not investigate;
the former penetrates deep into the marrow, the
    latter scratches the skin.
The arrow of abuse comes back to the man
who thinks to hurt. The opinion of others
is easily satisfied by the well-guided sword,
but an insulted heart heals with difficulty.

Goethe

158.*

A talent is formed in solitude,
A character in the stream of the world.

Goethe

159.*

The word hurts more easily than it heals.
And grief, forever repetitious, strives
In vain to bring back lost happiness.

Goethe

160.

Auf das empfindſame Volk hab ich nie was
gehalten; es werden
Kommt die Gelegenheit, nur ſchlechte Geſellen
daraus.   Goethe.

161.

Wie ſchal und abgeſchmackt iſt doch das Leben,
Wenn alles Regen, alles Treiben nur
Zu neuem Regen, neuem Treiben führt,
Und kein g e l i e b t e r Zweck uns endlich lohnt!
       Goethe.

162.

Bei einem Waſſerfalle mit einem
Regenbogen.

O wie ſchwebt auf dem grimmigen Waſſer=
ſturm der Bogen des Friedens ſo feſt. So ſteht
Gott am Himmel, und die Ströme der Zeiten
ſtürzen und reißen, und auf allen Wellen ſchwebet
der Bogen ſeines Friedens.   Jean Paul.

163.

An eine in der Sonne erblaſſende Roſe.

Bleiche Roſe, die Sonne gab dir die Farbe,
die glühende nimmt ſie dir wieder; du gleicheſt
uns. Wenn der Gott, der die Menſchenwange
glühen läßt, näher und heißer zu uns herunter=
kömmt, ſo erblaſſet ſie auch, und der Menſch
iſt entweder geſtorben oder entzückt.
       Jean Paul.

160.*

I never had much faith in sensuous people; they
      become,
When the occasion arises, only bad fellows.

Goethe

161.*

How stale and insipid is life
When all acting, all striving only
Leads to new acting, new striving,
And no beloved goal rewards us in the end!

Goethe

162.

A Waterfall with a Rainbow

Oh how on the grim raging water the arc of peace
hovers so firmly. Thus God stands in heaven, and the
currents of time pull and tear, and over all the waves hovers the arc of peace.

Jean Paul

163.

To a Rose Fading in the Sun

Pallid rose, the sun gave you color, and burning
takes it again away from you; you resemble us.
If the God who lets man's cheek glow descends to
us nearer and hotter, it also pales, and man is either
dead or entranced.

Jean Paul

164.

Was ist heilig? das ist's, was viele Seelen zusammen
Bindet; bänd' es auch nur leicht, wie die Binse
den Kranz.

Goethe.

165.

Was ist das heiligste? Das, was heut
und ewig die Geister
Tiefer und tiefer gefühlt, immer nur einiger
macht.   Goethe.

166.

Heuchler, ferne von mir! Besonders du
widriger Heuchler,
Der du mit Grobheit glaubst, Falschheit
zu decken und List.

Goethe.

167.

Glücklich ist der, dem sogleich die erste Ge=
liebte die Hand reicht,
Dem der lieblichste Wunsch nicht im Herzen ver=
schmachtet.   Goethe.

168.

Krone des Lebens, Glück ohne Ruh', Liebe
bist du!   Goethe.

169.

Immer strebe zum Ganzen, und kannst du
selber kein Ganzes
Werden, als dienendes Glied schließ an ein
Ganzes dich an.

Goethe.

164.*

What is sacred? that which binds many souls
      together;
Would it bound them as easily as bentgrass the
      wreath.

Goethe

165.*

What is the most sacred? That which today and ever,
felt more and more deeply, unifies the spirits.

Goethe

166.*

Hypocrite, away from me!
Especially you repugnant hypocrite
Who thinks you can cover up deceit
And cunning with rudeness.

Goethe

167.*

Happy is he to whom the first beloved immediately
      holds out her hand,
Who does not find his most precious wish smothered
      in his heart.

Goethe

168.*

Crown of life,
Bliss without cease,
You are love!

Goethe

169.*

Always strive towards the whole, and if you cannot
become a whole, then, as a serving link, attach yourself to
a whole.

Goethe

170.

Laß Neid und Mißgunst sich verzehren,
Das Gute werden sie nicht wehren,
Denn, Gott sei Dank, es ist ein alter Brauch:
So. weit die Sonne scheint, so weit erwärmt sie
auch.   Goethe.

171.

Nur demütig still getragen,
Was auch Gott noch auf dich legt,
Laß zu grübeln und zu fragen:
„Wird mir's nachten, wird mir's tagen,
Wenn dies Herz nun nicht mehr schlägt?"

Denk an Lohn nicht für Beschwerde,
Die im Grabe man vergißt;
Freu' dich, was aus dir auch werde,
Daß fortlebet froh die Erde
Und der Himmel ob ihr ist.
                            Justinus Kerner.

172.

T o a st.

Auf das Wohlsein der Poeten,
Die nicht schillern und nicht goethen,
Durch die Welt in Lust und Nöten,
Segelnd frisch auf eignen Böten.
                            Eichendorff.

173.

T r o st.

Wann dich die Lästerzunge sticht, so laß dir
dies zum Troste sagen:
Die schlecht'sten Früchte sind es nicht, woran die
Wespen nagen.
                            Bürger.

170.*

Let envy and ill will consume themselves,
They will not impede the good.
Because, thank God, it is an old custom!
As far as the sun shines,
It also warms.

Goethe

171.*

Bear with quiet humility whatever God still puts
upon you. Do not brood, do not ask: "Will it be dark, will
it be light when the heart will no longer beat?" Think not
of reward for the burdens which one forgets in the grave.
Be joyful that no matter what becomes of you, the earth
continues happily and heaven is above it.

Justinius Kerner

172.*[17]

A Toast

To the well-being of poets
Who do not imitate Schiller and Goethe,
Who sail through the world in joy or need
Fresh on their own boats.

Eichendorff

173.*

Consolation

If the slanderous tongue stings you,
Let this be a comfort to you:
It is not the rotten fruit on which the wasps feed.

Bürger

---

[17] The four lines have the same rhyme. The poet turns the names of Schiller
and Goethe into verbs.

174.

Was mir im Busen schwoll, mir unbewußt,
Ich konnt' es nicht verhindern, ward Gesang;
Zum Liede ward mir jede süße Lust,
Zum Liede jeder Schmerz, mit dem ich rang.

Chamisso.

175.

Die wenigsten jungen Leute, wenn sie auch
auf Akademien mehr leuchten als wetterleuchten,
wissen, was sie bloß lernen und worüber
sie weiter denken sollen. Sie lernen Gedanken,
allein sie lernen nicht denken; sie lernen
Philosophie, allein nicht philosophieren;
sie lernen die Gesetze, allein nicht das Recht.

Th. G. von Hippel.

176.

Wenn die deutschen Katholiken sich von Rom
lossagen, versöhnen sie nicht allein ihren Glauben
mit der Bildung der Zeit, sondern erweisen auch
ihrem Vaterlande einen wesentlichen Dank. Sie
entfernen einen äußeren Feind, der mindestens
so gefährlich ist, als es Rußland und Frankreich
sein können, und entwenden der inneren Rück=
schrittspartei einen nötigen Bundesgenossen.

Robert Blum.

177.

Bald ist das Epigramm ein Pfeil,
Trifft mit der Spitze;
Ist bald ein Schwert,
Trifft mit der Schärfe;
Ist manchmal auch — die Griechen liebten's so —
Ein klein Gemäld', ein Strahl, gesandt
Zum Brennen nicht, nur zum Erleuchten.

Klopstock.

174.*

What swelled my breast, unknown to me,
I could not prevent it, turned into song;
To song turned every sweet joy,
To song every ache with which I wrestled.

Chamisso

175.

Very few young people, even in an Academy, light
more than lightning, know what they are merely learning
and what they should continue to contemplate. They learn
thoughts, but they do not learn to think; they learn philosophy, but not to philosophize, they learn laws but not
justice.

Th. G. von Hippel

176.

When the German Catholics separate themselves
from Rome, they not only reconcile their faith with the
current of the present time but also render substantial service to their fatherland. They removed an outside enemy
who is at least as dangerous as Russia or France could be
and deprive the inner retrogressive party of an essential
confederate.

Robert Blum

177.*

Sometimes the epigram is an arrow,
Strikes with the tip;
Sometimes it is a sword,
Strikes with the edge;
Yet at other times—the Greeks loved it thus—
It is a small painting, a ray,
Sent not to burn, only to illuminate.

Klopstock

178.

Rat und Tat.

Wer dir viel Rat und wenig Tat gewähret,
Wenn dich die Last des schweren Kummers preßt,
Ist einer, der die Spinneweb' abkehret,
Und doch dabei die Spinne leben läßt.

A. Gryphius.

179.

Der Mai.

Dieser Monat ist ein Kuß, den der Himmel
gibt der Erde,
Daß sie jetzund seine Braut, künftig eine Mutter
werde.

A. Gryphius.

180.

Freundschaft.

Alten Freund für neuen wandeln,
Heißt für Früchte Blumen handeln.

A. Gryphius.

181.

Wohltaten.

Wer übertrifft den, der sich mild erzeigt?
Der seltne Freund, der es zugleich verschweigt.

Chr. Wernicke.

182.

Auf die Galathee.

Die gute Galathee! Man sagt, sie schwärz'
ihr Haar,
Da doch ihr Haar schon schwarz, als sie es
kaufte, war.

Lessing.

178.
Advice and Action
Whoever grants you a lot of advice but no action
When the burden of heavy cares oppresses you,
He is like one who sweeps away the cobwebs
While at the same time lets the spider live.

A. Gryphius

179.*
May
This month is a kiss which heaven gives to earth
So that it will now become its bride and later a
mother.

A. Gryphius

180.*
Friendship
To exchange old friends for new ones
Is like trading fruit for flowers.

A. Gryphius

181.*
Your Deeds
Who surpasses him who shows himself to be kind?
The rare friend who conceals his action.

Chr. Wernicke

182.*
About Galathea
The good Galathea! One says she colors her hair
black,
But her hair was already black when she bought it.

Lessing

183.
Mein Glaube.

Welche Religion ich bekenne? Keine von allen,
Die du mir nennst! — Und warum keine? Aus
Religion.

Schiller.

184.
Korrektheit.

Frei von Tadel zu sein ist der niedrigste
Grad und der höchste;
Denn nur die Ohnmacht führt, oder die Größe
dazu.   Goethe.

185.
Publikum.

Das Publikum das ist ein Mann,
Der alles weiß und gar nichts kann;
Das Publikum das ist ein Weib,
Das nichts verlangt als Zeitvertreib;
Das Publikum das ist ein Kind,
Heut so und morgen so gesinnt;
Das Publikum ist eine Magd,
Die stets ob ihrer Herrschaft klagt;
Das Publikum, das ist ein Knecht,
Der, was sein Herr tut, findet recht;
Das Publikum sind alle Leut',
Drum ist es dumm und auch gescheut.
Ich hoffe, das nimmt keiner krumm,
Denn einer ist kein Publikum.

Ludwig Richter.

183.*
My faith
Which religion do I profess? Not one of all those
You name! And why not one? Because of religion.

Schiller

184.*
Correctness
To be free of blame is the lowest degree and the
        highest;
For only faintness or greatness leads to it.

Goethe

185.*
The Public
The public is just like a man
Who knows it all but gets nothing done.
The public is a woman
Who asks only for amusement.
The public is a child,
Wanting this today and that tomorrow.
The public is a maid
Who always complains about her mistress.
The public is a servant
Who approves of everything his master does.
The public is all the people,
Therefore stupid and also bright.
I hope no one will take this seriously,
For one man is not a public.

Ludwig Richter

186.
Theophanie.

Zeigt sich der Glückliche mir, ich vergesse die
Götter des Himmels;
Aber sie stehn vor mir, wenn ich den Leidenden seh'.

Schiller.

187.
Unsterblichkeit.

Vor dem Tod erschrickst du! Du wünschest
unsterblich zu leben?
Leb im Ganzen! Wenn du lange dahin bist,
es bleibt.   Schiller.

188.
Das Werte und Würdige.

Hast du etwas, so teile mir's mit, und ich
zahle, was recht ist;
Bist du etwas, o, dann tauschen die Seelen
wir aus.   Schiller.

189.
An die Muse.

Was ich ohne dich wäre? Ich weiß es
nicht — aber mir grauet,
Seh' ich, was ohne dich Hundert' und Tausende sind.

Schiller.

190.
Das eigne Ideal.

Allen gehört, was du denkst; dein eigen ist
nur, was du fühlest.
Soll er dein Eigentum sein, fühle den Gott, den
du denkst.   Schiller.

186.*
Theophany

When a happy person shows himself to me,
I forget the gods in heaven;
But they stand before me
When I see someone suffer.

Schiller

187.*
Immortality

You are afraid of death! Do you want to live immortally?
Live for the whole! Long after you are gone, it
remains.

Schiller

188.*
Worth and Dignity

If you *have* something, then share it with me
and I pay whatever is just;
If you *are* something, oh, then we exchange our souls.

Schiller

189.*
To the Muse

What would I be without you? I do not know—but
I shudder
To see what hundreds and thousands are without you.

Schiller

190.*
The Proper Ideal

What you think belongs to everyone;
only what you feel remains your own.
To make it your property, feel the God of whom you
think.

Schiller

191.

Weisheit und Klugheit.

Willst du, Freund, die erhabensten Höh'n der
          Weisheit erfliegen,
Wag' es auf die Gefahr, daß dich die Klugheit
          verlacht.
Der Kurzsichtige sieht nur das Ufer, das dir
          zurückflieht,
Jenes nicht, wo dereinst landet dein mutiger Flug.

Schiller.

192.

Politische Lehre.

Alles sei recht, was du tust; doch dabei laß
          es bewenden,
Freund, und enthalte dich ja, alles, was recht
          ist, zu tun.
Wahrem Eifer genügt, daß das Vorhandne
          vollkommen
Sei; der falsche will stets, daß das Voll=
          kommene sei.

Schiller.

193.

Der beste Staat.

„Woran erkenn' ich den besten Staat?"
          Woran du die beste
Frau kennst — daran, mein Freund, daß man
          von beiden nicht spricht.

Schiller.

191.*

Wisdom and Cleverness

If you, friend, want to fly up to the loftiest heights
of wisdom,
do it but risk that cleverness will laugh at you.
The short-sighted only sees the shore which recedes
from you
but not where your courageous flight will some day
land.

Schiller

192.*

Political Lesson

Everything be right that you do, but leave it at that,
Friend, and abstain from doing all that is right.
True fervor is satisfied that what is at hand
be perfect;
False fervor always wants overall perfection.

Schiller

193.*

The Best State

How can I recognize the best state?
The same way you recognize the best woman—
when, my friend, one does not talk about either.

Schiller

194.

Licht und Farbe.

Wohne, du ewiglich Eines, dort bei dem
ewiglich Einen!
Farbe, du wechselnde, komm freundlich zum
Menschen herab.

Schiller.

195.

Nicht an wenig stolze Namen
Ist die Liederkunst gebannt!
Heilig achten wir die Geister,
Aber Namen sind uns Dunst;
Würdig ehren wir die Meister,
Aber frei ist uns die Kunst. Uhland.

196.

Der Stachelreim.

Erast, der gern so neu als eigentümlich spricht,
Nennt einen Stachelreim sein leidig Sinngedicht.
Die Reime hör' ich wohl; den Stachel fühl' ich
nicht. Lessing.

197.

Auf Lucinden.

Sie hat viel Welt, die muntere Lucinde,
Durch nichts mehr wird sie rot gemacht.
Zweideutigkeit und Schmutz und Schand' und
Sünde,
Sprecht, was ihr wollt: sie winkt euch zu und lacht.
Erröte wenigstens, Lucinde,
Daß nichts dich mehr erröten macht! Lessing.

194.*
Light and Color
Light, you eternal One, there with the eternal One!
Color, you changeable, kindly come down to man.

Schiller

195.*
The art of song is bound to many proud names!
We consider spirits holy, but names to us are
just vapor; we honor with dignity the masters,
but art to us is free.

Uhland

196.*
The Stinging Rhyme
Erast, who likes to use new and peculiar words, calls
his tiresome epigram a stinging rhyme.   I hear the rhyme
but do not feel the sting.

Lessing

197.*
About Lucinda
She has much worldliness, the gay Lucinda,
she does not blush at anything anymore.
Equivoque, and dirt, and shame, and sin —
talk as you wish, she winks at you and laughs.
Blush at least, Lucinda,
so that nothing will make you blush anymore!

Lessing

198.
Die Ewigkeit gewiſſer Gedichte.

Verſe, wie ſie Baſſus ſchreibt, werden un=
vergänglich bleiben:
Weil dergleichen Zeug zu ſchreiben, ſtets ein
Stümper übrigbleibt.

Leſſing.

199.
Auf das Jungfernſtift zu *.

Denkt, wie geſund die Luft, wie rein,
Sie um dies Jungfernſtift muß ſein!
Seit Menſchen ſich beſinnen,
Starb keine Jungfer drinnen.   Leſſing.

200.
Auf Frau Trix.

Frau Trix beſucht ſehr oft den jungen Doktor
Klette.
Argwohnet nichts! Ihr Mann liegt wirklich
krank zu Bette.

Leſſing.

201.
Die Wohltaten.

Wär' auch ein böſer Menſch gleich einer
lecken Bütte,
Die keine Wohltat hält: dem ungeachtet ſchütte —
Sind beides, Bütt' und Menſch nicht allzu morſch
und alt —
Nur deine Wohltat ein. Wie leicht verquillt ein
Spalt!   Leſſing.

198.*
The Immortality of Certain Poems
Verses like the ones Bassus writes will endure
Because a bungler will always remain to write such
stuff.

Lessing

199.*
About the Maiden Convent at....
Think how healthy the air, how pure
it is at this convent for young virgins!
As long as people remember,
no virgin died in that place.

Lessing

200.*
About Mrs. Trix
Mrs. Trix often visits the young doctor Klette.
Do not suspect anything! Her husband is really sick
in bed.

Lessing

201.*
Good Deeds
Even if a malicious person were like a leaking tub
which does not retain any good deed: neverthless
pour—
and if both, the tub and the person,
are not too decayed and old—
Pour in your good deed. How quickly a leak
can be closed!

Lessing

202.
Das böse Weib.

Ein einzig böses Weib lebt höchstens in der
Welt:
Nur schlimm, daß jeder sein's für dieses einz'ge
hält.　Lessing.

203.
Auf die Phasis.

Von weitem schon gefiel mir Phasis sehr:
Nun ich sie in der Nähe,
Von Zeit zu Zeiten sehe,
Gefällt sie mir — auch nicht von weitem mehr —.
Lessing.

204.
Das schlimmste Tier.

Wie heißt das schlimmste Tier mit Namen?
So fragt ein König einen weisen Mann.
Der Weise sprach: von wilden heißt's Tyrann,
Und Schmeichler von den zahmen.　Lichtenberg.

205.

Wir Protestanten glauben jetzt in sehr auf=
geklärten Zeiten in Absicht auf unsre Religion
zu leben. Wie, wenn nun ein neuer Luther
aufstände, vielleicht heißen unsre Zeiten noch
einmal die finstern; man wird eher den Wind
drehen oder aufhalten, als die Gesinnungen des
Menschen heften können.　Lichtenberg.

202.*
The Wicked Wife

One sole wicked wife at best lives in this world:
Too bad that each man assumes her to be his own.

Lessing

203.*
About Phasis

Even afar, Phasis pleased me very much.
Now that I see her from time to time nearby,
she does not further please me.

Lessing

204.*
The Worst Animal

What is the name of the worst animal?
Thus asked a king a sage.
The sage said: If wild, it is called tyrant,
and flatterer, if tame.

Lichtenberg

205.

We Protestants believe in these enlightened times to live according to our religion. How, if a new Luther should appear, perhaps our times will once again be called the dark age. It is easier to turn or stop the wind than to fasten the opinion of people.

Lichtenberg

206.

Weiß nicht, woher ich bin gekommen,
Weiß nicht, wohin ich werd' genommen,
Doch weiß ich fest: Daß ob mir ist,
Eine Liebe, die mich nicht vergißt.

Kerner.

207.

Um recht zu tun in der Welt, braucht man
nur sehr wenig zu wissen, aber um mit Sicher-
heit unrecht tun zu können, muß man die
Rechte studieren.　　　　　　　Lichtenberg.

208.

Wer aus sich herauslebt, tut immer besser,
als wer in sich hineinlebt.　　　J. G. Seume.

209.

Wo ein einziger Mann den Staat erhalten
kann, ist der Staat in seiner Fäulnis kaum der
Erhaltung wert.　　　　　　　J. G. Seume.

210.

Wer keine Ungerechtigkeiten vertragen kann,
gelangt selten zu Ansehn in der Gegenwart, und
wer es kann, verliert den Charakter für die
Zukunft.　　　　　　　　　　J. G. Seume.

211.

Wer die Krankheit hat, keine Ungerechtigkeiten ertragen zu können, darf nicht zum
Fenster hinaussehn und muß die Stubentür zu-
schließen. Vielleicht tut er auch wohl, wenn er
den Spiegel wegnimmt.　　　　J. G. Seume.

206.*

Don't know whence I came,
Don't know whither I will be taken,
But I know for certain: that above me
There is a Love which does not forget me.

Kerner

207.

To do justice in this world, one has to know very little, but to commit injustice with assurance one has to study law.

Lichtenberg

208.

He who lives outward, he whose life points outward, always does better than the one whose life points inward.

J.G. Seume

209.

When a single man can preserve a state, the state in its corruption is hardly worth preserving.

J.G. Seume

210.

He who cannot tolerate injustice, seldom receives recognition in the present, and he who can, loses his character for the future.

J.G. Seume

211.

A person who has the ailment of not being able to suffer any injustice must not look out of the window and must close the door to his room. Perhaps he would do well to remove a mirror.

J.G. Seume

212.

Der Erzeuger des Kunstwerkes der Zukunft ist niemand anderer als der Künstler der Gegenwart, der das Leben der Zukunft ahnt, und in ihm enthalten zu sein sich sehnt. Wer diese Sehnsucht aus seinem eigensten Vermögen in sich nährt, der lebt schon jetzt in einem besseren Leben, — nur einer aber kann dies: der Künstler.   Richard Wagner.

213.

Nein! Ich kann nicht, wenn ich auch wollte, und könnte ich's, so würd' ich hoffentlich nicht wollen: mir etwas vorspiegeln, nur um für mich Ruhe, mit andern Frieden zu behalten.
David Strauß.

214.

Ein Genie kann nur von einem Genie entzündet werden, und am leichtesten von so einem, das alles bloß der Natur zu danken zu haben scheint, und durch die mühsamen Vollkommenheiten der Kunst nicht abschreckt.   Lessing.

215.

Der spätere Mensch hält zu leicht das Ändern am Jüngern für ein Bessern desselben, aber, wie kein Mensch den andern ersetzen kann, so kann auch nicht einmal derselbe Mensch sich in seinen verschiedenen Altersstufen vertreten, am wenigsten der Dichter.   Jean Paul.

212.

The creator of the work of art of the future is none other than the artist of the present who divines the life of the future and longs to be part of it. He who nourishes this longing in himself with his innermost energy is already living in a better world—but only one person can achieve this: the artist.

Richard Wagner

213.

No! I can't, even if I wanted to, and if I could, then I hope I would not want to: keep up false pretenses, only to maintain tranquility for myself and peace with others.

David Strauss

214.

A genius can only be ignited by another genius, and most easily by one who seems to be indebted only to nature and is not deterred by the laborious perfections of art.

Lessing

215.

An older person too often considers a change in a younger one a change for the better, but, just as no man can represent another, so not even the same man can replace himself in his various stages of life, least of all the poet.

Jean Paul

216.

Wenn dich eine höhere Vorstellung durch=
dringt von einer Menschennatur, so zweifle nicht,
daß dies die wahre sei; denn alle sind geboren
zum Ideal, und wo du es ahnst, da kannst du
es auch in ihm zur Erscheinung bringen, denn
er hat gewiß die Anlage dazu. Wer das Ideal
leugnet in sich, der könnte es auch nicht ver=
stehen in andern, selbst wenn es vollkommen aus=
gesprochen wäre. Wer das Ideal erkannte in
andern, dem blüht es auf, selbst wenn jener es
nicht in sich ahnt.

Bettina [v. Arnim] (Zum zweiten Teil der Günderode).

217.

Denken ist beten.   Bettina v. Arnim.

218.

Schon greift die Überzeugung um sich, auf
welchem schwachen Grunde jene vor kurzem so
gepriesene Starkgeisterei, welche weder an
Wunder noch Mysterien glaubt, ruht, und man
sieht ein, daß ein stärkerer Geist dazu
gehört, an Wunder zu glauben, als
sie zu leugnen.   Solger (ungefähr 1820).

219.

Was die Gottheit sei, wirst du nicht er=
kennen, und wenn du alles erforschend umher=
gehst, wofern sie es dir nicht selbst offenbart.

Sophokles.

216.

If a higher conception of a human being permeates you, then do not doubt that it is the true one; for we are all born for an ideal, and wherever you suspect it in a person, you can make it visible because he surely has a natural faculty for it. He who denies the ideal in himself, cannot understand it in others, even if it were perfectly expressed. For him, who recognizes the ideal in others, it begins to flower even if the other expects it in himself.

Bettina [von Arnim]
(to the second part of *Günderode*)

217.

Thinking is praying.

Bettina von Arnim

218.

One has begun to realize on what weak grounds the so recently praised strong-mindedness, which believes neither in wonders nor mysteries, rests its case, and one comprehends that a stronger mind is necessary to believe in wonders than to deny them.

Solger (circa 1820)

219.

Even if you search far and wide, you will not recognize divinity if it does not reveal itself directly to you.

Sophocles

220.

Die Menschen kommen mir so unaussprech=
lich zerstreut vor, Alle reden und keiner horcht.

Jacobi.

221.

Tote heilen und Greise ermahnen, ist das=
selbe.   Diogenes.

222.

Unter der Tonkunst schwillt das Meer unsres
Herzens auf, wie unter dem Mond die Flut.

Jean Paul.

223.

Wenn ihr's nicht fühlt, ihr werdet's nicht
erjagen,
Wenn es nicht aus der Seele dringt,
Und mit urkräftigem Behagen,
Die Herzen aller Hörer zwingt.
Sitzt ihr nur immer! Leimt zusammen,
Braut ein Ragout von andrer Schmaus,
Und blast die kümmerlichen Flammen
Aus eurem Aschenhäuschen raus!
Bewunderung von Kindern und von Affen,
Wenn euch danach der Gaumen steht;
Doch werdet ihr nie Herz zum Herzen schaffen,
Wenn es euch nicht vom Herzen geht.

Goethe (Faust).

220.

People appear to me incredibly absent-minded.
Everyone talks and no one listens.

Jacobi

221.

Healing the dead and admonishing the aged is the
same thing.

Diogenes

222.

Under music the sea of our heart swells up like under the moon the flood.

Jean Paul

223.*

Unless you feel—your quest will be in vain.
Unless this feeling surges from your soul
With primal force of pleasure, to control
Your listeners' heart—if this you cannot gain—
Just sit forever! Patch and glue each bit,
From someone else's feast concoct a stew,
Puffing the wretched flame you've lit
Out of your own little ash-heap too!
To make apes and children gape and start
Is all very fine—if that is what you seek!
But you will never move from heart to heart
Unless it rises from the heart.

Goethe (Faust)

224.

Probatum est.

A.:

Man sagt: Sie sind ein Misanthrop!

B.:

Die Menschen hass' ich nicht. Gott Lob!
Doch Menschenhaß: er bließ mich an,
Da hab' ich gleich dazu getan.

A.:

Wie hat sich's denn sobald gegeben?

B.:

Als Einsiedler beschloß ich zu leben.

Goethe.

225.

Der Mund ist das L. S., auf das der Kuß
sein glühend Wachs drückt, zur Bestätigung des
Seeleneinklangs.

226.

Es gibt einen Grad der Technik, der zu Geist,
weil zur Vollkommenheit wird.

[1]) Signatur Joseph Joachims. Vgl. Vorwort S. VI.

57

224.*

Probatum est.

A.: One says you are a misanthrope!

B.: I do not hate people, thank God!
But misanthropy: it blew on me,
so I added it.

A.: What happened then?

B.: I decided to live as a hermit.

Goethe

225.[18]

The mouth is the L.S. on which the kiss presses its glowing wax as confirmation of the unison of the souls.

f.a.e.

226.

There is a degree of technique which, because of its perfection, becomes spiritual.

f.a.e

---

[18] In numbers 225 and 226, Joachim uses music notation for his signature f.a.e. See his entry in the Annotated List of Authors.

227.

Demut.

Seh' ich die Werke der Meister an,
So seh' ich das, was sie getan;
Betracht ich meine Siebensachen,
Seh' ich, was ich hätt' sollen machen.

Goethe.

228.

Jeder Künstler ist ein Ödipus; hält er sich
bei den Rätseln der Zeit auf, ohne sie zu lösen,
so wirft sie (die Sphinx) ihn in den Abgrund
der Vergessenheit, und er schreitet nicht an ihr
vorbei in die Zukunft der Unsterblichkeit.

229.

Künstler sollen nicht Diener, sondern
Priester des Publikums sein.   [J. Joachim.]

230.

Handwerker und Künstler.

Ihr, die ihr nur das zufällig Alltägliche auf=
greift und als modisch brauchbar Gerät wieder=
gebet, euch wird schon das nächste Geschlecht
euer Werk aus der Zeit in die Vergangenheit
nachschmeißen, es gegen neue modische Zier ver=
tauschen; aber ihr, die ihr fühlt, was durch alle
Zeiten dauernd zieht, Baumeister, die ihr mit

227.*
Humility
Looking at other masters' works,
I see what they have done;
Contemplating my own stuff,
I see what I should have done.

Goethe

228.[19]
Every artist is an Oedipus; if he dwells on the riddles of time without solving them, the sphinx will hurl him into the abyss of oblivion and he does not stride past her into the future of immortality.

   *f.a.e.*

229.
Artists should not be servants but priests of the public.

[J. Joachim]

230.[19]
Craftsman and Artist
You who seize only the accidental commonplace and render it as a fashionably usable implement, your work will be tossed after you into oblivion by the very next generation, which will exchange it for a newer, more fashionable decoration. But those of you, masterbuilders, who sense what will last through all times, you who create

---

[19] In numbers 228 and 230, Joachim's signature is given in music notation. He used Brahms's Notebooks to enter his quotations.

urewigen Steinen Tempel der Künſte ſchafft,
euer Werk werden auch ſpäte Völker, und
wär's als Ruine, halten lieb und wert.

(Beim Anblick einer Bergſchloß-Ruine.)

231.

Wir müſſen uns hüten, daß der Geiſt eines
geliebten Genius nicht für uns zur Flamme
werde, von der wir armen Schmetterlinge im
Umflattern untergehen.   f. a. e.

232.

Gott nur ſieht das Herz; eben darum, weil
                    Gott nur das Herz ſieht,
Sorge dafür, daß auch wir etwas Erträgliches
                    ſehn.   Schiller.

233.
Entſchuldigung.

Du verklagſt das Weib, ſie ſchwanke von
                    einem zum andern,
Tadle ſie nicht: ſie ſucht einen beſtändigen Mann.

Goethe.

234.

Wir denken gewöhnlich gleich zu viel an das
Herausgeben der Werke, ſtatt daran zu denken,
erſt unſer innerſtes Empfinden in dieſen aus der
Seele herauszugeben.   f. a. e.

temples of the arts with eternal stones, your work, even if in ruins, will be celebrated and loved by coming generations

(While looking at the ruin of a mountain castle.)

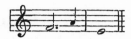

f.a.e.

231.*

We have to be careful that the spirit of a beloved genius does not become a flame for us through which we poor butterflies fluttering around it perish.

f.a.e.

232.*

God only sees the heart; therefore, just because
God sees only the heart,
Take care that we, too, see something tolerable.

Schiller

233.*

Apology

You accuse woman of swaying from one to another,
Do not blame her: she is looking for a constant man.

Goethe

234.

We are usually too much concerned with publishing our works instead of thinking of first publishing in them the innermost feelings of our soul.

f.a.e.

235.

Nur der Mensch ist ganzer Künstler, bei dem das Leben in die Kunst, diese in das Leben verherrlichend eingreift, der Mensch, dem die Kunst nichts Zufälliges ist, das er wie ein Ge= schmeide nach Belieben um= und abhängt.

f. a. e.

236.

Wenn wir den Keim eines Gedankens in uns spüren, so sind wir häufig nur zu ängstlich bemüht, ihn so schnell als möglich ans Licht zu fördern, und er verkümmert so, statt daß wir ihn erst mächtig in uns anschwellen ließen, bis er, von selbst unsre Brust zersprengend, als Ge= sang himmelwärts strebte.

f. a. e.

237.

Vor der Majestät des Gedankens von der Seele Gnaden beuge ich mich, wo ich sie finde, in der Erdhöhle des Zigeuners, oder auf dem Throne des Königs.

f. a. e.

238.

Wer sich vor der Welt ohne Haß verschließt, ist wie die weiße Mohnblüte, die, ihr Innerstes verhüllend, doch noch durch ihre Schönheit wohltut.

f. a. e.

239.

Lobet nicht, bewundert nicht: Liebet, ahmt nach!

f. a. e.

235.

Only that man is a total artist for whom life penetrates art; and art penetrates life in a glorious manner to whom art is not something casual which he may put on or take off like a piece of jewelry.

f.a.e.

236.

When we perceive in us the seed of a thought, we are often too anxiously eager to bring it to light as quickly as possible, so that it wastes away instead of our letting it swell mightily within us until by itself it bursts our breast as a song striving toward heaven.

f.a.e.

237.

I bow before the majesty of thinking of the grace of the soul, wherever I find it—in the cave of the gypsy or on the throne of a king.

f.a.e.

238.

He who shuts himself off from the world without hate resembles the blossom of a white poppy which hiding its innermost core still comforts by its beauty.

f.a.e.

239.

Do not praise, do not admire:
Love and imitate!

f.a.e.

240.

Werke hoher Menschen sind nur die Spuren, die sie auf ihrem Wege zur Vollendung zurück=
legen, nicht diese selbst.   f. a. e.

241.

Die Muschel rauscht auch fern von der See wie Wogengebraus; so tönt's dem echten Musiker auch fern vom Tongewoge im Innern wie Musik.
     f. a. e.

242.

Bei Schiller war die Spekulationsperiode nicht Gefühlskälte; sie war nur die notwendige Dämmerungskühle zwischen der Nacht der Un=
gewißheit und dem Licht der Vollendung.
     f. a. e.

243.

Da hetzen sie sich ab, einander das bißchen Ruhm und Gold abzujagen, und kommen nicht dazu, sich selbst das Kleinste abzugewinnen.
     f. a. e.

244.

Die Jünger, welche um einen Meister sich scharend, Schule bilden, sind an dem Himmel der Kunstgeschichte wie die Milchstraße; einzeln würden sie nicht bemerkt, zusammen geben sie freundlich hellen Glanz.   f. a. e.

245.

Wir erkennen nur Wahrheiten, nie die Wahr=
heit.   Jean Paul.

240.

The works of great men are only the traces which they leave behind on their way to perfection, not perfection itself.

f.a.e.

241.

Even far from the sea, the shell sounds like the roaring waves; and equally, the true musician finds, far from the sound of waves, music resounding in his heart.

f.a.e.

242.

With Schiller, the period of speculation was not coldness of feeling; it was a necessary coolness of twilight between the night of uncertainty and the light of perfection.

f.a.e.

243.

They exhaust themselves to snatch a bit of gold and fame from each other, yet they do not find the time for the smallest gain for themselves.

f.a.e.

244.

The disciples who congregating around the master form a school appear on the heaven of art history like the milky way; singly they would not be noticed, together they produce a bright and friendly lustre.

f.a.e.

245.

We recognize only truths, never the truth.

Jean Paul

246.

Haſt du was Großes im Sinn, ſo zeig' es
              nicht offen dem Volke
Noch im Keime; wie leicht wird es vom Pöbel
              gerafft!
Lieber bewahr' es ſtill und heg' es mit inniger
              Liebe
Tief in der Seele Verſchluß Tage wie Nächte
              hindurch,
Bis es im ſtillen erſtarkt und genähr: vom
              kräftigen Willen,
Kömmt in die Höhe der Welt, ſproſſet und
              blühet zur Frucht.

                              J. Zimmermann.

247.

Alle, die mit dem einmal Gelernten fertig
zu ſein glaubten, ſind klein geblieben; alle, die
immer wieder zu den Urprinzipien zurückkehrten
und Kenntniſſe und Fertigkeiten beobachtend,
lernend, übend ausbildeten, ſind tüchtig geworden.

                              F. v. Schlegel.

248.

Wer kann des Sängers Zauber löſen,
Wer ſeinen Tönen widerſtehn?
Wie mit dem Stab des Götterboten
Beherrſcht er das bewegte Herz,
Er taucht es in das Reich der Toten,
Er hebt es ſtaunend himmelwärts.

                              Schiller.

246.*

If you contemplate something great, do not show it openly to the people when it is still germinating; how easily the masses will snatch it up! It is better to keep it quiet and protect it with gentle love locked deep in your soul, night and day, until it grows strong, and nourished by the strong will comes up into the world, sprouts, and becomes fruit.

J. Zimmermann

247 = 492.

248.*

Who can decipher the singer's magic,
Who can resist his tunes?
With the wand of the gods' messenger
He dominates the agitated heart,
He dips it into the realm of the dead,
He lifts it with wonder heavenward.

Schiller

249.

Schickt nur Gefahr von Osten bis nach Westen,
Wenn Ehre sie von Nord nach Süden kreuzt,
Und laßt sie ringen: o, das Blut wallt mehr
Beim Löwenhetzen als beim Hasenjagen.

Shakespeare.

250.

Schreibe alles auf, von dem du fühlst, daß
es in dir wahr geworden, und wär's eine Re=
miniszenz.   f. a. e.

251.

Alles verwandelt sich; nichts stirbt.   In
schöner Verwandlung wird das Verlorene Gewinn.

Herder.

252.

Ich weiß, es wallt ob dieser
Dreifachen Nebelschicht
Die Sonne, und versendet
Durchs Ätherreich ihr Licht. —
Ich weiß, es thront ob jener
Endlosen Ätherschicht
Mein Schöpfer, und verströmet
Durchs Geisterreich sein Licht.
Bald, bald werd' ich durchbrechen
Dich, düstre Nebelschicht!
Auf endlich freien Schwingen
Mich nahn dem ew'gen Licht.

Elisabeth Kulmann (1825 in ihrem siebzehnten Jahre,
ihrem Todesjahre, geschrieben).

253.

Man kann ebensowohl unter der Schmeichelei
stehen als über ihr.   Wer niemandem traut,

249.*

Send danger from the east unto the west,
So honour cross it from the north to south,
And let them grapple: O! the blood more stirs
To rouse a lion than to start a hare!

Shakespeare [Henry IV,
Part I, Act I, scene 3]

250.

Write down everything which you feel has become
true for you, even if it were a reminiscence.

f.a.e.

251.

Everything is transformed, nothing dies. In beautiful transformation, loss becomes gain.

Herder

252.*

I know that above these three layers of fog there is
the sun sending its light through the ether realm. I know
that above that infinite ether stratum my creator dwells
and he pours forth his light throughout the realm of spirit.
Soon, soon I will break through the gloomy layers of fog,
to approach at last, on free wings, the eternal light.

Elisabeth Kulmann
[written in 1825, in her 17th year, the year of her death]

253.[20]

It is possible to be below flattery as well as above it.
One who trusts nobody will not trust sycophants. One

---

[20] Brahms quoted Macauley in German. The printed English is Macaulay's.

wird auch Schwätzern nicht trauen. Wer den
wahren Ruhm nicht wert hält, wird auch den
erlogenen nicht wert halten.

Macaulay (über Karl II. v. England).

254.

Tristan (als er Genoveva sieht).

Ein echtes deutsches Weib! Vor jedem Blick
Aus eines Mannes Aug' wird sie aufs neu'
Zur Jungfrau und verschließt sich in sich selbst!

Fr. Hebbel.

255.

Der Mensch ist das große Fragezeichen im
Buche der Natur.   Jean Paul.

256.

Um einen Gott zu glauben, bedarf es nur
zweier Menschen, wovon noch dazu der eine tot
sein kann, damit der Lebende ihn durchblättere
und studiere.   Tiedge.

257.

Wir sind nicht, um zu sein; wir werden, um
zu werden.   Tiedge.

258.

Durch nichts bezeichnen die Menschen mehr
ihren Charakter als durch das, was sie lächerlich
finden.   Goethe.

259.

Willst du dich selber erkennen, so sieh, wie
die andern es treiben;
Willst du die andern verstehn, blick' in dein
eigenes Herz.

Schiller.

who does not value real glory will not value its counter-
feit.

Thomas B. Macaulay,
The History of England vol.I, p.160

254.*
Tristan (when he sees Genoveva)
A true German woman! At every glance of a man's
eye, she becomes again a virgin and locks herself into herself.

Fr. Hebbel

255.
Man is the big question mark in the book of nature.

Jean Paul

256.
To believe in God, only two people are necessary of
whom, moreover, one of them may be dead so that the
living one can contemplate and study him.

Tiedge

257.
We are not in order to be; we come to be in order to
become.

Tiedge

258.
Nothing characterizes people more than what they
find ridiculous.

Goethe

259.*
Do you want to know yourself,
then see how the others live;
Do you want to understand the others,
then look into your own heart.

Schiller

260.

Eine edle Seele erträgt so wenig anhaltende Dissonanzen als das Ohr das Gekritzel eines Messers auf Glas.   Raupach.

261.

Wessen Wert nur im Besitz besteht,
Der mag für den Besitz auch alles wagen.
                    Raupach.

262.

Unrecht leiden schmeichelt großen Seelen.
                    Schiller (Don Carlos).

263.

Jeder Jüngling hat ein schönes Zeitalter, wo er kein Amt, und jede Jungfrau eines, wo sie keinen Mann annehmen will, dann ändern sich beide und nehmen oft sich einander noch dazu.   Jean Paul (Titan).

264.

Wahrlich, ich will ebenso gern im Angesicht des Hofes am Geburtstage der Fürstin zu einer Liebeserklärung öffentlich niederknien, als — denn man zeige mir doch den Unterschied — zwischen einem langen Vor= und Nachtrabe das trunkene Auge auf dich, Natur, meine Geliebte heften.   Jean Paul.

265.

Nicht der ist auf der Welt verwaist,
Dessen Vater und Mutter gestorben,
Sondern der für Herz und Geist
Keine Lieb' und kein Wissen erworben.
                    Rückert.

260.

A noble soul tolerates persevering dissonances as little as an ear the grating of a knife on glass.

Raupach

261.*

He whose only worth is in possessions
May also risk everything for the possessions.

Raupach

262.

To suffer injustice flatters great souls.

Schiller (Don Carlos)

263.

Every young man passes through a beautiful period when he will not accept any employment; and every young woman, when she will not accept any man; later both change and moreover often accept each other.

Jean Paul (Titan)

264.

Truly, I would just as gladly kneel down publicly at Court on the birthday of the Princess to declare my love— show me the difference—as to fasten my drunken glance, between a long preceding and following trot, on you, Nature, my beloved.

Jean Paul

265.*

Not he is an orphan in this world
Whose father and mother have died
But one who for his heart and mind
Has won no love and no learning.

Rückert

266.

Damit du nichts entbehrst, war Catos weise
Lehre,
Entbehre.   Voß.

267.
Würde und Wert.

Mein Guter, zwischen Würd' und Wert,
Ist eine große Kluft.
Dein Ehrenamt nur wird geehrt,
Dich selber nennt man — Schuft.   Voß.

268.
Freunde.

Jeder Freund ist des andern Sonne und
Sonnenblume zugleich; er zieht, und er folgt.
                                    Jean Paul.

269.
Die Leiden.

Ein kleines Leiden setzt uns außer uns,
ein großes in uns; eine Glocke mit einem
kleinen Risse tönt dumpf, wird er aber weiter
gerissen, so kehrt der helle Klang zurück.
                                    Jean Paul.

270.

Die Schmerzen der unerhörten Liebe und die
Schmerzen der Ehescheidung erinnern an die
Zähne, welche wehe tun, wenn sie kommen, und
wehe, wenn sie ausgezogen werden.
                                    Jean Paul.

266.

In order to lack nothing, Cato gave good advice: Renounce.

Voss

267.*
Dignity and Worth

My dear, there is a big gulf between dignity and worth. Your noble rank only is honored, you yourself are called a—scoundrel.

Voss

268.
Friends

Every friend is sun and sunflower at the same time for the other; he pulls, and he follows.

Jean Paul

269.
Sufferings

Minor suffering puts us beside ourselves, great suffering into ourselves; a bell with a small crack sounds dull, but when this crack widens, the clear ring returns.

Jean Paul

270.

The pains of unanswered love and the pains of divorce recall our teeth which hurt when they grow and hurt when they are extracted.

Jean Paul

271.

O die Tugend selbst gibt keinen Trost, wenn du einen Freund verloren hast, und das männliche Herz, das die Freundschaft durchstochen hat, blutet töblich fort, und aller Wundbalsam der Liebe stillt es nicht!   Jean Paul.

272.

Die jetzigen Schriftsteller zucken die Achsel am meisten über die, auf deren Achseln sie stehen; und erheben die am meisten, die an ihnen hinaufkriechen.   Jean Paul.

273.

Schwache und verschobene Köpfe verschieben und verändern sich am wenigsten wieder, und ihr innerer Mensch kleidet sich sparsam um; ebenso mausern Kapaune sich nie.   Jean Paul.

274.

Die, welche vom Völkerlichte Gefahren befürchten, gleichen denen, die besorgen, der Blitz schlag' ins Haus, weil es Fenster hat; da er doch nie durch diese, sondern nur durch deren Bleieinfassung fährt, oder an der Rauchwolke des Schornsteins herab.   Jean Paul.

271.

Oh, virtue itself does not console when you have lost a friend, and the masculine heart pierced by friendship continues to bleed fatally, and all the balm of love does not stanch it.

Jean Paul

272.

Today's writers shrug their shoulders mostly about those on whose shoulders they stand; and they elevate mostly those who crawl up on them.

Jean Paul

273.

Weak and confused heads shift and alter the least, and their inner person changes his clothes sparingly; just as capons never molt.

Jean Paul

274.

Those who fear danger from the national light resemble those who worry that lightning will strike a house because it has windows; but lightning never drives through the window but only through the lead frames or down through the smoke cloud in the chimney.

Jean Paul

275.

Der Liebende steht träge auf,
Zieht ein herr Jemine=Gesicht
Und wünscht, er wäre tot.
Der Morgen tut sich prächtig auf,
So silbern geht der Ströme Lauf,
Die Vöglein schwingen hell sich auf:
„Bad' Menschlein dich im Morgenrot,
Dein Sorgen ist ein Wicht!"   Eichendorff.

276.

Nimm dich in acht mit deinem Übermute!
Es ist leicht und angenehm, zu verspotten, aber
mitten in der Täuschung den großen, herrlichen
Glauben an das Bessere festzuhalten, und die
andern mit feurigen Armen emporzuheben, das
gab Gott nur seinen liebsten Söhnen.
                Eichendorff (Ahnung und Gegenwart).

277.

Das sind die rechten Leser, die mit und über
dem Buche dichten; denn kein Dichter gibt einen
fertigen himmel; er stellt nur die himmelsleiter
auf von der schönen Erde. Wer, zu träge und
unlustig, nicht den Mut verspürt, die goldenen,
losen Sprossen zu besteigen, dem bleibt der ge=
heimnisvolle Buchstabe ewig tot, und er täte
besser, zu graben oder zu pflügen, als so mit
unnützem Lesen müssig zu gehen.   Eichendorff.

275.*[21]

The lover arises lazily,
makes a godforsaken face,
and wishes he were dead.
The morning unfolds gloriously,
silver is the flow of the rivers.
The birds are soaring:
"Bathe, little man, in the red sunrise,
your worrying is a dwarf."

Eichendorff

276.

Be careful with your arrogance! Mocking is easy and
convenient, but to sustain in the midst of disappointment
the great glorious faith in something better, and to lift up
others with fiery arms, all this God only gave to his favorite
sons.

Eichendorff (Ahnung und Gegenwart)

277.

True readers are those who compose with and about
the book, for no poet presents a finished heaven; he only
erects a Jacob's ladder from the beautiful earth to heaven.
For him who is too lazy and unwilling, lacking courage to
mount the golden loose rungs, the secret letter will forever
remain dead and he would do better to dig or plow than to
waste his time with useless reading.

Eichendorff

---

[21] Folksy rhymes.

278.

Das Prinzip der individuellen Freiheit und
der politischen Freiheit ist in der unvertilgbaren
Überzeugung gewurzelt von der gleichen Be=
rechtigung des einigen Menschengeschlechts.

Alex. v. Humboldt.

279.

Vollkommenes Gedeihen und Freiheit sind
unzertrennliche Ideen auch in der Natur.

Alex. v. Humboldt.

280.

Man würze, wie man will, mit Widerspruch
die Rede,
Wird Würze nur nicht Kost und Widerspruch
nicht Fehde.   Lessing.

281.

Auf einen adeligen Dummkopf.

Das' nenn ich einen Edelmann!
Sein Ur=Ur=Ur=Ur=Älterahn
War älter einen Tag, als unser aller Ahn.

Lessing.

282.

Auf Dorinden.

Sagt nicht, die ihr Dorinden kennt,
Daß sie aus Eitelkeit nur in die Kirche rennt;
Daß sie nicht betet und nicht höret,
Und andre nur im Beten störet.
Sie bat (mein eignes Ohr ist Zeuge;
Denn ihre Schönheit geht allmählich auf die Neige),
Sie bat mit ernstlichen Gebärden:
„Laß unser Angesicht, Herr, nicht zuschanden
werden!"   Lessing.

278.

The principle of individual freedom and political freedom is rooted in the indestructible conviction of equal rights for a united mankind.

Alexander von Humboldt

279.

Perfect growth and freedom are inseparable ideas, even in nature.

Alexander von Humboldt

280.*

One can spice one's speech with contradictions as much as one wants, as long as the spice does not become the main dish and contradictions do not quarrel.

Lessing

281.*

About an Aristocratic Blockhead

This I call an aristocrat!
His great-great-great-great grandfather
Was one day older than the ancestor of all of us.

Lessing

282.*

About Dorinda

Do not say you who know Dorinda
That she runs to church only out of vanity;
That she does not pray and does not listen
And only disturbs others who are praying,
She asked (my own ear is witness;
For her beauty is slowly diminishing),
She asked with serious gestures:
"Lord, do not let our face become disgraceful."

Lessing

283.
Die große Welt.

Die Wage gleicht der großen Welt,
Das Leichte steigt, das Schwere fällt.

Leſſing.

284.
Für Jungfrauen.

Leſt in der Bibel fein,
Achtet euch klein,
Macht euch nicht gemein,
Haltet euch rein,
Seid gern allein!   Volksausſpruch.

285.

Marthen=Fleiß, Marien=Glut,
Schön wie Rachel, klug wie Ruth:
Frauenzimmer=Heiratsgut.

Volksausſpruch.

286.
Alte Sprüche.

In all' und jeder Zeit
Verknüpft sich Luſt und Leid;
Bleibt fromm in Luſt und seid
Dem Leid mit Mut bereit.

287.

Gut verloren, unverdorben,
Mut verloren, halb verdorben,
Ehre verloren, gar verdorben.

283.*
The Big World
A pair of scales is like the big world,
What is light, ascends; what is heavy, sinks.

Lessing

284.*
For Virgins
Read the Bible,
Consider yourself humble,
Do not become mean,
Keep yourself clean,
Be happy alone.

Popular Saying

285.*
Martha's diligence,
Mary's ardor,
Rachel's beauty,
Ruth's intelligence:
A woman's dowry.

Popular Saying

286.*
Old Sayings
At all times
Joy and sorrow are intertwined;
Remain virtuous in joy
And face sorrow with courage.

[no author]

287.*
Losing property, not damaged,
Losing courage, half damaged,
Losing honor, totally damaged.

[no author]

288.
Der Widerschein des Vesuvs im Meer.

„Seht, wie fliegen drunten die Flammen unter
die Sterne, rote Ströme wälzen sich schwer um
den Berg der Tiefe und fressen die schönen
Gärten. Aber unversehrt gleiten wir über die
kühlen Flammen, und unsre Bilder lächeln aus
brennender Woge." Das sagte der Schiffer er=
freut und blickte besorgt nach dem donnernden
Berg auf. Aber ich sagte: „Siehe, so trägt die
Muse leicht im ewigen Spiegel den schweren
Jammer der Welt, und die Unglücklichen blicken
hinein, aber auch sie erfreuet der Schmerz."

Jean Paul (Flegeljahre).

289.

„Ich kenne keine andern Ungerechtigkeiten
gewiß und genau als die ich an andern verübe.
Die so andere an mir begehen, können mir
wegen der Ungewißheit der Gesinnungen nie
ganz klar und entschieden sein. Aber es gibt
ja mehr Irrtümer des Geistes als der Liebe.
Wenn nun einmal eine Natur, welche die Anti=
these und Dissonanz der meinigen ist, existieren
sollte, wie von allem die Antithesen: so könnte
sie mir ja leicht begegnen; und da ich ebenso=
wohl ihre Dissonanz bin, als sie meine, so hab'
ich nicht mehr über sie zu klagen, als sie
über mich.   Jean Paul (Flegeljahre).

290.

O reiner starker Freund, die Poesie ist ja
doch ein Paar Schlittschuh, womit man auf dem

288.

The Reflection of Vesuvius in the Sea

"See, how the flames fly below the stars, red streams roll heavily around the deep mountain and devour the beautiful gardens. But unharmed we glide above the cool flames and our images smile out of the burning waves." This is what the sailor said and he looked up worried to the thundering mountain. But I said: "See, this is the way the Muse carries lightly in the eternal mirror the heavy misery of the world, and unhappy people look into it, but they find comfort in pain.

Jean Paul (Flegeljahre)

289.

I do not know other injustices as surely and exactly as those which I commit against others. Those which others do to me cannot ever be quite clear and definitive to me because of the uncertainty of the sentiments. But there are more errors of the spirit than of love. If once a nature could exist which is the antithesis and dissonance to mine, as it is the antithesis of everything, it could easily encounter me; and as I am in the same way its dissonance as it is mine, I cannot complain about it any more as it about me.

Jean Paul (Flegeljahre)

290.

Oh pure strong friend, poetry, after all, is a pair of skates with which one easily glides over the smooth, pure,

glatten, reinen, kriſtallenen Boden des Ideals
leicht fliegt, aber miſerabel forthumpelt auf
gemeiner Gaſſe.   Jean Paul (Flegeljahre).

291.

Es folgen ſich in jeder Sache, die man täg=
lich treibt, drei Perioden; in der erſten iſt ſie
neu, in der nächſten alt und langweilig, in der
dritten keines von beiden, ſondern gewohnt.
                                              Jean Paul.

292.

Die Liebe als Sphinx.

Freundlich blickt die fremde Geſtalt dich an,
und ihr ſchönes Angeſicht lächelt. Aber verſtehſt
du ſie nicht: ſo erhebt ſie die Tatzen.
                                              Jean Paul.

293.

Bei allen Mädchen entſchuldige ich es, wenn
ſie ſich ſchön finden, weil ſie ſich nur im Spiegel
ſehen, mithin, wie du aus der Katoptrik wohl
weißt, gerade in einer noch einmal ſo großen
Ferne, als der Fremde ſie; jede Ferne aber,
auch die optiſche, macht ſchöner.   Jean Paul.

294.

Ganz intolerant iſt auch kein Menſch; kleine
Irrtümer vergibt jeder, ohne es zu wiſſen.
Aber freilich ſieht der Eingeſchränkte, gleichſam
im Tal Wohnende, nur einen Weg; wer auf
dem Berge ſteht, ſieht alle Wege. Jean Paul.

the crystal floor of ideals, but only miserably limps along on the common street.

Jean Paul (Flegeljahre)

291.

In all matters done daily, three stages follow each other: in the first, it is new; in the next, old and boring; in the third, none of either but rather habitual.

Jean Paul

292.

Love as Sphinx

The unfamiliar figure gives you a friendly look and her beautiful countenance smiles. But if you do not understand her, then she raises her claws.

Jean Paul

293.

I forgive all girls when they consider themselves beautiful, for they see themselves only in the mirror, hence— as you well know from optic reflexion—at twice the distance the stranger sees her. Every distance, however, also the optical, makes things more beautiful.

Jean Paul

294.

No man is completely intolerant; everyone unwittingly forgives small errors. Yet surely a narrow-minded person, as if living in the valley, sees only one way; whoever stands on top of the mountain sees all ways.

Jean Paul

295.

Über Sachen kann man leicht die fremde Meinung borgen und glauben, aber nicht über Personen. Jean Paul.

296.

Und warum hat das Wörterbuch des Schmerzes so viele Alphabete und das der Entzückung und der Liebe so wenige Blätter? Bloß eine Träne, eine drückende Hand und eine Singstimme gab der Weltgenius der Liebe und der Entzückung und sagte: „sprecht damit!" Jean Paul.

297.

Freundschaftliche Eifersucht ist viel stärker als liebende, schon weil sie nicht, wie diese, ihren Gegenstand zu verachten vermag. Jean Paul.

298.

Ach, wer kann denn sagen im vielfach ver= worrenen Leben: ich bin rein. Das Schicksal hält uns im Zufalle den Vergrößerungsspiegel unsrer kleinsten Verirrung vor. — Ach, über dem leisen, leeren Wort, über sanften Klängen steht eine stille, bedeckte Höhe, aus der sie einen ungeheuren Jammer herunterziehen. (Ein Wort, ein Glockenton reißet oft die Lawine ins Fallen.) Jean Paul.

299.

Das Leben ein Traum.

In Silbernacht ich lag
Und träumt vom goldnen Tag;
Zum goldnen Tag erwacht,
Träumt ich von Silbernacht.

C. F. Scherenberg.

295.

It is easy to borrow and believe somebody else's opinion about things but not about people.

Jean Paul

296.

And why does the dictionary of sorrow have so many alphabets and that of love and rapture so few pages? The world genius gave to love and rapture only a tear, a handclasp, and a singing voice and said: "Speak with these!"

Jean Paul

297.

Jealousy of friendship is much stronger than that of love, if only because it cannot, as in the latter, feel contempt for its subject.

Jean Paul

298.

Alas, who in this multifarious intricate life can say: I am pure. Fate shows us by chance our smallest error in a magnifying glass.— Alas, above the soft empty word, above mild sounds there lies a quiet covered height from which they will pull down a tremendous misery. (One word, one tone of a bell often causes an avalanche to fall.)

Jean Paul

299.*

Life is a Dream

In the silvery night I lay
And dreamed of the golden day;
Waking to the golden day's light,
I dreamed of the silvery night.

C.F. Scherenberg

300.

Adlers Traum.

Tief im finstern Kerker gebannt, saß träumend
der Adler,
Hoch am eisernen Dach spielte verloren ein Strahl.
Lichtwärts hebt sich der Aar — tot liegt er am
Boden zerschmettert:
Toter, zerschlagener Aar! sage, was hast du ge=
träumt?

C. F. Scherenberg.

301.

Fürstenfehler.

Fehler der Fürsten vergleich' ich den wachsenden
Schrecken der Berge:
Oben in schwindelnder Höh', löst sich die Flocke
vom Firn,
Kaum daß dem Haupt sie entrollt, hängt flugs
sich an das Verwandte,
Bis sie, ein donnernder Ball, friedliche Täler
begräbt.

C. F. Scherenberg.

302.

„Unschuld, nur wenn du dich nicht kennst
wie die kindliche, dann bist du eine; aber dein
Bewußtsein ist dein Tod." So scheint gleichnis=
weise zermalmtes Glas ganz weiß, aber
ganzes ist beinahe gar unsichtbar.

Jean Paul (Flegeljahre .

303.

O es ist eine lächerliche und reine Zeit im
frühen Jünglingsalter, wo ein Jüngling die alte

300.*
Eagle's Dream
Deeply banished in a dark jail, the eagle sat dreaming,
High up on the iron roof, a lost ray played.
The eagle rises toward the light—dashed to pieces he
    lies dead on the ground.
Dead, smashed eagle! Tell me what you dreamed?

C.F. Scherenberg

301.*
Princely Errors
I compare errors of princes to the growing horrors of
    mountains:
Up on dizzy heights a flake detaches itself from the
    icy snow.
Barely rolling away from the head, it quickly clings to
    its kinsfolk
Until, a thundering ball, it buries peaceful valleys.

C.F. Scherenberg

302.
"Innocence, only if you do not know yourself, like
the childish one, are you true, but your consciousness is
your death." Thus, in a simile, ground glass seems completely white, whereas whole glass is nearly invisible.

Jean Paul (Flegeljahre)

303.
Oh, it is a ridiculous and pure period in early youth
when a youngster renews the French knighthood with its

französische Ritterschaft mit ihrer heiligen Scheu
erneuert, und wo der Kühnste grade der Blödeste
ist, weil er seine Jungfrau, für ihn eine vom
Himmel geflogene, eine nach dem Himmel
fliegende Gestalt, so ehret wie einen großen
Mann, dessen Nachbarschaft ihm der heilige
Kreis einer höheren Welt ist und dessen berührte
Hand ihm eine Gabe wird. — Unselig, schuld=
voll ist der Jüngling, der niemals vor der Schön=
heit blöde war.   Jean Paul.

304.
Dult:

Was Raphaelens Tränen anlangt — glaube
mir, die Weiber haben größere Schmerzen
als die, worüber sie weinen.
                                             Jean Paul.

305.

Der sanfteste Mensch wird spornstetig,
sobald man seiner Freiheit statt zu schmeicheln,
droht. (So sagt man von Pferden, welche das
Spornen zu nichts bringt als zum Stehen.)
                                             Jean Paul.

306.

Es ist auffallend, wie oft auch ich schon seit
Jahren geschworen, mich meiner Herkunft zu
entsinnen, wenn ich im Publikum bedeutend in
die Höhe und Dicke wüchse . . . . Man kann
nicht früh genug anfangen, sich bescheiden zu
gewöhnen, weil man nicht weiß, wie unendlich
viel man noch wird am Ende.   Jean Paul.

sacred modesty, and where the bravest is precisely the most stupid because he honors his maiden — for him a figure flown down from heaven, flying up to heaven — as if she were a great man whose neighborhood is for him the holy circle of a higher world and whose touched hand becomes for him a gift.— Infelicitous, guilty is the youth who never was stupid facing beauty.

Jean Paul

304[22]

Vult:

As for Raphael's tears—believe me, women have bigger pains than those over which they weep.

Jean Paul

305.

The gentlest man becomes stubborn as soon as one threatens instead of flattering his freedom. (Thus one speaks of horses who just stand still when spurred.)

Jean Paul

306.

It is remarkable how often and for how many years I have sworn to remember my origin if I grew big in height and weight in public.... One cannot begin early enough to practice modesty because one never knows how infinitely much one will become in the end.

Jean Paul

---

[22] Vult and Walt, who figure in numbers 304, 308, and 309, are the protagonists in Jean Paul's novel *Flegeljahre*.

307.

Vielleicht wird der Druck einer niedrigen Abstammung nie schmerzlicher empfunden als in den geselligen Festen, zu welchen die dürftige Erziehung nicht mit Künsten der Freude aus= rüstete, wie Tanz, Gesang, Reiten, Spiel, fran= zösisches Sprechen sind. Jean Paul.

308.
Aus Dults Brief über Kritik.

Er erklärte die gewöhnliche Regelgeberei bei Männern, wie z. B. Goethe, für ebenso unnütz als eine zurechtweisende Sonnenuhr auf der Sonne. Jean Paul.

309.

„Armut", antwortete Walt, „ist die Mutter der Hoffnung; gehe mit der schönen Tochter um, so wirst du die häßliche Mutter nicht sehen. Aber ich will gern dein Simon von Kyrene sein, der dir das Kreuz tragen hilft." „Bis nämlich auf den Berg," versetzte Dult, „wo man mich daran schlägt." Jean Paul.

310.

Ein Ball en masque ist vielleicht das Höchste, was der spielenden Poesie das Leben nach= zuspielen vermag. Wie vor dem Dichter alle Stände und Zeiten gleich sind, und alles Äußere nur Kleid ist, alles Innere aber Lust und Klang: so dichten hier die Menschen sich selber und das Leben nach. Jean Paul.

307.

The pressure of humble descent is perhaps never felt more painfully than at social festivities, for which the poor education has not provided any training in the arts of pleasure such as dancing, singing, riding, playing, or conversing in French.

Jean Paul

308.

From Vult's Letter on Criticism:

He declared the usual rule-giving by men, e.g., Goethe, to be just as useless as a corrective sundial on the sun.

Jean Paul

309.

"Poverty," Walt answered, "is the mother of hope; keep company with the beautiful daughter and you won't see the ugly mother. But I shall gladly be your Simon of Kyrene who helps you carry the cross." Vult answered: "Namely, till the mount where they will nail me to the cross."

Jean Paul

310.

A ball *en masque* is perhaps the highest manner in which life can imitate playful poesy. Just as the poet finds all ranks and times alike, and everything external only a garment, but everything internal joy and song, so do the people here poeticize themselves and life.

Jean Paul

311.

Kaiſer Heinrich:

Narr, der ſelbſt beſchreibt, was er getan —
der Klüg're überläßt es andern.

Agnes:

Das Weib ſieht tief, der Mann ſieht weit.
Euch iſt die Welt das Herz, uns iſt das Herz
die Welt.   Grabbe, Kaiſer Heinrich VI.

312.

Kaiſer Heinrich:

Iſt auch Ofterdingen
Gefallen auf dem Kreuzzug meines Vaters?

Diephold:

Nein, Herr, er lebt in Ungarn, um bei Klingsohr,
Dem Zaubrer, ſeine Kunſt noch zu verbeſſern.

Kaiſer Heinrich:

Die Dichtkunſt auch, die erſte Zauberin,
Bedarf noch andern Zaubers? — Nun, ſo gibt's
Nicht einen Sel'gen unter dieſer Sonne,
Iſt der Dichter nicht beglückt in ſeinen Träumen,
Wie wären wir's im Wachen?
                    Grabbe, Kaiſer Heinrich VI.

313.
Don Juan.

Jedes Ziel iſt Tod: Wohl dem, der ewig
ſtrebt, ja Heil, Heil ihm, der ewig hungern
könnte.   Grabbe.

77

311.

Emperor Henry: A fool who himself describes what he has
                  done—
                  a wiser man leaves it to others.
Agnes: Woman sees deep while man sees far.
                  For you the world is the heart,
                  for us the heart is the world.

Grabbe, Emperor Henry VI

312.

Emperor Henry: Has Ofterdingen also been killed in my
                  father's crusade?
Diephold: No, sir, he lives in Hungary in order to
                  improve his art at Klingsohr the
                  magician's.
Emperor Henry: Does poetry, too, the primal magician, need
                  some other magic?—
                  Well, so nobody is blessed under this sun.
                  If the poet is not happy in his dreams,
                  how could we be while awake?

Grabbe, Emperor Henry VI

313.

Don Juan

Every aim is death: Good for him who strives eternally, yes, blessed, blessed he who could hunger eternally.

Grabbe

314.

Fauſt.

Aus Nichts ſchafft Gott, wir ſchaffen aus
Ruinen! Erſt zu Stücken müſſen wir uns
ſchlagen, eh' wir wiſſen, was wir ſind, und was
wir können.   Grabbe.

315.

Fauſt.

Wozu Menſch, wenn du nach Über=
menſchlichem nicht ſtrebſt?   Grabbe.

316.

Die Ruinen.

Wandrer! es ziemet dir wohl, in der Burg
Ruinen zu ſchlummern,
Träumend bauſt du vielleicht herrlich ſie wieder
dir auf.   Uhland.

317.

Mutter und Kind.

Mutter:

Blicke zum Himmel, mein Kind! Dort wohnt
dir ein ſeliger Bruder;
Weil er mich nimmer betrübt, führten die Engel
ihn hin!

314.
Faust

God creates out of nothing, we create out of ruins.
We have to shatter ourselves to pieces before we know
what we are and what we can do.

Grabbe

315.

Why human if you do not strive for the superhu-
man?

Grabbe

316.*
The Ruins

Wanderer! It well behooves you to slumber in the
ruins of the castle. Dreaming you perhaps gloriously re-
build it for you.

Uhland

317.*
Mother and Child

Mother Look up to heaven, my child! There lives for you
a blessed brother.
The angels led him there so he can nevermore grieve
me!

Kind:

Daß kein Engel mich je von der liebenden
Brust dir entführe,
Mutter, so sage du mir, wie ich betrüben dich
kann.   Uhland.

318.

Märznacht.

Horch! wie brauset der Sturm und der
schwellende Strom in der Nacht hin!
Schaurig süßes Gefühl! Lieblicher Frühling,
du nahst!   L. Uhland.

319.

Die Schlummernde.

Wann deine Wimper neidisch fällt,
Dann muß in deiner innern Welt
Ein lichter Traum beginnen:
Dein Auge strahlt nach innen!

                         L. Uhland.

320.

Meist findet man das, was man Offenheit
nennt, im höchsten Grade just bei den leicht=
fertigsten und gedankenlosesten Menschen; das,
was man Verschlossenheit nennt, gerade
bei den tiefsten, reichsten und treuesten Gemütern
und wirklich: ich teile mich gern mit und liebe
ein volles, freies Ergießen des Gesprächs beim
Becherklange; alles, was ich Edles gedacht, sei

Child: So that no angel will ever carry me off from
         your loving bosom,
    Mother, tell me how I may grieve you.

Uhland

318.*
March Night

Hark! how the storm roars at night and the swollen
stream! Horrid sweet feeling! Lovely spring is near!

L. Uhland

319.*
The Slumbering Girl

When your eyelid enviously drops,
Then in your inner world
A light dream must begin:
Your eye shines inward!

L. Uhland

320.

One often finds what is called *frankness* to the highest degree in the most frivolous and thoughtless people; and what is called *reserve* in the most profound, richest, and truest people, and really: I like to communicate my thoughts, and love a full, free flow of conversation over a glass of wine; all my noble thoughts should not be for me

nicht für mich; es sei, wo möglich, für die
ganze Welt erobert. Aber dennoch gibt's ein
A l l e r h e i l i g ſt e s im Gemüt. Was dort im
innerſten Kern im Verborgnen prangt, das mag
ich nicht hervorheben und im allgemeinen Licht
des Tages eitel und kindiſch glitzern laſſen. Es
bleibe da in heiliger Nacht! Selbſt meinem
Seelenfreunde, ſei er der edelſte Mann, ſelbſt
meiner Geliebten (wenn ich eine hätte) darf ich
in dürren Worten nicht Kunde davon geben.
Weshalb? Ich könnte einen einzigen ſchiefen
Ausdruck brauchen, der andre könnte einen
einzigen Ausdruck ſchief faſſen, und mein Götter=
bild, von einem Hohlſpiegel reflektiert, würde
zur Fratze, entweder gemein und alltäglich oder
gar mißgeſtaltet und lächerlich. Was hätte der
Menſch überhaupt am Menſchen zu ſinnen und
zu forſchen, wenn jeder ſich gleich bis zum
innerſten Grund ſeines Weſens, wie ein Ein=
maleins auswendig herſagen könnte? Was
hätte der Menſch am Menſchen zu **l i e b e n**,
wenn nicht das Unausgeſprochene, nie ganz Er=
forſchte? Vom Heiligen in uns, direkt aus=
einanderſetzend, Bericht zu erſtatten iſt eine
ſchamloſe Entweihung. Hat der andre ein
geiſtiges Auge, das würdig iſt, es zu ſchauen,
ſo möge er ſtill einen jener ſeligen Augenblicke
erwarten, wo der Wolkenvorhang zerreißt und
ein raſcher, faſſender Blick ins Innerſte des
Tempels dem Würdigen gegönnt iſt. Was er
da in mir anſchaut und erkennt, das iſt ſein,
ſo gut als mein, aber mehr geahnt als haus=
backen begriffen; in ſolchen Augenblicken wird

alone; they have been conquered, if possible, for the whole world. Yet there exists something most sacred in the soul. I cannot take out what shines hidden in the innermost soul and let it vainly and childishly glisten in common daylight. Leave it there in sacred night! Even to my dearest friend, be he the noblest man, even to my beloved (if I had one) must I not talk about it in barren words. Why? Because I might use one oblique expression, the other might obliquely interpret one expression, and my divine image, reflected in a concave mirror, would become a grimace, either common or ordinary, or even mangled and ridiculous. What could a human being study and explore in another human being when everyone would recite by heart, like a multiplication table, himself down to the very roots of his being? What would remain to be loved in a human being if not the unsaid, the never completely fathomed? It is a shameless sacrilege to report, with an explanation added, what is most sacred to us. If the other person possesses spiritual vision, worthy to see it, let him quietly wait for that blissful moment when the curtain of clouds tears asunder and a quick comprehending glance into the innermost part of the temple is granted to him who is worthy of it. What he sees and recognizes in me is his as well as mine, more guessed than duly understood; such moments celebrate the high feast of friendship as of love. But I must not reveal any of it in words except in

das hohe Fest der Freundschaft wie der Liebe
gefeiert. Ich selbst aber darf in Worten nichts
davon offenbaren, außer in der D i c h t u n g.
Da darf ich es, denn da geschieht es auf eine,
mir unbegreifliche, göttliche Weise; und überdies
ist die Dichtung kein ums Maul geschmierter
Brei, sondern auch wieder nur Hieroglyphe, die
nur der Würdigste sich ahnungsvoll zu deuten
weiß.   Aus: Friedr. Sallet, Kontraste und Paradoxen.

321.

Es ist mir von jeher total sinnlos und voll=
kommen unbegreiflich erschienen, in ein und
demselben, konkret g a n z e n Individuum, den
D i c h t e r, vom s i t t l i c h e n M e n s c h e n zu
trennen, beide zu vergleichen, oder gar einander
gegenüberzustellen. Denn was in aller Welt
ist denn ein Dichter a n d e r s als das, wohinein
er sein ganzes Fühlen und Denken ausgeströmt,
worin er die Quintessenz seines Ich verkörpert
oder versinnbildlicht hat, nämlich seine W e r k e?
Und was in aller Welt sind denn diese seine
Werke anders als er s e l b s t? Woher hat er
sie genommen? Etwa aus dem Monde, oder
aus der Champagnerflasche? O nein! Seien
Sie versichert, was nicht in ihm war, als sein
innerster Kern, von Ursprung an, das vermag er
auch nicht als K u n s t w e r k (als P f u s c h e r e i
könnte einer es allerdings) außer sich hin=
stellen.
       Ich will sagen: Wer imstande ist, uns im
Kunstwerk w a h r h a f t (dies Wörtlein ist wohl
zu beachten) Hohes, Edles, Göttliches zu geben,
der gibt's a u s s i c h, der ist h o c h, edel, gött=
lich s e l b s t.

poetry. There it is permitted, because there it happens in a divine way, incomprehensible to me; moreover, poetry is not much smeared around the mouth but again a hieroglyph which only the worthiest knows how to interpret with awe.

From: *Friedr. Sallet, Kontraste und Paradoxen*

321.

It has always appeared to me totally unreasonable and entirely incomprehensible to separate in one and the same, concrete, whole individual the poet from the moral person, to compare the two and even place them in opposition. For what else in all the world is a poet but that into which he has poured all his feeling and thinking, that which embodies or symbolizes the quintessence of his self, namely, his works? And what else in the world are his works other than himself? From where did he take them? Perhaps from the moon or a bottle of champagne? Oh no! Be assured, what was not in him as his innermost kernel, from the very beginning, he cannot present as a work of art (but somebody could produce a hodgepodge).

I want to say: an individual capable of giving us in a work of art truly (note carefully this little word) high,

323.

Gewisse Menschen haben gerade im Punkte der Zerfließung den Anschein und die Anlage der Verhärtung am meisten, wie der Schnee kurz vor dem Zerschmelzen gefriert. (Albano.)
                                                    Jean Paul.

324.

Ach du Lieber, der Mensch, besonders der rosenwangige, hält, betrogen, so leicht Bereuen für Bessern, Entschlüsse für Taten, Blüten für Früchte, wie am nackten Zweige des Feigenbaums scheinbare Früchte sprießen, die nur die fleischigen Hüllen der Blüte sind!
                                                    Jean Paul.

324.

Ach du Lieber, was wird denn schmerzlicher und länger gesucht als ein Herz? Wenn der Mensch von dem Meere und auf Gebirgen und vor Pyramiden und Ruinen und vor dem Unglücke steht und sich erhebt, so strecket er die Arme nach der großen Freundschaft aus. Und wenn ihn die Tonkunst und der Mond und der Frühling und die Freudentränen sanft bewegen, so zergeht sein Herz und er will die Liebe. — Und wer beide nie suchte, ist tausendmal ärmer, als wer beide verlor.   Jean Paul.

325.

Die fortgehende moralische Entkräftigung und Verfeinerung wird alle unsre Außenseiten noch so absäubern und ausgleichen — und zwar nach demselben Gesetze, wonach physische Schwächung die Hautausschläge zurückjagt und in die edleren Teile verweist —, daß

noble, and divine qualities, giving them from himself, he is himself high, noble, and divine.

Sallet

322.[23]
[no such number in Krebs]

323.
Certain people have exactly at the point of dissolving the appearance and disposition of hardening just as snow freezes shortly before melting. (Albano.)

Jean Paul

324.
Oh my dear, a man, especially the starry-eyed, easily takes, when deceived, repentance for improvement, resolutions for deeds, blossoms for fruit, just as on the naked branch of the fig tree *fruits* appear to be growing which are really only the the meaty shells of the *blossoms.*

Jean Paul

324 [a].
Oh my dear, what is searched more painfully and longer than a heart? When man stands at the sea and on mountains and before pyramids and ruins and before misfortune, and exalts, then he stretches out his arms to the great *friendship.* And when music and the mood and the spring and the tears of joy move him gently, his heart melts and he wants *love.*—And he who has never looked for both, is a thousand times poorer than he who has lost both.

Jean Paul

[23] Rather than copying many more pages from Sallet, Brahms in his Notebooks merely refers to the page numbers in the editon of Sallet's complete works. Krebs went to the trouble of finding and printing them.

wahrhaftig ein Engel und ein Satan zuletzt in
nichts zu unterscheiden sind als im Herzen.

Jean Paul.

326.

Es ist dem Menschen leichter und geläufiger,
zu schmeicheln als zu loben.   Jean Paul.

327.

Das Alter ist nicht trübe, weil darin unsre
Freuden, sondern weil unsre Hoffnungen aufhören.

Jean Paul.

328.

Habt Mitleiden mit der Armut, aber noch
hundertmal mehr mit der Verarmung! Nur
jene, nicht diese macht Völker und Individuen
besser.   Jean Paul.

329.

Es gibt einen gewissen edlen Stolz, durch
welchen mehr als durch Bescheidenheit Verdienste
heller glänzen.   Jean Paul.

330.

Nicht nach den Kinderjahren, sondern nach
der Jünglingszeit würden wir uns am sehn=
süchtigsten umkehren, wenn wir aus dieser so
unschuldig wie aus jener herkämen.

Jean Paul.

331.

Nicht an unmännlichen Charaktern entzückt
die Milde, sondern an männlichen; wie nicht
an unweiblichen die Kraft, sondern an weib=
lichen.   Jean Paul.

325.

The progressive moral enfeeblement and refinement will so cleanse and equalize all our externals—namely, following the same law according to which physical weakening chases away skin irritations and transports them to the nobler parts—that truly in the end an angel and a devil will not be distinguishable except in the heart.

Jean Paul

326.

It is easier for human beings to flatter fluently than to praise.

Jean Paul

327.

Old age is dim not because our pleasures but because our hopes come to an end.

Jean Paul

328.

Have pity on the poor but a hundred times more on the impoverished! Only poverty, not impoverishment, improves nations and individuals.

Jean Paul

329.

There is a certain noble pride which, more so than modesty, makes accomplishments glow brighter.

Jean Paul

330.

We would long to return, not to the years of childhood, but to the time of youth if only we came out of the latter as innocent as out of the former.

Jean Paul

331.

Gentleness delights, not in unmanly characters, but in manly, just as strength delights, not in unfeminine characters, but in feminine.

Jean Paul

332.

Frühe Hochzeiten, lange Liebe. Ich habe immer gesehen, daß Ehen, die frühe geschlossen wurden, am glücklichsten waren. In späteren Jahren ist gar keine solche Andacht mehr im Ehestande als in der Jugend. Eine gemein= schaftlich genossene Jugend ist ein unzerreißliches Band. Die Erinnerung ist der sicherste Grund der Liebe.

Novalis (Der Großvater im „Heinrich von Ofterdingen").

333.

Die Natur ist das Ideal. Das wahre Ideal ist möglich, wirklich und notwendig zugleich.

Novalis.

334.

Sprechen und hören ist befruchten und empfangen.

L. Tieck.

335.

Aus Ritter Blaubart.

Agnes:

Was ist denn aber am Ende der menſch= liche Verstand?

Simon:

Ja, das können wir mit unſerm eignen Ver= stande nicht leicht begreifen, aber er hat gewiß, wie eine Zwiebel, eine Menge von Häuten, jede dieser Häute wird auch Verstand genannt, und der letzte inwendige Kern ist der eigentliche beste Verstand. Recht verständig sind nun also

332.

Early weddings, long love. I have always noticed that early marriages became the happiest ones. In later years marriage contains no longer the same devotion as in youth. Days of youth enjoyed together are a solid bond. Recollection is the securest foundation of love.

Novalis (The Grandfather in
Heinrich von Ofterdingen)

333.

Nature is the ideal. The true ideal is possible, real, and necessary at the same time.

Novalis

334.

Speaking and hearing is fertilizing and conceiving.

L. Tieck

335.

From *Ritter Blaubart*

Agnes: What really is human intelligence?

Simon: Yes, we cannot grasp it easily with our own intelligence, but it certainly has, like an onion, many skins, each one of these skins is also called intelligence, and the last innermost core is the real best intelligence. Truly intelligent people are those people who have trained in long practice their onion-like intelligence so that they can think about every idea not only with their outer skins but also

die Menschen, die ihren zwiebelartigen Verstand durch lange Übung so abgerichtet haben, daß sie jede Idee, nicht nur mit den äußern Häuten, sondern auch mit dem innern Kern denken. — Bei den meisten Leuten aber, wenn sie auch die Hand vor den Kopf halten, ist nur die oberste Haut in einiger Bewegung, und sie wissen es gar nicht einmal, daß sie noch mehrere Arten von Verstand haben. **L. Tieck.**

336.

Ich muß lachen, wie fromm und moralisch plötzlich unsre Regierungen werden; der König von X. läßt unsittliche Bücher verbieten! Da darf er seine Biographie nicht erscheinen lassen, denn die wäre das Schmutzigste, was je ge= schrieben worden. **Aus G. Büchners Briefen.**

337.

Worte sind an Taten nur Sägespäne von der Herkulessäule. **Jean Paul (Schoppe, im Titan).**

338.
Linda im Titan.

Ich liebe dich fort, wenn du mich liebst. Bist du die Giftblume, so bin ich die Biene und sterbe in dem süßen Kelch. **Jean Paul.**

339.

Wie anders sind die Leiden des Sünders als die des Frommen! Jene sind eine Mond=

with the innermost core! With most people, however, even when they are holding the head with their hands, only the uppermost skin is in some motion, and they do not even know that they possess still more kinds of intelligence.

L. Tieck.

336.

I have to laugh how pious and moral our governments become all of a sudden; the King of X forbids indecent books! Then he cannot permit the publication of his biography, for it would be the dirtiest ever written

From *G. Büchner's Letters*

337.[24]

Words are to deeds merely chippings from the Pillar of Hercules.

Jean Paul (Schoppe in *Titan*)

338.

Linda in *Titan*

I continue to love you when you love me. If you are the poisonous flower, then I am the bee and die in the sweet cup.

Jean Paul

339.

How different are the sufferings of a sinner from those of a pious man! The former are a lunar eclipse by which black night becomes still wilder and blacker. The latter are a solar eclipse which cools and romantically shad-

---

[24] Schoppe is a character in Jean Paul's novel *Titan*.

finſternis, durch welche die ſchwarze Nacht noch
wilder und ſchwärzer wird; dieſe ſind eine Sonnen=
finſternis, die den heißen Tag abkühlt und
romantiſch beſchattet und worin die Nachtigallen
zu ſchlagen anfangen. Jean Paul (Titan, Bd. III).

340.

Wenn die Weiber von Weibern reden, ſo
zeichnen ſie beſonders an der Schönheit den Ver=
ſtand, und am Verſtande die Schönheit aus, am
Pfau die Stimme, das Gefieder an der Nachtigall.

Jean Paul.

341.

Der Menſch darf nicht bei jeder leiſeſten
unſanften Berührung die Fühlhörner einziehen,
wie ein ſchüchternes überempfindliches Käferlein.

E. T. A. Hoffmann (Serapions Brüder).

342.

Danton vor ſeinem Tode.

Das Volk iſt wie ein Kind, es muß alles
zerbrechen, um zu ſehen, was darin ſteckt.

Georg Büchner (Dantons Tod).

343.

Ich ſage euch, wenn ſie nicht alles in hölzernen
Kopien bekommen, verzettelt in Theatern,
Konzerten und Kunſtausſtellungen, ſo haben ſie
weder Augen noch Ohren dafür. Schnitzt einer
eine Marionette, wo man den Strick herein=
hängen ſieht, an dem ſie gezerrt wird, und deren

ows the hot day and during which the nightingales begin to sing.

Jean Paul (Titan III)

340.

When women talk about women, they single out intelligence in beauty, and beauty in intelligence, the voice of a peacock and the feathers of a nightingale.

Jean Paul

341.

A human being should not, like a shy over-sensitive little insect, pull in his feelers at the slightest ungentle touch.

E.T.A. Hoffmann
(Serapionsbrüder)

342.

Danton before his Death

People are like children, they have to break everything to see what lies inside.

Georg Büchner

343.

I am telling you, if they are not given everything in wooden copies, squandered in theatres, concerts, and art exhibits, then they have neither eyes nor ears for it. If someone carves a marionette where one sees the string hanging down which tugs it, and whose joints creak at each step in five-foot iambs, what a character, what consistency!

Gelenke bei jedem Schritt in fünffüßigen Jamben krachen, welch ein Charakter, welche Konsequenz! Nimmt einer ein Gefühlchen, eine Sentenz, einen Begriff und zieht ihm Rock und Hose an, macht ihm Hände und Füße, färbt ihm das Gesicht und läßt das Ding sich drei Akte hindurch herumquälen, bis es sich zuletzt verheiratet oder sich totschießt — ein Ideal! — Fiedelt einer eine Oper, welche das Schweben und Senken im menschlichen Leben wiedergibt wie eine Tonpfeife mit Wasser die Nachtigall, — die Kunst! — Setzt die Leute aus dem Theater auf die Gasse — die erbärmliche Wirklichkeit! — Sie vergessen ihren Herrgott über seine schlechten Kopisten. Von der Schöpfung, die glühend, brausend und leuchtend in ihnen sich jeden Augenblick neu gebiert, hören und sehen sie nichts. Sie gehen ins Theater, lesen Gedichte und Romane, schneiden den Fratzen darin die Gesichter nach und sagen zu Gottes Geschöpfen: wie gewöhnlich! — Die Griechen wußten, was sie sagten, wenn sie erzählten, Pygmalions Statue sei lebendig geworden, habe aber keine Kinder bekommen.

Georg Büchner (Dantons Tod).

344.

An dem Meere ging ich und suchte mir
　　　　Muscheln, in einer
Fand ich ein Perlchen; es bleibt nun mir am
　　　Herzen verwahrt.

Goethe.

If somebody takes a spoonful of emotion, a sentence, an idea, and dresses it up with coat and trousers, makes hands and feet for it, adds some makeup, and lets this thing suffer through three acts, until it finally marries or commits suicide—an ideal!

If somebody fiddles an opera which renders the ups and downs of a human life just as a clay pipe filled with water the song of a nightingale—what art!

Put the people out of the theatre into the street, the disgusting reality! They forget God over his poor copyists!

Of the creation which glowing, roaring, shining, reveals itself to them every moment, they do not hear or see anything. They go to the theatre, they read poems and novels, imitate the faces of those caricatures, and say to Gods' creatures: how common!

The Greeks knew what they were saying when they told that Pygmalion's statue came to life but did not bear any children.

Georg Büchner (Danton's Death)

344.*

I wandered beside the ocean and searched for shells,
    in one
I found a little pearl; it now remains close to my
    heart.

Goethe

345.

Welch ein Mädchen ich wünsche zu haben?
Ihr fragt mich? Ich hab' sie,
Wie ich sie wünsche, das heißt, dünkt mich, mit
wenigem viel.   Goethe.

346.

Seltsam ist Propheten Lied;
Doppelt seltsam, was geschieht.
                         Goethe.

347.

Stets wandle fort auf diesem heil'gen Pfad,
Der dich zum Himmel führt; gut bist du schon,
Und mehr will ich dich lehren; schau hinauf
Zum Firmamente, dorten thront die Macht,
Die Erd der Schemel ihrem Fuße; lern es
Und üb es, wer so hoch hinauf will steigen,
Muß erdwärts keiner Lust sein Auge neigen.
Aus: Die Geburt des Merlin, Shakespeare, Suppl.=Bd. I,
                         Ortlepp.

348.

Was übrigens die sogenannte Unsittlichkeit
meines Buches (Dantons Tod) angeht, so
habe ich folgendes zu antworten: Der dramatische
Dichter ist in meinen Augen nichts als ein Ge=
schichtsschreiber; steht aber über letzterem da=
durch, daß er uns die Geschichte zum zweiten=
mal erschafft, und uns gleich unmittelbar, statt
eine trockne Erzählung zu geben, in das Leben
hinein versetzt, und statt Charakteristiken
Charaktere und statt Beschreibungen Gestalten

345.*

Which girl I would want to have? You ask me?
    I have her
Just as I like her, which means, I think, much with
    small means.

Goethe

346.*

Strange is the prophets' song,
Doubly strange what comes to pass.

Goethe

347.*25

Walk forward on this holy path
Which leads you to heaven; you are already good,
And I want to teach you more. Look up
To the firmament, there thrones the power,
Earth its footstool. Learn
And practice it, he who wants to climb so high
Must not turn down his eye to any desire.

From: *The Birth of Merlin,*
Shakespeare

348.

What concerns the so-called immorality of my book
(*Danton's Death*), I have to answer the following:

The dramatic poet in my eyes is nothing but a historian but stands above him by creating the story for a
second time and transposes us directly into life instead of
telling a dull tale and by giving us characters instead of
characterizations, people instead of descriptions.—His

25The source Brahms indicates is puzzling. *Die Geburt des Merlins* (The
Birth of Merlin), whatever it may be, is not by Shakespeare.

gibt. — Sein Buch darf weder sittlicher noch unsittlicher sein als die Geschichte selbst; aber die Geschichte ist vom lieben Herrgott nicht zu einer Lektüre für junge Frauenzimmer geschaffen worden, und da ist es mir auch nicht übel zu nehmen, wenn mein Drama ebensowenig dazu geeignet ist.

Der Dichter ist kein Lehrer der Moral, er erfindet und schafft Gestalten, er macht vergangne Zeiten wieder aufleben, und die Leute mögen denn daraus lernen, so gut wie aus dem Studium der Geschichte und der Beobachtung dessen, was im menschlichen Leben um sie herum vorgeht. *Aus G. Büchners Briefen.*

349.

Ich verachte niemanden, am wenigsten wegen seines Verstandes oder seiner Bildung, weil es in niemands Gewalt liegt, kein Dummkopf oder kein Verbrecher zu werden, — weil wir durch gleiche Umstände wohl alle gleich würden, und weil die Umstände außer uns liegen. Der Verstand nun gar ist nur eine sehr geringe Seite unsers geistigen Wesens und die Bildung nur eine sehr zufällige Form desselben. Wer mir eine solche Verachtung vorwirft, behauptet, daß ich einen Menschen mit Füßen träte, weil er einen schlechten Rock anhätte. Es heißt dies, eine Roheit, die man einem im Körperlichen nimmer zutrauen würde, ins Geistige übertragen, wo sie noch gemeiner ist. Ich kann jemanden einen Dummkopf nennen, ohne ihn deshalb zu verachten. Die Dumm=

book must be neither more nor less moral than history itself; but the story has not been produced by our Lord God as reading matter for young females, and neither should it be taken amiss if my dramas are just as unfit for it.

The poet is not a teacher of morals, he invents and creates figures, brings the past back to life, and people may learn as much from him as from the study of history or from the observation of human life around them.

From *Büchner's Letters*

349.

I scorn nobody, least of all because of his intelligence or his education, because it lies in nobody's power not to become a fool or a criminal, because equal circumstances would make all of us equal, and because the circumstances lie beyond us. Intelligence, anyway, is only a very minor part of our spiritual being, and education only a very incidental form of it. Whoever charges me with such a contempt asserts that I am kicking a person for wearing a poor coat. This means transferring a rudeness which one would not impute to a person in the physical world into the spiritual world, where it is even meaner. I can call somebody stupid without therefore scorning him. Stupidity belongs to the common qualities of human affairs; I am not responsible for its existence, but no one can forbid me to call everything that exists by its name and to

heit gehört zu den allgemeinen Eigenschaften
der menschlichen Dinge; für ihre Existenz kann
ich nichts, es kann mir aber niemand wehren,
alles, was existiert, bei seinem Namen zu nennen,
und dem, was mir unangenehm ist, aus dem
Wege zu gehen. Jemanden kränken, ist eine
Grausamkeit, ihn aber zu suchen oder zu meiden,
bleibt meinem Gutdünken überlassen. — D a h e r
erklärt sich mein Betragen gegen alte Bekannte;
ich kränkte keinen und sparte mir viel Lange=
weile; halten sie mich für hochmütig, wenn ich
an ihren Vergnügungen oder Beschäftigungen
keinen Geschmack finde, so ist es eine Ungerechtig=
keit; mir würde es nie einfallen, einem andern
aus dem nämlichen Grunde einen ähnlichen Vor=
wurf zu machen. Man nennt mich einen
S p ö t t e r. Es ist wahr, ich lache oft, aber ich
lache nicht darüber, w i e jemand ein Mensch,
sondern nur darüber, d a ß er ein Mensch ist,
wofür er ohnehin nichts kann, und lache dabei
über mich selbst, der ich sein Schicksal teile.
Die Leute nennen das Spott, sie vertragen es
nicht, daß man sich als Narr produziert und sie
duzt; sie sind Verächter, Spötter und Hochmütige,
weil sie die Narrheit nur außer s i c h suchen.
Ich habe freilich noch eine Art von Spott, es
ist aber nicht der der Verachtung, sondern der
des Hasses. Der Haß ist so gut erlaubt als
die Liebe, und ich hege ihn im vollsten Maße
gegen die, w e l c h e v e r a c h t e n. Es ist deren
eine große Zahl, die im Besitze einer lächerlichen
Äußerlichkeit, die man Bildung, oder eines toten
Krams, den man Gelehrsamkeit heißt, die große

avoid what is disagreeable to me. It is cruel to insult somebody, but it is up to me to search him out or avoid him.

    This explains my behaviour toward old acquaintan-
ces; I offended nobody and saved myself a lot of bore-
dom. If they consider me arrogant because I have no taste
for their amusements and occupations, they are unjust; I
would never think of similarly reproaching anybody for
such a reason. One calls me a mocker. True, I often laugh,
but do not laugh at *how* he is but only *that* he is human,
for which he anyway is not responsible, and besides laugh
at myself for sharing his fate. People call this mockery,
they do not tolerate that one presents oneself as a fool on
the same level with them. They are scorners, mockers,
and snobs, because they look for foolishness only outside
themselves.

    I have, it is true, also another kind of mockery, but
not that of contempt but of hate. Hate is as well permitted as love, and I cherish it fully against those who nurse
contempt. There are many of them who, possessing a lu-
dicrous externality called education or a dead rubbish called
scholarship, sacrifice the large mass of their brothers to
their egotistic contempt. Aristocratism is the most shame-
ful contempt for the sacred spirit in man; against it I turn

Maſſe ihrer Brüder ihrem verachtenden Egoismus
opfern. Der Ariſtokratismus iſt die ſchändlichſte
Verachtung des heiligen Geiſtes im Menſchen;
gegen ihn kehre ich ſeine eigenen Waffen; Hoch=
mut gegen Hochmut, Spott gegen Spott. — Ihr
würdet euch beſſer bei meinem Stiefelputzer nach
mir umſehen, mein Hochmut und Verachtung
Geiſtesarmer und Ungelehrter fände dort wohl
ihr beſtes Objekt. Ich bitte, fragt ihn einmal . . .
Die Lächerlichkeit des Herablaſſens werdet ihr
mir doch wohl nicht zutrauen. Ich hoffe noch
immer, daß ich leidenden, gedrückten Geſtalten
mehr mitleidige Blicke zugeworfen als kalten,
vornehmen Herzen bittere Worte geſagt habe.

                          Aus G. Büchners Briefen.

350.

Wie es mit dem Streite der Schweiz mit
Frankreich gehen wird, weiß der Himmel. Doch
hörte ich neulich jemand ſagen: „Die Schweiz
wird einen kleinen Knicks machen, und Frank=
reich wird ſagen, es ſei ein großer geweſen."
Ich glaube, daß er recht hat.

                          Aus G. Büchners Briefen.

351.

„Ich bete dich an, Vernunft, Tochter Gottes,
Schirmherrin der Männer, Atem der Seele! Ich
bete dich an im Geiſt und in der Wahrheit.
Du erſchütterſt mir Herz und Nieren; führe
mich, bleibe bei mir bis an das Ende meiner

its own weapons, haughtiness against haughtiness, mockery against mockery.—

You would not, I trust, suspect me of the ridiculousness of condescension. I still hope to have cast more glances of sympathy at suffering, oppressed figures than said bitter words to cold, noble hearts.

From *G. Büchner's Letters*

350.

Heaven only knows what will happen to the quarrel between Switzerland and France. But the other day I heard someone say: "Switzerland will make a small curtsy, and France will say it was a big one." I believe he is right.

From *G. Büchner's Letters*

351.

I worship you, reason, God's daughter, men's protector, the soul's breath! I worship you in spirit and in truth. You shake my heart and kidneys; lead me, stay with me until the end of my days! A simple, colorless prayer, a prayer like a servant! I shall try to manage with it."

Immermann
Münchhausen (at the end of volume 2)

Tage! Ein schlichtes, farbloses Gebet, ein Gebet
in Knechtsgestalt! Ich will damit auszukommen
suchen."

Immermann (Münchhausen zum Schluß des 2. Bandes).

352.

Ein feierliches Lied, der beste Tröster zur
Heilung irrer Phantasie.   Shakespeare (Sturm).

353.

(Schauspieler kommen mit Flöten.)

Hamlet:

O die Flöten! Laßt mich eine sehn. Um
Euch insbesondere zu sprechen!

(Nimmt Güldenstern beiseite.)

Weswegen geht Ihr um mich herum, um
meine Witterung zu bekommen, als wolltet Ihr
mich in ein Netz treiben?

Güldenstern:

O gnädiger Herr, wenn meine Ergebenheit
allzu kühn ist, so ist meine Liebe ungesittet.

H.:

Das versteh' ich nicht recht. Wollt Ihr auf
dieser Flöte spielen?

G.:

Gnädiger Herr, ich kann nicht.

H.:

Ich bitte Euch.

G.:

Glaubt mir, ich kann nicht.

352.*
A solemn air and the best comforter
To an unsettled fancy, cure the brains.

Shakespeare
The Tempest V/I, 58-59.

353.[26]
Enter players, with recorders.

Hamlet: O! the recorders: let me see one. To withdraw with
you: why do you go about to recover the wind of me,
as if you would drive me into a toil?

Guildenstern: O! my lord, if my duty be too bold, my love
is too unmannerly.

Hamlet: I do not well understand that. Will you play upon
this pipe?

Guildenstern: My lord, I cannot.

Hamlet: I pray you.

Guildenstern: Believe me, I cannot.

Hamlet: I do beseech you.

Guildenstern: I know no touch of it, my lord.

---

[26] Brahms quotes in German.

H.:

Ich ersuche Euch darum.

G.:

Ich weiß keinen einzigen Griff, gnädiger Herr.

H.:

Es ist so leicht wie lügen. Regiert diese Windlöcher mit Euren Fingern und den Klappen, gebt der Flöte mit Eurem Munde Odem, und sie wird die beredteste Musik sprechen. Seht Ihr, dies sind die Griffe.

G.:

Aber die habe ich eben nicht in meiner Gewalt, um irgendeine Harmonie hervorzubringen; ich besitze die Kunst nicht.

H.:

Nun seht Ihr, welch ein nichtswürdiges Ding Ihr aus mir macht? Ihr wollt auf mir spielen, Ihr wollt in das Herz meines Geheimnisses dringen, Ihr wollt mich von meiner tiefsten Note bis zum Gipfel meiner Stimme hinauf prüfen, und in dem kleinen Instrument hier ist viel Musik, eine vortreffliche Stimme, dennoch könnt Ihr es nicht zum Sprechen bringen. Wetter! denkt Ihr, daß ich leichter zu spielen bin als eine Flöte? Nennt mich, was für ein Instrument Ihr wollt, Ihr könnt mich zwar verstimmen, aber nicht auf mir spielen.   Shakespeare.

Hamlet: 'Tis as easy as lying; govern these ventages with finger
and thumb, give it breath with your mouth, and it
will discourse most eloquent music. Look, these are
the stops.

Guildenstern: But these cannot I command to any utterance
of harmony; I have not the skill.

Hamlet: Why, look you know, how unworthy a thing
you make of me. You would play upon me; you
would seem to know my stops; you would pluck out
the heart of my mystery; you would sound me from
the lowest note to the top of my compass; and there
is much music, excellent voice, in this little organ, yet
cannot you make it speak. 'Sblood, do you think I
am easier to be played on than a pipe? Call me
what instrument you will, though you can fret me,
you cannot play upon me.

Shakespeare

354.

Die Scheerauer Konzerte sind bloß in Musik gesetzte Stadtgespräche und prosaische Melodramen, worin die Sesselreden der Zuhörer wie gedruckter Text unter der Komposition hinspringen.　　　　　　　　　Jean Paul.

355.

Von jeher machte ein fortbebender Ton mich traurig.　　　　　　　　　Jean Paul.

356.

Ich habe mir oft gewünscht, nur so reich zu werden, daß ich mir (wie die Griechen taten) einen eigenen Kerl halten könnte, der so lange musizierte, als ich schriebe. — Himmel! welche opera omnia sprössen heraus! Die Welt erlebte doch das Vergnügen, daß, da bisher viele poetische Flickwerke (z. B. die Medea) Anlaß zu musikalischen Musikwerken waren, sich der Fall umkehrte, und daß musikalische Nieten poetische Treffer gäben.　　　　Jean Paul.

357.

Drüben in der Abendgegend brauste am Himmel statt des Vogelgesangs das himmlische Pedal, der Donner.　　　　Jean Paul.

358.

In kalten Ländern ergötzen die Vögel mit einer schönen Stimme, in warmen nur mit schönem Gefieder.　　　　　　　Jean Paul.

354.

The concerts in Scheerau are nothing but city gossip put in music and prosaic melodramas in which the listeners' chair-conversations like printed text jump below the composition.

Jean Paul

355.

A continuous vibrating tone has always made me sad.

Jean Paul

356.

I have often wished that I would become just rich enough so that I, like the Greeks, could afford to have a servant make music while I write. Heavens, what *opera omnia* would result! The world would have the pleasure to see that, instead of the many poetic patchworks (e.g., Medea) which were the occasion for musical masterworks, the situation would be reversed and musical flops would produce high-ranking poetry.

Jean Paul

357.

Over there toward sunset, replacing birdsong, on the sky roared the heavenly pedal, thunder.

Jean Paul

358.

In cold countries birds entertain with a beautiful voice, in warm climates only with beautiful feathers.

Jean Paul

359.

Darum wird ja diese Erde alle Tage ver=
finstert, wie Käfige der Vögel, damit wir im
Dunkeln leichter die höheren Melodien fassen.

Jean Paul.

360.

So lässet eine Frau ihre Meinung, sobald
sie auch der Mann annimmt, fahren: sogar in
der Kirche singen die Weiber, um mit den
Männern in nichts eintönig zu sein, das Lied
um eine Oktave höher als diese. Jean Paul.

361.

Wie Nachtigallen am liebsten vor einem Echo
schlagen, so spricht unser Herz am lautesten vor
Tönen.

Jean Paul.

362.

Mir ist bei der Musik, als hörte ich eine
laute Vergangenheit oder eine laute Zu=
kunft. Die Musik hat etwas Heiliges, sie
kann nichts als das Gute malen, verschieden
von andern Künsten.

Jean Paul.

363.

Echo das Mondlicht des Klanges.

Jean Paul.

364.

Wenn Töne schon ein ruhendes Herz er=
schüttern, wie weit mehr ein tief bewegtes. Als
der volle Baum der Harmonie über ihm (Walt,

359.

This earth is darkened every day like bird cages so that in the dark we can more easily reach the higher melodies.

Jean Paul

360.

A woman discards her opinion as soon as the man adopts it: even in church the women sing the melody one octave higher than the men, so as never to be in unison with them.

Jean Paul

361.

Just as nightingales most like to sing before an echo, so our heart speaks most loudly before tones.

Jean Paul

362.

When there is music, it is as if I heard a resounding past or a resounding future. Music possesses something sacred, it can depict only the good, differing from other arts.

Jean Paul

363.

Echo, the moonlight of sound.

Jean Paul

364.

When tones already affect a heart at rest, how much more so a deeply agitated one. When the full tree of harmony rustled above him (Walt in *Flegeljahre)*, there de-

in den Flegeljahren) rauſchte, ſo ſtieg daraus
ein neuer, ſeltſamer Geiſt zu ihm herab, der
weiter nichts zu ihm ſagte als: weine!

Jean Paul.

365.

Man verſteht das Künſtliche gewöhnlich
beſſer als das Natürliche. Es gehört mehr Geiſt
zum Einfachen als zum Kompliزierten, aber
weniger Talent.   Novalis.

366.

Ich weiß, wir werden durch das Lied
Die Freiheit nicht erſingen, —
Doch in des Volkes Seele zieht
Der Mut auf Liederſchwingen!

Hermann Rollet.

367.

Singen kann ich nicht wie du,
Und wie ich nicht der und jener,
Kannſt du's beſſer, ſing friſch zu!
Andre ſingen wieder ſchöner,
Droben an dem Himmelstor
Wird's ein wunderbarer Chor.

Eichendorff.

368.

Verklagt die Mitwelt bei der Nachwelt nicht;
In Bergesklüften ſchläft der Widerhall
Und ſchläft in aller Herzen, wem ein Gott
Die Macht verliehen hat, der ruft ihn wach.
Und das iſt Sängerslohn.   Chamiſſo.

scended upon him a new strange spirit which said nothing else to him but: weep!

Jean Paul

365.

One usually understands the artificial better than
the natural. Greater spirit is needed for simple than for
complicated things, but less talent.

Novalis

366.*

I know that with a tune
Our liberty will not be won, —
But in the people's soul
Courage moves on the wings of song.

Hermann Rollet

367.*

I cannot sing like you,
And like me not this one and that one.
If you can do it better, sing freely!
Others sing more beautifully,
It becomes a wonderful chorus
At the gates of heaven above.

Eichendorff

368.*

Do not accuse the present at the court of the future;
Resonance is sleeping in mountainous chasms
And in all hearts. To whom a God has conferred the
        power,
He will awaken it, this is the singer's reward.

Chamisso

369.
Die Tonkunst.

O Töne, ohne Worte
Sprecht zu den Herzen ihr,
Erreget allgewaltig
Der Seele Tiefen mir.

Geheimnisvoll und dennoch
Wie Menschenworte klar,
Ist eure Geistersprache,
Prophetisch, ernst und wahr.

Oft weckt aus ihrem Grabe
Ihr die Vergangenheit,
Und rüttelt nah vors Auge
Mir Szenen künft'ger Zeit.

Elisabeth Kulmann (1822, in ihrem 14. Jahr geschrieben).

370.

Wie überall, besonders im Brautstand gegen
den Ehestand, halten die Menschen, wie in der
Musik, den Vorschlag länger und stärker als
die Hauptnote.   Jean Paul (Flegeljahre).

371.

Meide die große Welt möglichst, ihre Hops=
tänze sind aus F=Moll gesetzt.   Jean Paul.

372.

Dichter bauen, wie die afrikanischen Völker,
ihre Brotfelder am liebsten unter Musik und
nach dem Takte an.   Jean Paul.

369.*
Music

Oh tones, without words
You speak to the heart,
Stir forcefully
The depth of my soul.

Secret and yet
Clear like human words
Is your language of spirits,
Prophetic, serious, and true.

Often you wake from its grave
The past,
And shake before my eye
Scenes of a future time.

Elisabeth Kulmann (1822,
written in her 14th year)

370.

Everywhere, especially in an engagement as opposed
to marriage, do people, as in music, hold the suspension
longer and stronger than the resolution.

Jean Paul (Flegeljahre)

371.

Avoid the big world as much as possible, its skip-
dances are in F-minor.

Jean Paul

372.

Poets like Africans like to cultivate their fields with
music and in time.

Jean Paul

373.

Im unermeßlichen Äther der Tonkunst kann alles fliegen und kreisen, die schwerste Erde, das leichteste Licht, ohne zu begegnen und an= zustoßen.   Jean Paul (Flegeljahre).

374.

Die Tonkunst ist die heilige, die Madonna unter den Künsten; sie kann nichts gebären und darstellen als das Sittliche. Selig ist eine Priesterin dieser Madonna und ihr Gesang ist nur ein anderes Gebet.   Jean Paul.

375.

O bringt die Töne weg, wenn das Herz voll ist und doch nicht überfließen soll.
                                    Jean Paul.

376.

Alle Glieder veraltern am Menschen, aber doch nicht das Herz. Und wenn, wie in der Haydnschen Symphonie [1]), ein Konzertist um den andern sein Licht auslöscht und mit dem Instru= ment hinausgeht, und ich etwa der Kontrabassist

---

[1]) Jean Paul denkt hier an die sogenannte „Abschieds= symphonie", die Haydn 1772 in Esterház schrieb, als der Fürst seinen Aufenthalt auf dem Lande gar zu lange ausdehnte, während die Kapellmusiker sich nach ihren Familien in Eisen= stadt sehnten. Das Aufbrechen eines Künstlers nach dem andern sollte ihre Ungeduld, wegzukommen, ausdrücken. Der Fürst ver= stand auch, was Haydn wollte, und sagte ihm am Schluß: „Ich habe Ihre Absicht wohl durchschaut, die Musiker sehnen sich nach Hause — nun gut — morgen packen wir." Übrigens spielt nicht, wie Jean Paul annimmt, der Kontrabassist zuletzt, sondern zwei Geigen.

373.

In the infinite ether of music, everything, the heaviest planet, the lightest light, can fly and circulate without meeting and colliding.

Jean Paul (Flegeljahre)

374.

Music is the saint, the madonna among the arts; it can give birth and represent nothing that is not ethical. Blessed is a priestess of this madonna, and her song is only another prayer.

Jean Paul

375.

Oh take away the tones when the heart is full and yet must not overflow.

Jean Paul

376.[27]

All members of the human body age except the heart. And when, as in Haydn's Farewell Symphony, one musician after the other puts out his light and leaves with his instrument, and if I were the doublebass who is the last one to play—but no, I shall extinguish my light earlier

---

[27] In a long footnote, Krebs refers to the Farewell Symphony and corrects Jean Paul's statement that the double bass ends the composition, rather than two violins.

sein soll, der zuletzt spielt, — ach nein, ich werde
schon eher mein Licht ausblasen und die Noten
einstecken; aber wär's auch, wir kommen doch
alle, wie in dem Haydnschen Stücke, mit unsern
Lichtern wieder. Jean Paul.

377.

Die Tonkunst.

Chladni bauet mit Tönen Gestalten aus
Steinchen, Amphion aus Steinen, Orpheus aus
Felsen, der Tongenius aus Menschenherzen, und
so bauet die Harmonie die Welt. Jean Paul.

378.

Dreiklang.

Das Leben, das Sterben, die Unsterblichkeit;
diese drei bilden den Dreiklang der menschlichen
Endlichkeit. Jean Paul (Aus einem Traum: der Tod
in der letzten zweiten Welt).

379.

Nur die Töne allein konnten sich nicht verändern, denn sie sind selber Seelen. Sie waren
schon auf der alten tiefen Erde bei uns gewesen und waren uns nachgegangen durch die
Sonne, durch den Sirius und den unendlichen
Sternenweg; sie waren die Engel Gottes, die
uns von seinen Himmelshöh'n erzählten, daß
das Herz vor lauter Sehnsucht in seinen eigenen
Tränen starb. Jean Paul.

and take the music with me; but even so, all of us, as in the Haydn symphony, come back again, bringing our lights.

Jean Paul

377.
Music

Chladni with tones builds shapes from pebbles, Amphion from stones, Orpheus from rocks, the musical genius from human hearts, and thus harmony builds the world.

Jean Paul

378.
Triad

Life, death, immortality, these three form the triad of human finiteness.

Jean Paul (From a Dream:
Death in the Last Second
World.)

379.

Only tones could not change, for they are themselves souls. They were with us already on the old deep earth and went with us through the sun, through Sirius, and the infinite way of the stars. They were God's angels who told us of his heavenly vault so that the heart, filled with desire, died in its own tears.

Jean Paul

380.

Vor die Stürme stelle eine Äolsharfe, aber
kein brennendes Licht. (Leidenschaften.)

Jean Paul.

381.

O Natur, mit deinem Hauche läutere die
Seele, daß sie
Widerhalle rein dein Glockenspiel, das reine!
Gib, daß in den großen Einklang deiner
Stimme, jedes
Menschenherz harmonisch schmelze, ob es jauchz',
ob weine! Rückert.

382.

„Kann nicht der Mann, was er will?" So
trotzet der schwärmende Jüngling,
Während der Weise zuletzt immer nur will, was
er darf. v. Brinckmann.

383.

Der kalt und einseitig urteilenden Welt ist
nicht zu verargen, wenn sie alles, was phan=
tastisch hervortritt, für lächerlich und verwerf=
lich achtet; der denkende Kenner der Menschheit
aber muß es nach seinem Werte zu würdigen
wissen. Goethe.

384.

Nicht das hochauffahrende Wogen, sondern
die glatte Tiefe spiegelt die Welt. Jean Paul.

380.

In the way of approaching storms, place an Aeolian
harp but not a burning light. (Passions.)

Jean Paul

381.*

Oh nature, with your breath purify the soul so that
Pure it resonate your chime, the pure!
Give that in the great unison of your voice every
Human heart melt harmonically, whether it exult or
    weep!

Rückert

382.*

"Can a man not do what he wants?" Thus defies the
fervent youth, while the sage at the end always only wants
what is allowed.

von Brinckmann

383.

One cannot blame the cold and biased world when
it rejects all that appears fanciful as ridiculous or objec-
tionable; but the intelligent connoisseur of mankind must
know to judge everything according to its worth.

Goethe

384.

Not the highrising wave but the smooth depth mirrors the
world.

Jean Paul

385.

Greif, Sänger, wieder in den eignen Busen,
In deines eignen teuren Volks Geschichte!
Da oder nirgends wohnen deine Musen.

G. Herwegh.

386.

Vor jedem steht ein Bild des, was er
                        werden soll,
Solang' er das nicht ist, ist nicht sein Friede voll.

Rückert.

387.

Es gibt keine Regel, die ich nicht zum Besten
des Effekts aufgeopfert hätte.   Gluck.

388.

Es sterbe Streit und Hader!
Doch, nicht zu früh! denn wie aus Kontra=
                        punkten
Der Musika, so muß aus Kampf und Streit,
Des Geistes Einklang mit sich selbst entstehn.

3. Werner.

389.

Und wie die Welt, so ist ihr Lohn,
Es reut mich jeder Liedeston,
Der aufs verworrene Getriebe,
Der Zeit sich wandt' und nicht auf Liebe.

Rückert.

390.

Gerade das Erhebendste wird der gewöhn=
lichen Welt am leichtesten unbedeutend.

Thibaut.

385.*

Reach, singer, again into your own bosom,
Into the story of your own dear people!
There or nowhere is the abode of your muses.

G. Herwegh

386.*

Everyone has a vision of what he shall become.
As long as he has not embodied it, he is not fully at
        peace.

Rückert

387.

There is no rule which I would not have sacrificed
in the interest of effect.

Gluck

388.*

Death to struggle and discord!
But not too soon! For as from counterpoints
In music, so must arise from conflict and struggle
the unison of the spirit with itself.

Z. Werner

389.*

As the world is, so is its reward.
I regret each tone of a song
Which turned to the chaos of the time
And not to love.

Rückert

390.

It is particularly the sublime which for the common
world most readily becomes insignificant.

Thibaut

391.

Ja Menschenstimme hell aus froher Brust
Du bist doch die gewaltigste und triffst
Den rechten Grundton, der verworren anklingt,
In all den tausend Stimmen der Natur.

Eichendorff.

392.

Reich und vielfach beglückt ist der Sterbliche,
                        welcher die Weisheit
Sich zur Führerin wählt, und zur Gefährtin
                        die Kunst. Jacobi.

393.

Der Aar steigt einsam, doch das Volk der
Krähen schart sich.   Byron.

394.

Musik ertönet durch das Schilf des Weihers,
Musik auch in des Bächleins Widerspiel,
Musik in allem — wollte man nur hören!
Die Erd ist Widerhall von Himmelschören.

F. Schlegel.

395.

Laßt unverzagt uns vorwärtsschreiten,
Es schlummern in den goldnen Saiten,
Noch unbekannte Kräfte viel.   F. Schlegel.

396.

Das Liederwesen,
Ich meine so der Ton, die Melodie,
Das tut uns, mein' ich, not wie Brot und Wasser.

3. Werner.

391.*

Yes, the human voice, clear voice, clear from a happy
       breast,
You are the mightiest, you hit
The right fundamental tone which sounds confused
In all the thousand voices of nature.

Eichendorff

392.*

Rich and happy in many ways is the mortal who
chooses wisdom as his guide and art as his companion.

Jacobi

393.*28

An eagle rises alone:
But the band of crows congregates.

Byron

394.*

Music is heard in the reeds of the pond,
Music, too, in the ripple of the brook;
Music in everything—if only one wanted to hear!
The earth is the echo of heavenly choirs.

F. Schlegel

395.*

Let us bravely move forward.
In the golden strings
Many still unknown forces are slumbering.

F. Schlegel

396.*

The existence of song, I mean tone and melody, is
as essential to us, I mean, as bread and water.

Z. Werner

---

28 In the Notebook, Byron is cited as the author, but the quotation is from
John Webster's *The Duchess of Malfi*, V/2.

397.

O wie soll der Nachtigallen
Seele denn ins Ohr dir fallen,
Wenn dir immer noch vor Ohren
Summet das Geschwätz von Toren?

Rückert.

398.

Wo aber die natürliche Musika durch die
Kunst geschärft und poliert wird, da siehet und
erkennt man erst zum Teil (denn gänzlich kann's
nicht begriffen noch verstanden werden) mit
großer Verwunderung die große und vollkommene
Weisheit Gottes in seinem wunderbarlichen Werke.

Luther.

399.

O blicke nicht nach dem, was jedem
fehlt;
Betrachte, was noch einem jeden bleibt.

Goethe.

400.

Nicht mit Unrecht kann man sagen, daß der
Fleiß wie ein Magnet durch fortgesetztes Tragen
unglaublicher Lasten immer mächtiger wird,
während die Trägheit ein Stahl in der Scheide
ist, den zuletzt doch der Rost zernagt.

Immermann.

401.

Wer das Tiefste gedacht, liebt das Lebendigste,
Hohe Tugend versteht, wer in die Welt geblickt,
Und es neigen selbst die Weisen
Oft am Ende zum Schönen sich.   Hölderlin.

397.*

How can the soul of nightingales fill your ear
When your ears still buzz with the chatter of fools?

Rückert

398.

When natural music is sharpened and polished by
art, only then with great astonishment one sees and recognizes in part (for wholly it cannot be conceived nor
understood) the great and perfect wisdom of God as shown
in his wondrous work.

Luther

399.*

Oh, do not look for that which everyone lacks,
Do consider that which everyone still has.

Goethe

400.

One can rightly say that diligence like a magnet grows
more powerful by uncreasingly carrying incredibly heavy
loads, while indolence is a sword in a scabbard which is
finally corroded by rust.

Immmermann

401.*

He who has thought the deepest thoughts loves what
is most alive.
He who has looked into the world understands high
virtue.
And even wise men bow
Often at the end before beauty.

Hölderlin

402.

Ich kann mein Werk nicht nach der Mode
meißeln und zuschneiden, wie sie's haben wollen:
das Neue und Originelle gebiert sich selbst, ohne
daß man daran denkt. Beethoven.

403.

Die Spielleut' grüßen manch fernes Land,
Sind überall willkommen und wohlbekannt,
Finden überall offne Ohren und Hände,
Und schäumende Becher und Beifallsspende.
A. Grün.

404.

Den lieben Gott laß in dir walten,
Aus frischer Brust nur treulich sing!
Was wahr in dir, wird sich gestalten,
Das andre ist erbärmlich Ding.
Eichendorff.

405.

Denn Kunst, die zwar ihr sichres Erbteil
droben
Im Himmel hat, bedarf, so lange sie
Auf Erden geht, des ird'schen Schutzes wohl.
Rückert.

406.

Stets soll sich frei und stolz der Künstler
fühlen!
Drum, bläht vor dir ein reicher Geck sich auf,
Und mißt er dich mit seinem Blick,
So ruf' ihm froh aus voller Brust entgegen:
Behalt' dein Gold! Die Kunst belohnt sich selbst.
v. Collin.

402.

I cannot cut and chisel my work according to the latest fashion, as they want to have it: the new and original gives birth to itself without one's thinking about it.

Beethoven

403.*

Minstrels greet many a foreign land,
Are everywhere welcome and well known,
Find everywhere open ears and hands,
And foaming goblets and bountiful applause.

A. Grün

404.*

Let God rule inside you,
Just sing faithfully from your fresh breast!
What is true in you will find form,
The other is a miserable thing.

Eichendorff

405.*

Art which has its secure inheritance up in heaven needs, as long as it walks on earth, terrestrial protection.

Rückert

406.*

The artist shall always feel free and proud!
Hence, if a rich fop puffs himself up in front of you
And measures you with his glance,
Just call to him cheerfully from your full breast:
Keep your gold! Art is its own reward.

von Collin

407.

Den Sänger ſchützt
Der Gott, der ihn zum Liebling ſich erwählt,
Ihm lohnt der Ton, der aus der Kehle dringt,
Er borget nichts von ird'ſcher Majeſtät.

Chamiſſo.

408.

Viele Boten gehn und gingen
Zwiſchen Erd' und Himmelsluſt,
Solchen Gruß kann keiner bringen,
Als ein Lied aus friſcher Bruſt.

Eichendorff.

409.

Man muß an die Einfalt, an das Einfache,
an das Urſtändig-Produktive glauben, wenn
man den rechten Weg gewinnen will. Dieſes
iſt aber freilich nicht jedem gegeben.

Goethe.

410.

Nicht einen Hauch vergeuden ſie, nicht einen,
Nein, alles wird gleich für den Markt geboren,
Kein Herzensſchlag geht ohne Zins verloren,
Die Herren machen Brot aus ihren Steinen.

G. Herwegh.

411.

Was du geſtern friſch geſungen,
Iſt doch heute ſchon verklungen,
Und beim letzten Klange ſchreit
Alle Welt nach Neuigkeit.   Eichendorff.

412.

Ohne Zuſammenhang, ohne die innigſte Ver=
bindung aller und jeder Teile, iſt die Muſik ein

407.*

The singer is protected by God who has chosen him
as his favorite. He is rewarded by the tone which issues
from his throat, he borrows nothing from secular majesty.

Chamisso

408.*

Many messengers go and went
Between the earth and the joy of heaven,
Nobody can carry a greeting
Like a song from a fresh breast.

Eichendorff

409.

One has to believe in the simple, the uncomplicated,
originally-productive if one wants to find the right way.
This, of course, is not given to everybody.

Goethe

410.*

They do not waste a breath, not one,
No, everything is quickly brought forth for the
        market.
No heartbeat is lost without dividend,
Those gentlemen make bread out of their stones.

G. Herwegh

411.*

What you freshly sang yesterday,
Today has already faded away,
And at the last sound,
The whole world shouts for something new.

Eichendorff

412.

Without coherence, without the most intimate con-
nection of all and each part, music is a mere sandpile,

eitler Sandhaufen, der keines dauernden Ein=
drucks fähig ist; nur der Zusammenhang macht
sie zu einem Marmor, an dem sich die Hand
des Künstlers verewigen kann.

Leſſing (Dramaturgie).

413.

Die Grenzen sind noch nicht gesteckt, die dem
Talent und Fleiß entgegenriefen: bis hierher
und nicht weiter.   Beethoven.

414.

Gerade die größten Genies haben das Eigne,
daß sie nicht immer billig gut schaffen, wie die
Mittelmäßigen, sondern auch wohl einmal recht
matt arbeiten, wenn ihr Geist vor einer großen
Schöpfung ausruhen muß.   Thibaut.

415.

Ist denn die Sonne verdunkelt, weil Mücken
darin fliegen? Der Adler läßt kleine Vögel ganz
ruhig singen und bekümmert sich nicht darum,
was sie damit wollen.

Beethoven und Roſſini, Schumann und Meyerbeer[1]).

416.

Valentin:

O Silvia! Wenn ich nicht bei dir bin, so ist
keine Musik in dem nächtlichen Lied der Nachtigall,
und wenn ich dich bei Tage nicht sehe, so sehe ich
keinen Tag.   Shakeſpeare (Die beiden Veroneſer).

---

[1]) Bemerkung von Brahms.

incapable of leaving a lasting imprint;   only coherence transforms it to marble which can immortalize the artist's hand.

Lessing (Dramaturgie)

413.

The boundaries are not yet fixed which would call out to talent and diligence: up to here and no further.

Beethoven

414.

Especially the greatest geniuses have the peculiarity of not always easily producing good works, like mediocre talents, but at times they work feebly when their minds must rest before a great creation.

Thibaut

415.[29]

Is the sun blacked out because gnats are flying about? The eagle leaves small birds to their singing and is not concerned with their intentions.

[Beethoven and Rossini, Schumann and Meyerbeer]

Author unknown

416.*

Valentine: Except I be by Silvia in the night,
There is no music for the nightingale;
Unless I look on Silvia in the day,
There is no day for me to look upon.

Shakespeare,
(The Two Gentlemen of Verona)

---

[29] Brahms added the names Beethoven and Rossini, Schumann and Meyerbeer, thinking the quote sounded like them.

417.

Hermia:

Die Nacht, die uns der Augen Dienst entzieht,
Macht, daß dem Ohr kein leiser Laut entflieht.
Was dem Gesicht an Schärfe wird benommen,
Muß doppelt dem Gehör zugute kommen.

Shakespeare (Sommernachtstraum).

418.

Grübelt den Künsten nicht nach. Sehr wenigen
Augen
Wurde der Blick, sie zu sehn — grübelt nicht,
aber genießt.

Klopstock.

419.

Was mit des Himmels Flammen dich durch=
glühet,
Was dir so stürmend in der Brust geschlagen,
Es waren Gottes Stimmen, welche riefen,
Sein sel'ger Atem, der in dir gesprühet.

Aus: Zedlitz, „Totenkränze".

420.

Des volle Brust nur Stimme sucht und Klänge,
Um auszusprühn, was ihm das Herz bewegt:
Er, der bald jauchzen möcht, und wieder weinen,
Den stets des Augenblicks Gewalt erregt,
Wie soll er wandeln in dem Weltgedränge,
Wo niemand ist und alle wollen scheinen?

Aus: Zedlitz, „Totenkränze".

417. *

Hermia: Dark night, that from the eye his function takes,
    The ear more quick of apprehension makes;
    Wherein it does impair the seeing sense,
    It pays the hearing double recompense.

                                Shakespeare
                      (A Midsummer-Night's Dream III/2)

418.*

Do not ponder over the arts. Very few eyes only were
      granted
The gift to perceive them—do not brood, but enjoy!

                                Klopstock

419.*

What glowed through you with heavenly flames,
What beat your breast with storms,
They were the voices of God which called,
His blessed breath which sparkled in you.

                From: *Zedlitz, Totenkränze*

420.*

He whose breast seeks only voice and sounds
To scatter what moves his heart;
He who now wants to shout with joy, now to weep,
Whom the force of the moment always agitates,
How shall he wander in the crush of the world
Where nobody is and everybody wants to shine?

                From: *Zedlitz, Totenkränze*

421.

Ist es kein Glück, ist es nicht edle Wonne,
Wenn unsre Werke, ob wir selbst geendet,
Heilbringend durch die allerfernsten Zeiten
Im Licht des Ruhmes schreiten?   Zedlitz.

422.

Was göttlich lauterm Herzen sich verkündet,
Es wird bestehn trotz aller Macht des Schlechten,
Begeisterung wird's mit edler Glut verfechten,
Mit Glut, von reiner Flamme nur entzündet!
                                         Zedlitz.

423.

Ob sich die Blüten oder nicht entfalten,
In Gottes Händen lieget das Gelingen,
Doch edel sei das Ringen!   Zedlitz.

424.

Soll euch der Kranz umwallen,
Schlagt euer Joch ans Kreuz und lernt ertragen!
                                         Zedlitz.

425.

Die Musik ist die Kunst des Gemüts, welche
sich unmittelbar an das Gemüt selber wendet.
                                         Herbart.

426.

Musik soll mit den ew'gen Sphären tönen,
Alle Lebenstöne der Natur versöhnen.
                                         Rückert.

421.*

Is it not happiness, is it not noble bliss
When our works, after we are gone,
Move beneficially through remotest times
In the light of fame?

Zedlitz

422.*

What announces itself to a divine pure heart,
It will endure in spite of the forces of evil,
It will fight for enthusiasm with noble ardour,
Ardour inflamed by a pure fire!

Zedlitz

423.*

Whether the blossoms unfold or not,
Success lies in God's hands,
But our wrestling be noble!

Zedlitz

424.*

If you expect a laurel wreath,
Nail your yoke to the cross and learn to suffer!

Zedlitz

425.

Music is the art of the soul which appeals directly to
the soul.

Herbart

426.*

Music shall sound with the eternal spheres,
Reconciling all living tones of nature.

Rückert

427.

Wenn du leuchten willst mit Himmelsglanz,
Mußt du leisten auf der Erde Frucht Verzicht.

Rückert.

428.

Was unsterblich im Gesang soll leben
Muß im Leben untergehn.   Schiller.

429.

Die Totalwirkung bleibt immer das Dä=
monische, dem wir huldigen.   Goethe.

430.

Auch in dem schwächsten Kunstwerk ist neben
allen Versäumnissen eine poetische Leistung: keines
ist ganz feste Masse, es lebt irgendein Geist in
ihm. Diesen zitiere die Kritik.

Aber — es gibt auf dem Kunstmarkte Werke,
die gar nicht einmal welche sind, sondern nur
Konglomerate von Natur= und Kunststoff. Sie
verhalten sich wie Nagelfluh zum Felsen. Diese
sind unter aller Kritik, weil sie in einer Region
erst beginnen, in welche jene nicht einmal reicht.

Aus: Menzels Kunstblatt[1]).

431.

Man schilt oft den Ausspruch: er ist kein
Gluck, Haydn, unverständig, unbillig, wenn er
über neuere Künstler ausgesprochen wird. Wenn
er aber aus der wohltuenden Empfindung hervor=
geht, daß manches schätzbare Talent auf ganz
verkehrtem Weg ist, ganz anderen Prinzipien

---

[1]) Vgl. die Angaben im Autorenverzeichnis.

427.*

If you wish to shine in heavenly splendor,
You must renounce terrestrial fruit.

Rückert

428.*

What immortally should live in song
Must perish in life.

Schiller

429.

The total effect remains always the demoniacal, to
which we pay homage.

Goethe

430.

Even the weakest work of art contains, apart from
omissions, a poetic accomplishment: none is wholly solid
mass, some spirit lives in it, and this quality is what critics
should cite.

But—there are works on the art market which cannot even be called thus, for they are only conglomerates
of natural and artificial substances. They are like surface
stones to a rock. They are below all criticism because they
begin in a region to which criticism does not even extend.

From: *Menzel's Kunstblatt*

431.

One often rebukes the saying, "He is no Gluck,
Haydn," as being unreasonable, unfair, when applied to
newer artists. But when the saying arises from the salu-
tary feeling that many an estimable talent is on a totally
wrong path, follows quite different principles, considers

folgt, sich für zu vornehm hält, den klassischen
Meistern nachzueifern, sie in ihren Grundsätzen,
in den Geheimnissen ihres Schaffens angestrengt
forschend zu begleiten, nachzufühlen, nachzuahmen,
dann ist der Vorwurf nicht ungerecht, er tadelt
mehr das Nichtwollen als das Nichtkönnen.

Wie könnte man etwas erreichen, zu dem
Neigung, Studium, Übung die Richtung gar
nicht nehmen. Es blühen noch herrliche Kränze
dem ernsten Streben, nur muß man nicht er=
warten, daß diese die Zeitmenschen ihm reichen
werden.   Kunstblatt 1836.

432.

Im Gemeinen und Mittleren gibt die Be=
mühung besser aus als im Höheren. Darum
trifft man dort die meisten Virtuosen. In allen
Zweigen der Dicht= und bildenden Kunst haben
die Genremeister die glänzendsten Siege errungen.
                                           Kunstblatt.

433.

Wer wird zweifeln, daß der Kunst eine
reinigende Kraft innewohne? Ist sie ja selbst
ein gereinigtes Leben konzentriert erhöht. Wer
in der Kunst lebt, der sucht sie im Leben geistig,
sittlich, ästhetischsittlich nachzuahmen. Von der
Kunst lernt man Klarheit, Wirksamkeit, Ob=
jektivität, Ruhe, Fixierung des Blickes, Einheit
und Stil des Lebens. Was die Menschen im
Leben mit Anteil erfüllt, ergreift, trägt immer
ein künstlerisches Moment in sich, und wenn
wir uns selbst genügen, so ist unser Tun und

himself too noble for emulating classical masters, for ac-
companying them, sympathizing with them, imitating
them, then the rebuke is not unjust, it chides more the
indolence than the incompetence.

How can one reach something toward which inclination, study, practice are not at all directed? Gorgeous
wreaths are still blooming for serious effort, only one must
not expect that the contemporaries will offer them.

Kunstblatt 1836

432.

On a common and mediocre level, effort is more
effective than on a higher one. Therefore one encounters
there most virtuosi.   In all branches of poetry, painting,
and sculpture, the conquerors of a genre have gained the
most brilliant victories.

Kunstblatt

433.

Who can doubt that art contains a purifying power?
For art is itself a purified life heightened by concentra-
tion. Who lives in art seeks to imitate it in life spiritually,
morally, and aesthetically. From art we learn clarity, effec-
tiveness, objectivity, calmness, fixation of the sight, unity
and style of life. Whatever moves and impresses people
always carries an artistic element in it; and when we are
self-sufficient, then our coming and going, our giving and

Laſſen, Geben und Aufnehmen ein künſtleriſches, kunſtgerechtes im höchſten Sinn.

Manche ſehen die Welt für eine Schaubühne an, die Menſchen für ihr Publikum, teilen ſich eine Rolle zu und gebärden ſich immer thea= traliſch. Das iſt die K a r i k a t u r der Sache und ein verfehlter Weg; die Wirklichkeit in die Kunſt zu überſetzen iſt ein Beſtreben, das nur dem geiſtig ſittlichen Geſchmack gelingt.

Kunſtblatt.

434.

Das Kunſtwerk iſt ſeinem rechten Weſen nach eine Blüte der Geſamtkunſtkraft ſeines Meiſters, eine Blume des günſtigſten Moments. An der Wurzel, am Stamme, am Aſte blüht der Baum nicht, und während der Roſenſtrauch wächſt und Zweige und Blätter ſchießt, trägt er noch keine Roſen.

Wer eigentlich etwas anderes tun ſollte, während er ein Kunſtwerk zu erſchaffen glaubt, der fördert gewiß ein ſchlechtes Werk zur Welt. Das künſtleriſche Produzieren iſt wie eine Ehren=, ſo auch eine Gewiſſensſache. Manches, was uns erheitern, erheben will, iſt ein Produkt der Er= niedrigung, ein Erzeugnis fehlerhafter Empfin= dung, unſittlicher Regung, leichtſinniger Pflicht= verletzung, wo nicht verbrecheriſcher Lebens= verhältniſſe, und wären alle, die ſich der Kunſt widmen, ſtrenge gegen ſich und gewiſſenhaft, wir würden uns nicht von einem Schwall von unreifen Sachen überſchwemmt ſehen. So iſt alſo die täglich wachſende Flut ſchlechter Dicht=

taking are in the highest sense artistic.

Some see this world as a stage, the people as their audience, they assign themselves a role, and always behave in a theatrical manner. That is the caricature of the situation and a false road; the translation of reality into art is an endeavor in which only a spiritual ethical taste succeeds.

Kunstblatt

434.

A work of art is properly a blossom of the total creative power of its master, a flower of the most propitious moment. The tree does not blossom at the root, trunk, or branch, and while the rosebush grows and develops twigs and leaves, it does not yet carry any roses.

Whoever actually should do something else while believing that he is creating a work of art, he certainly will produce a poor work. Artistic production involves not only honor but also conscience. Much that is meant to cheer and inspire us is a product of abasement, the result of faulty sentiment, immoral impulse, frivolous violation of an obligation if not also of criminal conditions of life. If all who dedicate themselves to art were severe toward themselves and conscientious, we would not find ourselves inundated by a deluge of immature things. Thus the daily swelling flood of bad poetry and art works is an expand-

und Kunstwerke eine wachsende Sündflut in dem
Sinn, daß sie aus Dünkel, Eigennuß, sinnlichen
Genüssen, Frivolität, Geistesfaulheit entspringt.

Kunstblatt.

435.

Soll mich das musikalische Kunstwerk be=
friedigen, so fordere ich ein Gefühl jenem gleich,
wenn man in ein neues, hohes, fremdes Haus
tritt, mit glänzenden Statuen im Vorsaal —
alles wie noch nie gesehen und doch bekannt,
und wie schon früher geahnet.

436.

Jeder kann nur, was er gelernt hat. Diese
Gemeinwahrheit gewinnt für mich, je älter ich
werde, desto mehr Bedeutung. Wie vieles wird
allerorten behauptet, gelehrt, getrieben, dar=
gestellt — was man doch nicht weiß und kann,
weil man es nicht gelernt hat. Manches braucht
50 Jahre an Beobachtung, Schule, Übung, bis
man es kann, bis es recht gelingt. Je länger
man lebt, desto mehr schäßt man die Leute, die
etwas Tüchtiges können — weil sie es gelernt
haben.

Kunstblatt.

437.

Das Meisterliche reizt unsre Einbildungskraft
schon durch wenige charakteristische Züge, es mit
Leben auszufüllen, — das Verfehlte oder Fabrik=
mäßige bleibt mit allem Aufwand von Stoff
leblos. Das Meisterliche ist auf jeder Stufe
organisch, dieses in Anfang, Mittel, Ende; das
Manierierte ist ein Neben= und Aufeinander.

ing punishing flood in the sense that it originates in arrogance, selfishness, sensuous pleasures, frivolity, and spiritual sluggishness.

Kunstblatt

435.

For a musical work of art to satisfy me, I demand a feeling like entering a new, lofty, strange house with splendid statues in the entrance hall—everything like never seen before and yet familiar, and as if earlier apprehended.

[Kunstblatt]

436.

Everyone knows only what he has learned. This common truth gains more importance for me the older I get. How much is everywhere asserted, taught, carried on, presented—which one does not know and cannot do because one has not learned it. Some matters need 50 years of observation, schooling, practice, until one knows them perfectly, until one succeeds. The longer one lives, the more one values people who know something practical—because they have learned it.

Kunstblatt

437.

Masterworks stimulate our power of imagination with only a few characteristic strokes which bring them to life—the failed or commercial piece remains lifeless, no matter how much material it employed. The masterly piece is organic on each step, in the beginning, midddle, end; the mannered piece is a disorderly mixture. This

Dieſes zeigt ſich auch beim Umgekehrten des
Werdens, beim Zerſtören; ein Fabrikwerk iſt
es bei rauher Berührung, leichter Beſchädigung,
ein Meiſterwerk verrät auch ſeinen Meiſter im
letzten Moment der Verwüſtung.   Kunſtblatt.

438.

Der Philiſter gar poſſierlich iſt,
Zumal wenn er vom Nektar frißt.
Eichendorff.
Reißiger, Lachner, Lindpaintner, Mo (unleſerlich) uſw.[1]

439.

Großen Seelen ziehen Schmerzen nach, wie
den Gebirgen die Gewitter; aber an ihnen
brechen ſich auch die Wolken, und ſie werden
die Wetterſcheide der Ebene unter ihnen.
Jean Paul.

440.

Im Herzen ſchöne Heiterkeit
Und milden Ernſt im Geiſt,
So ſei gewiß, daß du den Schmerz,
Der läutern muß ein jedes Herz,
In Luſt zu kehren weißt!
Herm. Rollet (aus: Jucunde).

441.

Wenn jemand liebt und im Vertraun
Davon zu andern ſpricht er,
Wird er die Hörer ſchlecht erbaun,
Oder er iſt ein Dichter.   Rückert.

---

[1] Bemerkung von Brahms.

shows in the reverse of creation, in destruction. A commercial piece is destroyed by a rough touch, or light damage, a masterwork reveals its master even in the last moment of devastation.

Kunstblatt

438.*[30]
The philistine is droll
Particularly when gorging on nectar.

Eichendorff

439.
Great souls attract pain like mountains which attract thunderstorms. But against them the clouds break up, and they become the weather divide of the plain below them.

Jean Paul

440.*
In the heart beautiful serenity,
And mild seriousness in the spirit,
Thus you may be certain that you will know
How to transmute the ache,
Which must purify every heart
Into joy.

Herm. Rollet (from: *Jucunde*)

441.*
When someone is in love and confidentially
Speaks of it to other people,
He will poorly edify the hearers
Unless he is a poet.

Rûckert

---

[30] Parody of a popular verse. Brahms added to this entry: Reissiger, Lechner, Lindpaintner, etc.

442.

Die Poesie ist freilich Zauberei;
Ob aber der Poet
Mehr Zauberer, mehr halb bezaubert sei?
Ist, was in Frage steht.   Rückert.

443.

Wenn die Wässerlein kämen zu Hauf,
Gäb es wohl einen Fluß,
Weil jedes nimmt seinen eignen Lauf,
Eins ohne des andern vertrocknen muß.
                    Rückert.

444.

Nullen, tretend hinter eine Eins,
Würden Tausende zählen;
Weil sie den Führer nicht wählen,
Zählen sie alle zusammen keins.
                    Rückert.

445.

                    Närrisches Kind!
Du sollst ja nur etwas, nicht alles, werden;
Wie kannst du dich denn so erstaunt gebärden,
Zu sehn, daß a n d r e a u c h etwas sind.
                    Rückert.

446.

Wahrheit ist das leichteste Spiel von allen.
Stelle dich selber dar,
Und du läufst nie Gefahr,
Aus deiner Rolle zu fallen.   Rückert.

442.*

Poetry is magic, certainly,
But whether the poet be more
Magician or half under the spell of magic,
That is the question.

Rückert

443.*

If little brooks were to pile up,
We would have a river.
Because each one runs its own course,
One without the other must dry up.

Rückert

444.*

Zeros stepping behind a one,
Would count thousands.
Because they do not choose the leader,
All together they amount to nothing.

Rückert

445.*

Foolish child!
You will become something, not everything;
How can you be so amazed
To see that other people also are something.

Rückert

446.*

Truth is the easiest play of all,
Present your self
And do not run the danger
Of stepping out of your role.

Rückert

447.

Kuckuck als Virtuose.

Einstmals in einem tiefen Tal
Der Kuckuck und die Nachtigall
Täten ein Wett anschlagen
Zu singen um das Meisterstück:
Wer's gewönn aus Kunst oder durchs Glück,
Dank sollt er davon tragen.
Der Kuckuck sprach: „So dir's gefällt,
Ich hab zur Sach ein Richter erwählt",
Und tät den Esel nennen:
„Denn weil er hat zwei Ohren groß,
So kann er hören desto baß
Und was Recht ist erkennen."
Sie flogen vor den Richter bald.
Wie ihm die Sachen ward erzählt,
Schuf er, sie sollten singen.
Die Nachtigall sang lieblich aus,
Der Esel sprach: „Du machst mir's kraus,
Ich kann's in Kopf nit bringen."
Der Kuckuck drauf anfing geschwind:
Kuckuck! sein G'sang durch Terz, Quart, Quint,
Und tät die Noten brechen;
Er lacht auch drein nach seiner Art.
Dem Esel g'fiel's; er sagt: „Nun wart!
Ein Urteil will ich sprechen.
Wohl sungen hast du Nachtigall;
Aber, Kuckuck, du singst Choral
Und hältst den Takt fein immer.
Des sprich' ich nach mein' hoh'n Verstand;
Und kostet's gleich ein ganzes Land,
So laß ich dich's gewinnen."

447.*

Cuckoo as Virtuoso

Once in a deep valley
The cuckoo and the nightingale
Made a bet
To sing a masterpiece;
Who wins by art or luck
Will gain gratitude.
The cuckoo said: "If you agree,
I have chosen a judge,"
And named the donkey:
"Because he has two big ears,
He can hear all the better
And recognize what is right."
They flew before the judge,
When the affair was told him,
He ordered them to sing.
The nightingale sang beautifully.
The donkey said: "You confuse me,
I can't get it into my head."
The cuckoo promptly began:
Cuckoo! singing through third, fourth, and fifth,
And broke up the notes;
He also giggled in his manner.
The donkey liked it; he says: "Now wait!
I will pass judgment.
You nightingale have sung well,
But cuckoo, you sing chorale
And always keep time.
I pronounce according to my high intelligence;
And even if it costs a whole country,
I let you win."

Solch' Richter das sind diese G'sellen,
Die von der Musik Urteil fällen,
Die sie doch gar nicht känten.
Ein solcher Narr schwieg leichter still,
Der von der Sach' will plappern viel,
Wie von der Farb' die Blinden.

Aus: Des Knaben Wunderhorn.

448.

Dichterlos.

Wenn ich die Lerche sehe, wie sie langsam
Mit süßem Sang sich in die Lüfte hebt,
Und dann schnell abwärts zu dem Boden stürzt,
So macht's mich traurig. — Mühsam schwingt
der Dichter
Wohl auch sich auf zu höheren Regionen;
Doch zieht das Leben schleunig ihn zurück. —
Er bleibt ein Mensch und haftet an dem Boden!

Heinr. Jos. v. Collin.

449.

Einem strebet nur nach! Versöhnet die Kunst
mit dem Leben;
Wirklichkeit und Ideal schreite nicht länger getrennt.
Wäre das alles? Nun gut. Ein Kleines gewähret uns voraus:
Hebt nur das Leben zuerst! — Selbst wohl be-
flügelt sich Kunst.

v. Collin.

NB. Siehe in Collins Gedichten die
„Künstlerentzückung".

Such justices are these fellows
Who pass judgment on music
Which they do not know at all.
Such a fool had better keep silent
Who wants to prattle about this matter,
Like a blind man about color.

From: *Des Knaben Wunderhorn*

448.*

A Poet's Fate

When I see the lark slowly rising into the air
With sweet song
And then abruptly plunging down to the ground,
It makes me sad.—Laboriously the poet, too,
Swings himself up to higher regions;
But life quickly pulls him back.
He remains a human and adheres to the ground.

Heinr. Jos. von Collin

449.*[31]

Strive for only this! Reconcile art with life;
Let reality and ideal no longer move separately.
Would this be all? Well enough. Grant us something
Little in advance: Lift life first! Art will find its own
       wings.

von Collin

[31] Brahms added this comment: NB. See in Collin's poems his "Künstlerentzückung." Krebs printed the entire poem (five pages) in his edition of
the Notebooks.

450.

Es sitzt auf dunkler Klippe
Die lichte, gewaltige Fei,
Sang strömt von süßer Lippe
Der süßen Lorelen.
Wohl alle können's hören,
Doch viele fassen's nicht.
„Laß, Knabe, dich nicht betören!"
Die graue Klugheit spricht.
Dort unten auf den Wellen
Arbeitend, rudern viel;
Daß sie nur nicht zerschellen,
Das ist ihr höchstes Ziel.
Sie schließen der Sangeswonne,
Verstockt die störrische Brust
Und meinen viel gewonnen,
Entrannen sie der Lust.
Das Lied von süßem Tone
Vernehmen sie nimmermehr,
Ihr Los ist ew'ge Frohne
Und Ruderarbeit schwer.
Wem aber warmes Leben
Und Mut im Busen wallt,
Der hat sich ganz ergeben
Der hohen Sangesgewalt.

450.*

On a dark cliff
Sits the light, mighty fairy.
Song pours from the sweet lips
Of the sweet Loreley.
All can hear it
But many do not grasp it.
"Do not, boy, let yourself be deceived!"
Grey prudence speaks.
Down there on the waves
At work, many row;
Not to be wrecked
Is their highest goal.
They obdurately close to the rapture of song
Their stubborn breast
And think to have gained much
By escaping the bliss.
They nevermore hear
The sweet tone of the song.
Their fate is eternal labor
And heavy rowing.
But whose breast is filled
With warm life and courage
He has fully yielded
To the high power of the singing.

Der läßt das Ruder fallen
Und achtet's nicht für Not,
Wenn von des Wirbels Wallen
Verschlungen wird das Boot.
Nun ruht er, weich umkoset,
Tief unten im süßen Traum;
Des Lebens Müh' vertoset,
Im stillen Kristallenraum.
Und in die Träume mengt sich
Das Lied der Lorelen,
Und Märchenwonne drängt sich
In süßem Gewirr herbei.
Wohl mir, daß mich mit Schäumen
Der heil'ge Strom verschlang,
Ich liege schon lang in Träumen
Und horche dem Wundersang.

Friedr. v. Sallet (aus Novelle: Kontraste und Paradoxen).

451.

Solange der Virtuose Anschläge faßt, Ideen
sammelt, wählet, ordnet und Pläne verteilt: so
lange genießt er die sich selbst belohnenden
Wollüste der Empfängnis. Aber sobald er einen
Schritt weiter gehet und Hand anleget, seine
Schöpfung auch außer sich darzustellen: sogleich
fangen die Schmerzen der Geburt an, welchen
er sich selten ohne alle Aufmunterung unterzieht.

Lessing (Vorrede zu den Fabeln).

452.

Angela (in den Feldblumen):

Ich bin nicht Kennerin genug, um anders
als nach meinem Eindrucke zu urteilen; aber

He lets drop the oar
And does not worry
When the boat is swallowed up
By the swell of the whirlpool.
Now he rests softly caressed
Down deep in a sweet dream;
Life's trouble fades
In the silent crystal room.
And into the dreams blends
The song of the Loreley,
And fairyland happiness
Presses forward in sweet confusion.
I am blessed that the holy stream
Swallowed me in its foam.
I have been lying in a dream
Listening to the wonderful song.

> *Friedr. von Sallet* (from story:
> *Contrasts and Paradoxes*).

451.

As long as the virtuoso has a project, collects ideas, makes order, and distributes plans: for the time being he enjoys the self-rewarding voluptuosness of reception. But as soon as he takes one further step and tries to present his creation also outside himself, immediately labor pains set in to which he rarely subjects himself without much encouragement.

> *Lessing* (Preface to the *Fables*)

452.

Angela (in the *Feldblumen*)

I am not experienced enough to judge otherwise than by my impressions; but I am carried away where, as in

mich reißt es hin, wo, wie in der Natur, großartige Verschwendung ist. Mozart teilt mit
freundlichem Angesichte unschätzbare Edelsteine
aus und schenkt jedem etwas; Beethoven aber
stürzt gleich einen Wolkenbruch von Juwelen
über das Volk; dann hält es sich die Hände
vor den Kopf, damit es nicht blutig geschlagen
wird, und geht am Ende fort, ohne den kleinsten
Diamanten erhascht zu haben.   Adalbert Stifter.

453.

Manfred (Alpenreigen in der Ferne):

Horch, der Ton! Des Alpenrohrs natürliche
                 Musik —
Denn hier ward nicht zu bloßer Hirtendichtung
Die Patriarchenzeit — in freien Lüften
Vermählt dem Klinggeläute muntrer Herden;
D i e Töne trinkt mein Geist. —
O wär' ich doch
Solch sanften Klanges ungeseh'ner Geist,
Lebend'ge Stimme, atmende Harmonie,
Leiblose Wonne, —
Sterbend wie geboren
Im sel'gen Tone, der mich zeugte!
                Lord Byron (Manfred, Akt I).

454.

O ihr unbefleckten Töne, wie so heilig ist
eure Freude und euer Schmerz! denn ihr froh-
lockt und wehklagt nicht über irgendeine Be-
gebenheit, sondern über das Leben und Sein,
und eurer Tränen ist nur die Ewigkeit würdig,

nature, magnificent extravagance rules. Mozart distributes priceless gems with a friendly face and gives something to everyone; Beethoven, however, pours a thunderstorm of jewels over the people; they, shielding their heads with their hands in order not to be beaten bloody, leave in the end without having caught the smallest diamond.

Adalbert Stifter

453.*[32]

Manfred: (the shepherd's pipe in the distance is heard)
    Hark! the note,
    The natural music of the mountain reed
    (For here the patriarchal days are not
    A pastoral fable) pipes in the liberal air,
    Mix'd with the sweet bells of the sauntering herd;
    My soul would drink those echoes.—Oh, that I were
    The viewless spirit of a lovely sound,
    A living voice, a breathing harmony,
    A bodiless enjoyment—born and dying
    With the blest tone which made me!

Byron (Manfred, Act I)

454.

Oh you immaculate tones, how sacred is your joy and your pain! For you exult and lament not over any kind of event but over life and being, and only eternity is worthy of your tears whose Tantalus is man. How else

---

[32] Brahms quotes in German; the printed text is by Byron.

deren Tantalus der Menſch iſt. Wie könntet
ihr denn, ihr Reinen, im Menſchenbuſen, den
ſo lange die erdige Welt beſetzt, euch eine heilige
Stätte bereiten oder ſie reinigen vom irdiſchen
Leben, wäret ihr nicht früher in uns als der
treuloſe Schall des Lebens, und würde uns euer
Himmel nicht angeboren vor der Erde.

Jean Paul (Flegeljahre).

455.

Dult (ſich ſelbſt beſchreibend):

Und doch ſo beſcheiden, wie ſchon geſagt.
Der Muſikdirektor der Sphärenmuſik werd' ich
doch nie, ſagt er einſt, ſich verbeugend, die Flöte
weglegend, und meinte wahrſcheinlich Gott.

Jean Paul.

456.

Dult:

Aber wie hörteſt du? Voraus und zurück
oder nur ſo vor dich hin? Das Volk hört wie
das Vieh nur Gegenwart, nicht die beiden
Polarzeiten, nur muſikaliſche Silben, keine
Syntax. Ein guter Hörer des Worts prägt ſich
den Vorderſatz einer muſikaliſchen Periode ein,
um den Nachſatz ſchön zu faſſen. Jean Paul.

457.

Dult:

Denn wie Muſik entheiligt wird — obgleich
jede Kunſt überhaupt, das höre. Tafelmuſik
laß ich noch gelten, weil ſie ſo ſchlecht iſt wie
Tafelpredigten, die man in Klöſtern ins Käuen

could you, who are pure, prepare in the human breast, long occupied by the terrestrial world, a holy place or purify it from secular life if you had not been within us earlier than the faithless sound of life, and if your heaven were not born within us ahead of the earth.

Jean Paul (Flegeljahre)

455.[33]

Vult (describing himself)

And yet so modest, as already said. I shall never become the music director of the music of the spheres, he once said, taking a bow, putting away the flute, and he probably meant God.

Jean Paul

456.

Vult:

How did you listen? Forward or backward, or just to what strikes your ear? People like beasts hear only the present, not the two polar times, only musical syllables, no syntax. The good listener of the word fastens his mind on the first phrase of a musical period in order to grasp beautifully the second phrase.

Jean Paul

457.

Vult:

Hear now how music—actually every art—is desecrated. I shall let dinner music pass because it is as bad as table sermons in convents added to chewing; anger does

---

[33] Vult is a main character in Jean Paul's novel *Flegeljahre* (see nos. 455 to 460).

hineinhält; von verfluchten, verruchten Hof-
konzerten, wo der heilige Ton wie ein Billard-
sack am Spieltische zum Spielen spielen und
klingeln muß, red' ich gar nicht vor Grimm, da
ein Ball in einem Bilderkabinett nicht toller
wäre; aber das ist Jammer, das ich in Konzert-
sälen, wo doch jeder bezahlt, mit solchem Recht
erwarte, er werde für sein Geld etwas empfinden
wollen, allein ganz umsonst. Sondern damit
das Klingen aufhöre, ein paarmal und endlich
ganz, — deswegen geht der Narr hinein. Hebt
noch etwas den Spießbürger empor am Ohr,
so ist's zwei=, höchstens dreierlei: 1. wenn aus
einem halbtoten Pianissimo plötzlich ein Fortissimo
wie ein Rebhuhn aufknattert; 2. wenn einer,
besonders mit dem Geigenbogen, auf dem höchsten
Seile der höchsten Töne lange tanzt und rutscht,
und nun kopfunten in die tiefsten herunter-
klatscht; 3. wenn gar beides vorfällt. In
solchen Punkten ist der Bürger seiner nicht
mehr mächtig, sondern schwitzt vor Lob.

Jean Paul.

458.

Denn ich bleibe dabei, Wirklichkeit in die
Kunst zu kneten zum Effekt, ist so eine Mischung
wie an manchen Deckengemälden, in welche der
Perspektive wegen noch wirkliche Gipsfiguren
geklebt sind. (Dult.)

Jean Paul.

459.

Gäb' es nichts Unerklärliches mehr, so möcht'
ich nicht mehr leben, weder hier noch dort.
Ahnung ist später als ihr Gegenstand; ein

not let me talk of the accursed, atrocious court concerts where the sacred tone like the pocket on a billiard table has to accompany the play by playing and tingling, a dance in a painting cabinet would not be more absurd. But this is the misery that in concert halls where everyone pays admission, I rightly expect he would want to feel something for his money, but all in vain. Rather in order to stop the tingling, a few times and finally altogether—therefore, the fool enters. Two or, at best, three things can pull the ear of the philistine: 1. when out of a half-dead pianissimo all of a sudden a fortissimo like a partridge roars up; 2. when someone, especially with the violin bow, dances long and slides on the highest rope of the highest tones and now headfirst splashes down into the lowest; 3. when both happens. In such instances, the citizen is no longer master of himself but sweats full of praise.

Jean Paul

458.

For I stick to it, kneading reality into art for effect is a mixture such as can be found in certain painted ceilings onto which, for the sake of perspective, real plaster figures have been pasted.

Jean Paul

459.

If there were nothing inexplicable any more, then I would not want to continue to live, neither here nor there. Presentiment is later than its object; eternal thirst is a con-

ewiger Durst ist ein Widerspruch, aber auch
ein ewiges Trinken ist einer. Es muß ein
Drittes geben, so wie die Musik die Mittlerin
ist zwischen Gegenwart und Zukunft.
Jean Paul.

460.

Einige Menschen sind Klaviere, die nur ein=
sam zu spielen sind, manche sind Flügel, die in
ein Konzert gehören[1]).
Jean Paul.

461.
Sang und Sänger.

Des Sängers Leben ist sein Sang,
Sein Herz und Odem sein Lied,
Und wenn sein letztes Lied verklang,
Gings letzte Leben mit.
Und wer er ist, das frag' ihn nicht,
Nicht wo? wohin? woher?
Denn was er weiß, sein Lied dir spricht,
Und drüber weiß er nichts mehr. —
Was kümmert ihn des Lebens Zeit
Und was des Lebens Traum?
Er träumt des Lebens Wirklichkeit
Und lebt des Lebens Traum. Scherenberg.

462.

O Gott, wie kann ein Mensch nicht in har=
_monischem Strome untersinken, sondern daraus
noch etwas vorstecken, besonders die Zunge.
Jean Paul (Flegeljahre).

---

[1]) Mit Klavieren sind hier die sehr schwach klingenden
Clavichorde des 18. Jahrhunderts gemeint, im Gegensatz zu den
tonreicheren, rauschenden Kielflügeln.

tradition, and so is eternal drinking. There must be a third, just as music is the mediator between present and future.

Jean Paul

460.

Some people are clavichords and should only be played in solitude, others are pianos which belong in a concert hall.

Jean Paul

461.*

Song and Singer

The singer's life is his singing,
His heart and breath are his song.
And when his last song fades away,
His last life goes with it.
And who he is, do not ask him,
Not where? whither? whence?
For what he knows, his song tells you,
And beyond this he knows nothing more.—
Life's span does not worry him,
Nor life's dream!
He dreams life's reality
And lives life's dream.

Scherenberg

462.

Oh God, how can a man not sink down in the harmonic stream but even let something stick out of it, especially the tongue.

Jean Paul (Flegeljahre)

463.

Wenn die Tonkunst, welche schon in die gemeine feste Welt gewaltsam ihre poetische einschiebt, vollends eine offene bewegte findet, so wird darin statt des Erdbebens ein Himmels=beben entstehen, und der Mensch wird sein wie Walt, der das Ufer mit stillen Dankgebeten und lauten Freudenrufen umlief und seine Herzens=welt, so oft die Flöte sie ausgesprochen, immer von neuem und verklärter erschuf.

Jean Paul.

464.

Die Musik und Poesie mögen wohl ziemlich eins sein und vielleicht ebenso zusammengehören wie Mund und Ohr, da der erste nur ein be=wegliches und antwortendes Ohr ist.

Novalis (Heinrich [von] Ofterdingen).

465.

Man sollte plastische Kunstwerke nie ohne Musik sehen, musikalische Kunstwerke dagegen nur in schön dekorierten Sälen hören.

Novalis (Fragmente).

466.

Die Natur ist eine Äolsharfe, ein musikalisches Instrument, dessen Töne wieder Tasten, wieder Töne höherer Saiten in uns sind.   Novalis.

467.

Unsere Seele muß Luft sein, weil · sie von Musik weiß und daran Gefallen hat. Ton ist Luftsubstanz, Luftseele, die fortpflanzende Luft=

463.

When music, which violently inserts into the common fixed world its poetic world, finds at last an open flexible world, there will issue from it instead of an earthquake a heavenly quake, and man will be like Walt who ran around the shore with silent prayers of thanksgiving and loud shouts of joy, creating his heart's world, as often as the flute had pronounced it, always afresh and transfigured.

Jean Paul

464.

Music and poetry might well be one and perhaps belong together like mouth and ear, as the former is only a movable and responding ear.

Novalis (Heinrich [von] Ofterdingen)

465.

One should never see plastic works of art without music, on the other hand hear artful music only in beautifully decorated halls.

Novalis (Fragmente)

466.

Nature is an Aeolian harp, a musical instrument, of which the tones are again keys, again tones of higher strings within us.

Novalis

467.

Our soul must be air, because it knows of music and finds pleasure in it. Tone is air substance, air soul, the

bewegung ist eine Affektation der Luft durch
den Ton. Im Ohre entsteht der Ton von
neuem.   Novalis.

468.

Ein Märchen ist wie ein Traumbild ohne
Zusammenhang. Ein Ensemble wunderbarer
Dinge und Begebenheiten, z. B. eine musikalische
Phantasie, die harmonischen Folgen einer Äols=
harfe, die Natur selbst.   Novalis.

469.

Sonett.

In ewigen Verwandlungen begrüßt
Uns des Gesangs geheime Macht hienieden;
Dort segnet sie das Land als ew'ger Frieden,
Indes sie hier als Jugend uns umfließt.

Sie ist's, die Licht in unsre Augen gießt,
Die uns den Sinn für jede Kunst beschieden,
Und die das Herz der Frohen und der Müden
In trunkner Andacht wunderbar genießt.

An ihrem vollen Busen trank ich Leben;
Ich ward durch sie zu allem, was ich bin,
Und durfte froh mein Angesicht erheben.

Noch schlummerte mein allerhöchster Sinn,
Da sah ich sie als Engel zu mir schweben
Und flog, erwacht, in ihrem Arm dahin.
              Novalis (steht vor Heinrich [von] Ofterdingen).

spreading air motion is an affectation of the air by the tone. In the ear, the tone is reborn.

Novalis

468.

A fairytale is like a dream without coherence. An ensemble of miraculous things and events, e.g., a musical fantasy, the harmonic sequences of an Aeolian harp, nature itself.

Novalis

469.*

Sonnet

In eternal transformations
The secret power of song greets us here;
There it blesses the land as eternal peace,
While here it flows around us as youth.

It is this power which pours light into our eyes,
Which has granted us the sense for every art,
And which is relished in intoxicated devotion
By the heart of the cheerful and the tired.

I drank life at its full blossom;
Through it I became everything I am,
And could cheerfully lift up my countenance.

My highest sense was still slumbering
When I saw it hovering over me like an angel,
And awakened I flew away in its arm.

Novalis
(Heinrich [von] Ofterdingen.[34]*)*

---

[34] *Heinrich von Ofterdingen* is the novel by Novalis in which the hero sets out to find the blue flower.

470.

Ein Tänzermädchen
Kam wie ein Rofenblatt, das Zephir lockt,
Als hing's an unsichtbaren Sommerfädchen;
Bewegung floß durch ihre zarten Glieder
Harmonisch wie ein fortgetragner Klang.
Wer hätte da gesagt, sie tanzte, sprang?
Sie flog empor, und Amor trug sie nieder.

Hermann Grimm (Traum und Erwachen).

471.

Aus dem Abcbuch des Onkels
Holofernes.

NB. Wenn du nicht mit dem gleichen Gefühl
der Befriedigung eine reife Weintraube essen
kannst, wie du in die Abendröte blickst, so bist
du ein Schwächling.

Es ist nicht genug, daß du den Ton in dir
trägst; soll er wahrhaft da sein, so ist nötig,
das du ihn spielst. Dazu aber gehört eine
Geige, die aus Holz gefügt, und Saiten, die
aus Schafsdarm gedreht sind.
Das vergiß nicht!

NB. Träume nicht in Orangenhainen, und
halte es nicht für ein Verdienst, wenn dir eine
unwillkürliche Wonneträne im Auge zittert. Die
Welt soll nicht auf dir spielen, sondern du auf
ihr. Deshalb überwinde und kenne sie. Er=
klimme den Berg und den Baum mit eigener
Kraft und Anstrengung, dann schau hinab und
genieße von oben den schönen Frieden des Tales.

470.*

A dancing girl
Came like a rose leaf enticed by zephyr,
As if hanging on invisible summer threads;
Motion flowed through her gentle limbs
Harmonically like a transported sound.
Who could have said, she danced, jumped?
She flew up, and Amor carried her down.

Hermann Grimm (Dream and Awakening)

471.[35]

from the *ABC Book of Uncle Holofernes*

N.B. If you cannot eat a ripe grape with the same feeling of contentment as when you look at the sunset, then you are a weakling.

* * *

It is not enough to carry the tone within you; if it should be really here, then it is necessary that you play it. But for that you need a violin, fashioned of wood, and strings twisted of catgut.

Don't ever forget this!

* * *

N.B. Do not dream in orange groves and do not regard it a merit when an involuntary tear of bliss trembles in your eye. The world should not play upon you, but you upon it. Therefore, conquer and know it. Climb the mountain and tree with your own force and effort, then look down and enjoy from above the beautiful valley.

---

[35] Uncle Holofernes, in 471 and 472, is the author's fanciful invention.

Kräftige deinen Arm fürs Schwert und zum
mächtigen Umfassen eines geliebten Wesens, übe
deinen Mund zu Rede und Kuß, trinke **keinen**
Mondschein, sondern Rheinwein.

Leute, die sich einbilden oder der Welt weis=
machen, sie schwämmen in der Luft, ganz nahe
beim Monde, auf seligen Inseln, voll süßer
Seufzerhauche, umher, nennt man wohl zuweilen
Dichter. Aber wer jenen Mann erkannt hat,
auf dessen Götterstirn das gewaltigste, geistigste
Anschaun, auf dessen attisch lächelnder Lippe das
vollste, keckste Genießen der ganzen Welt thronte,
und der dastand mit festen, markigten Knochen
auf der wohlgegründeten dauernden Erde, wer
den erkannt hat, der nennt sie **Fasler.** Ver=
tiefe und verliebe dich nicht ins Blumen= und
Früchtepflücken, schau auch einmal wieder auf
zu den Sternen.

Iß Beefsteak und fliehe das gedankenlose
Brüten.

Das Gefühl ist gut; aber es ist nur Farben=
schmelz. Der Gedanke ist die Zeichnung und
offenbart allein den Geist des Meisters fest und
erkennbar.

Du wirst dich nicht in die Göttlichkeit hinein=
faulenzen und empfindeln.

Versage deinem Geist die kühnsten Flüge
nicht, sollten sie auch an Tollheit grenzen. Welch
eine kecke Tollheit wäre für den trockenen
Nüchterling das Dasein des Weltalls, wenn er

Strengthen your arm for the sword and the mighty embrace of a beloved being, exercise your mouth for discourse and kiss, drink no moonlight, but Rhinewine

People who imagine by themselves or spin a yarn to the world that they swim around in the air, close to the moon, on happy isles full of sweet sighs, are sometimes called poets. But he who has recognized the man whose divine brow shows the most intense spiritual gaze, on whose attic smiling lips thrones the fullest, most daring enjoyment of the whole world, and who stood with firm strong bones on the established lasting earth, if he has recognized such a man, he calls the others drivelers. Do not become absorbed and infatuated plucking flowers and fruit, look up for a change to the stars.

* * *

Eat beefsteak and flee thoughtless brooding.

* * *

Sentiment is good, but it is only a crucible of colors. Thought is the design, and it alone reveals the firm and recognizable spirit of the master.

* * *

You will not intrude upon divine perfection by idleness and sentimentality.

* * *

Do not deny to your spirit the most daring flights even when they border on madness. How impudently mad would the existence of the world appear to the dry and sober person if he could understand too well

die Shakespearesche Komposition und Unergründ=
lichkeit darin zu sehr verstünde!

Bete nicht, sondern denke! das heißt:
Bete! aber dein Denken sei hoch, rein und
mutig, daß Gott sich daran freue.

Aus Sallet, Kontraste und Paradoxen.

472.

Holofernes (in demselben Buch):

Ja leben, leben! Das ist die Haupt=
sache, das macht den Kerl; das hat den hier
gemacht (hier schlug er mit der Hand auf den
Deckel der Folioausgabe Shakespeares). Er hat
den Sommernachtstraum geschaffen, hätte er
ihn aber selbst träumen wollen, dann wär'
er ein Duckmäuser geworden, eine Mondschein=
pastete und nicht der größte Held, der je Kühnes
ersonnen.　　　　　　　Sallet, Kontraste und Paradoxen.

473.

Jean Paul im Titan nennt die Nachtigall
„eine geflügelte Zwergorgel", „sie riß
auf einmal alle Flötenregister heraus, daß Liane
im Vergessen ihrer Blindheit niederblickte".

Alonso:

O es ist gräßlich! gräßlich!
Mir schien, die Wellen riefen mir es zu,
Die Winde sangen mir es, und der Donner,
Die tiefe, grause Orgelpfeife sprach
Den Namen Prospero, sie rollte meinen Frevel.

Shakespeare im Sturm (III, 3).

Shakespeare's unfathomable composition!

Don't pray, but think! Which means, pray! But your thinking must be high, pure, and courageous to please God.

From *Sallet, Kontraste und Paradoxen*

472.

Holofernes (in the same book)

Yes, living, living! This is the main thing, this makes the man; this has made this one (here he struck with his hand the cover of Shakespeare's folio volume). He created the Midsummer-Night's Dream, but if he had wanted to dream it himself, then he would have turned into a coward, a moonlight paste, and not the greatest hero who ever imagined audacious adventures.

Sallet, Kontraste und Paradoxen

473.[36]

Jean Paul in *Titan* calls the nightingale "a winged dwarf organ," "she once tore out all flute registers so that Liane looked down forgetting her blindness."

Alonso

O, it is monstrous! monstrous!
Methought the billows spoke and told me of it;
The winds did sing it to me; and the thunder,
That deep and dreadful organ-pipe, pronounc'd
The name of Prosper: it did bass my trespass.

Shakespeare (The Tempest III/3)

---

[36] Brahms quotes a German translation. The English text printed here is the original.

474.

Echte Mathematik ist das eigentliche Element
des Magiers. In der Musik erscheint sie förm=
lich als Offenbarung, als schaffender Idealismus.
Hier legitimiert sie sich als himmlische Ge=
sandtin. — Aller Genuß ist musikalisch, mithin
mathematisch. Das höchste Leben ist Mathematik.

Novalis.

475.

Aus „Peter und die schöne Magelone".

Die Musik floß wie ein murmelnder Bach
durch den stillen Garten, und er sah die Anmut
der Prinzessin auf den silbernen Wellen der
Harmonie hoch einherschwimmen, wie die Wogen
der Musik den Saum ihres Gewandes küßten
und wetteiferten, ihr nachzufolgen: wie die
Morgenröte schien sie in die dämmernde Nacht
hinein, und die Sterne standen in ihrem Laufe
still, die Bäume hielten sich ruhig, und die Winde
schwiegen, die Musik war jetzt die einzige Be=
wegung, das einzige Leben in der Natur, und
alle Töne schlüpften so süß über die Grasspitzen
und durch die Baumwipfel hin, als wenn sie
die schlafende Liebe suchten und sie nicht wecken
wollten, als wenn sie so wie der weinende
Jüngling zitterten, bemerkt zu werden.
   ... Jetzt erklangen die letzten Akzente, und
wie ein blauer Lichtstrom versank der Ton, und
die Bäume rauschten wieder, und Peter erwachte
aus sich selber und fühlte, daß seine Wange
von Tränen naß sei.

Ludwig Tieck.

474.

Pure mathematics is the magician's proper element. In music it appears formally as revelation, as creative idealism. Here it legitimates itself as a celestial ambassador.— All bliss is musical, hence mathematical.   The highest form of life is mathematics.

Novalis

475.[37]

From Peter and the Beautiful Magelone

The music flowed like a murmuring brook through the quiet garden, and he saw the charm of the Princess swimming high on the silvery waves of harmony, saw how the billows of music kissed the hem of her dress and competed in following her: like sunrise she shone into the dawning night, and the stars stood still in their course, the trees kept quiet, and the winds were still, music was now the sole motion, the sole life in nature, and all tones slipped so sweetly over the grass tips and through the tree tops as if they were in search of sleeping love and did not wish to wake it, as if they trembled like the weeping youth lest they be noticed.

....Now sounded the last accents, and the tone sank like a blue stream of light, and the trees rustled again, and Peter woke up and felt that his cheek was wet with tears.

Ludwig Tieck

[37] Tieck's "Love Story of the Beautiful Magelone and the Count Peter von Provence" heightens the prose narration in a characteristic romantic fashion by the insertion of many poems. Brahms, in his late twenties, composed fifteen of them to form a cycle, which earned him early recognition as a song writer. For his notebooks, he copied these two long passages.

476.

Im Schlafe fah fie (Magelone) fich in einem
fchönen und luftigen Garten; der hellfte Sonnen=
fchein flimmerte auf allen grünen Blättern, und
wie von Harfenfaiten tönte das Lied ihres Ge=
liebten aus dem blauen Himmel herunter, und
goldbefchwingte Vögel ftaunten zum Himmel
hinauf und merkten auf die Noten; leichte
Wolken zogen unter der Melodie hinweg und
wurden rofenrot gefärbt und tönten wieder.

Dann kam der Unbekannte aus einem dunklen
Gange, er umarmte Magelonen und fteckte ihr
einen noch köftlicheren Ring an den Finger,
und die Töne vom Himmel herunter fchlangen
fich um beide wie ein goldnes Netz, und die
roten Lichtwolken umkleideten fie, und fie waren
von der Welt getrennt nur bei fich felber und
in ihrer Liebe wohnend, und wie ein fernes
Klagegetön hörten fie Nachtigallen fingen und
Büfche flüftern, daß fie von der Wonne des
Himmels ausgefchloffen waren.   Ludwig Tieck.

477.

„Wie kommt's," fagte Julienne, „daß im
Freien und nachts auch die unbedeutendfte Mufik
gefällig und rührend wird?" „Vielleicht, weil
unfre innere heller und reiner dazu mittönt,"
fagte Idoine.

„Und weil vor der Sphärenmufik des Uni=
verfums menfchliche Kunft und menfchliche Ein=
falt am Ende gleich groß find," fetzte Albano
dazu.   Jean Paul (Titan, Bd. IV).

476.

In her sleep, Magelone saw herself in a beautiful and cheerful garden; the brightest sunshine glittered on all green leaves, and as on harp strings the song of her lover sounded down from the blue sky, and golden-winged birds looked amazed up to the sky and marked the notes; light clouds passed below the melody and became colored like red roses and sounded anew.

Then came the unknown man out of a dark passage, he embraced Magelone and put a still costlier ring on her finger, and the tones from heaven wound themselves around both like a golden net, and the red bright clouds dressed them, and they were separated from the world and only by themselves and dwelling in their love, and they heard like a distant lamentation the nightingales singing and the bushes whispering that they were excluded from the bliss of Heaven.

Ludwig Tieck

477.

"How is it," said Julienne, "that outdoors and at night even the most insignificant music becomes agreeable and touching?"

"Perhaps because our inner music, clearer and purer, resonates with it," said Idoine.

"And because in the end the spheral music of the universe and human art and human simplicity are equally great," Albano added.

Jean Paul (Titan IV)

478.

Wie Menschen zugleich harthörig unter dem gemeinen Lebensgetöse sein können und doch den feinsten musikalischen Lauten offen (z. B. der Kapellmeister Naumann [1]), so waren Schoppens innere Ohren verhärtet gegen das Volksgepolter des allgemeinen Treibens, aber durstig zogen sie alle weiche, leise Melodien der heiligen Seelen ein.   Jean Paul.

479.

Am Morgen.

Endlich trat die Sonne wie ein Musengott in den Morgen und nahm die Erde als ihr Saitenspiel in die Hand und griff in alle Saiten.
                    Jean Paul.

480.

Omar:

Die Welt ist ein Gesang, wo ein Ton den andern verschlingt und vom nächsten verschlungen wird.   Tieck (Abdallah).

481.

Sternbald:

Ich fühle es jedesmal, wie Musik die Seele erhebt und die jauchzenden Klänge wie Engel mit himmlischer Unschuld alle irdischen Begierden und Wünsche fern abhalten.

Wenn man an ein Fegefeuer glauben will, wo die Seele durch Schmerzen geläutert und

---

[1] Johann Gottlieb N., 1741—1810, seit 1776 Hofkapell-meister in Dresden, geschätzter Opernkomponist.

478.[38]

Just as people amidst the common noise of life can at the same time be hard of hearing and yet open to the subtlest musical sounds (e.g., Kapellmeister Naumann), so were Schoppe's inner ears hardened against the raucousness of people in their common doings, but thirsty they drew in all mild soft melodies of the sacred souls.

Jean Paul

479.

In the Morning

At last the sun stepped like a god of the Muses into the morning and took the earth in its hand for its harp and touched all strings.

Jean Paul

480.

Omar:

The world is a song where one tone devours the other only to be devoured by the next one.

Tieck (Abdallah)

481.

Sternbald:

I feel it every time how music elevates the soul and how the jubilant sounds like angels in heavenly innocence ward off all earthly desires and wishes.

If one wants to believe in purgatory, where the soul is purified and purged by suffering, then music, on the

---

[38] Schoppe is a character in Jean Paul's novel *Titan*. In a footnote, Krebs identifies Johann Gottlieb Naumann (1741-1810) as music director in Dresden and a highly regarded opera composer.

gereinigt wird, so ist im Gegenteil die Musik
ein Vorhimmel, wo diese Läuterung durch weh=
mütige Wonne geschieht.   Tieck (Sternbald).

482.

Die Form ist etwas durch tausendjährige
Bestrebungen der vorzüglichsten Meister Ge=
bildetes, das sich jeder Nachkommende nicht
schnell genug zu eigen machen kann. — Ein
höchst törichter Wahn übelverstandener Ori=
ginalität würde es sein, wenn da jeder wieder
auf eigenem Wege herumsuchen und herum=
tappen wollte, um das zu finden, was schon in
großer Vollkommenheit vorhanden ist.
Die Form wird überliefert, gelernt, nach=
gebildet, denn sonst könnte ja überall von keinem
Studium, von keinem Fortschreiten in der Kunst
die Rede sein; jeder müßte wieder von vorn
anfangen. Die Kunst aber ist lang und das
Leben kurz, und man tut daher wohl, seine
Kräfte nicht unnütz zu zersplittern und zu ver=
schwenden.   Eckermann (Beiträge zur Poesie).

483.
Über Form.

Was uns aber zu strengen Forderungen, zu
entschiedenen Gesetzen am meisten berechtigt, ist,
daß gerade das Genie, das angeborene Talent
sie am ersten begreift, ihnen den willigsten
Gehorsam leistet. Nur das Halbvermögen wünschte
gern seine beschränkte Besonderheit an die Stelle
des unbedingten Ganzen zu setzen und seine

contrary, is a foretaste of heaven, where this purification happens by bliss.

Tieck (Sternbald)

482.

Form is something shaped through thousand-year-old efforts by the most excellent masters, which every successor cannot assimilate quickly enough.—It would be extreme folly of misunderstood originality if everyone would search around anew and grope along on his way in order to find what already exists in great perfection.

Form is handed down, learned, imitated because otherwise one could never speak of study or advance in art; for everyone would have to start at the beginning again. But art is long and life is short, and one does well not unnecessarily to splinter and waste one's powers.

Eckermann (Beiträge zur Poesie)

483.[39] [= 617]
On Form

But what mostly justifies our strict demands and definite laws, is that it is precisely genius, the inborn talent, which grasps them first, and yields them the most willing obedience. Only mediocrity would fain substitute its limited specialty for the unlimited whole and glorify

---

[39] Brahms must have particularly liked this passage, for he copied it again as number 617.

falschen Griffe unter Vorwand einer unbezwing=
lichen Originalität und Selbständigkeit zu be=
schönigen. Das lassen wir aber nicht gelten,
sondern hüten unsere Schüler vor
allen Mißtritten, wodurch ein großer
Teil des Lebens, ja manchmal das
ganze Leben verwirrt und zerpflückt
wird. Mit dem Genie haben wir am liebsten
zu tun, denn dies wird eben von dem guten
Geist beseelt bald erkennen, was ihm nutz ist.
Es begreift, daß Kunst eben darum Kunst
heiße, weil sie nicht Natur ist. Es
bequemt sich zum Respekt, sogar vor dem, was
man konventionell nennen könnte: denn was
ist dieses anders, als das die vorzüg=
lichsten Menschen überein kamen, das
Notwendige, das Unerläßliche für
das Beste zu halten? Und gereicht es nicht
überall zum Glück?   Goethe.

484.
Form.

Unsere Geringschätzung der Form vernichtet
uns eine Anzahl geistvoller Talente. Ich glaube
nicht, daß es außerhalb Deutschland so viel
literarische Selbstmorde gibt als bei uns. Der
Geist, und was man poetischen Geist nennt,
ist unter uns mit einem unseligen Übermute
getränkt. Er hält es unter seiner
Würde, nach einer angemessenen Ge=
stalt zu trachten, und behandelt den Begriff
der Form verächtlich, und was gar im weitesten

its wrong ideas under the pretense of an incontrolable originality and independence. This, however, we do not let
pass, but we protect our pupils against all false steps,
whereby a great part of life, nay, often the whole life becomes confused and broken up. We love best to deal with
genius, for he is specially animated by the good spirit of
recognizing quickly what is useful to him. He sees that
Art is called Art, precisely because it is not Nature. He
accommodates himself to proper respect even for that
which might be called conventional, for what else is this
but that the best men have agreed to regard the necessary,
the inevitable, as the best? And does it not everywhere
lead to good fortune?

Goethe
(Wilhelm Meister's Years of Travel)

484.
Form

Our undervaluing form destroys a number of spir-
ited talents. I do not believe that outside Germany there
are so many literary suicides as with us. The spirit, and
what one calls poetic spirit, is soaked with a fatal wanton-
ness by us. One considers it below one's dignity to find
an appropriate shape and treats the concept of form with
contempt. And what in the widest sense of the word is

Sinn des Wortes Technik genannt wird, das
ist ihm fast eine Unwürdigkeit.

Obwohl innerhalb der irdischen Bedingungen
denkend und selbst im Denken eingeschlossen,
meint er doch ungestraft die irdische Formen=
welt überspringen zu können, ein Mensch, der
ohne Körper ein ausgezeichneter Mensch sein
will; der Idealismus bleibt unsere
Krankheit. Umsonst zeigt Lessing an so
vielen Orten, welch ein mächtiger Geist in den
literarischen Formen ruhe, und welch ein geist=
voller Sieg es sei, sich dieser Formen bemächtigen
zu können; umsonst zeigt der Briefwechsel zwischen
Schiller und Goethe, wie tiefsinnig diese beiden
großen Schriftsteller dem Studium der Form
nachgegangen, umsonst! Man greift die Resul=
tate dieser Männer, aber ihre Wege läßt man
unbeachtet.

Man wird es begreiflich finden, daß ein
wohlhabender Mann Platz, Steine, Kalk, Holz,
Wiesen und Bäume in reichlichem Maße zur
Hand haben und deshalb doch noch nicht Schloß
und Park errichten kann, wenn er nicht einen
Riß entworfen und die Arbeit nach richtiger
Folge betrieben, wenn er nicht über Handwerk,
Anlage und Kunst gebieten kann.

Die Schriftsteller mögen aber gar nicht be=
greifen, daß es nicht genug sei, reichliches
Material zur Hand zu haben.   Laube.

485.

Es gehört zu den traurigsten Irrtümern der
Zeit, wenn geglaubt wird, nicht nur, daß die

called technique, for him it is almost unworthy of consideration.

Although thinking within earthly conditions and himself included in the thinking, he yet believes to be able to jump with impunity over the earthly world of forms, a man who without body wants to be an excellent man. Idealism remains to be our illness. In vain Lessing shows in many places that a forceful spirit lies in literary forms and that it is a spiritual victory to master these forms; the correspondence between Goethe and Schiller shows in vain how intelligently these two great authors pursued the study of form, in vain! One grabs the results of these men but ignores their ways.

It is comprehensible that a rich man can have at his disposal a place, stones, quicklime, wood, meadows, and trees in abundance and yet cannot raise a castle and park if he has not drafted a design, arranged the work in proper order, if he cannot control labor, plan, and art. Authors, however, do not want to understand that having rich material on hand does not suffice.

Laube

485.

One of the saddest errors of our time is the belief not only that art can spare the luminescence of higher

Kunſt die Leuchten der höheren Einſicht ent=
behren könne, ſondern auch, daß ſie von ihrem
Einfluſſe ſchädlich berührt und in ihrem un=
befangenen Streben beirrt werde, daß ihr
Enthuſiasmus das Denken ausſchließe, in den
Armen beſonnener und tiefer Erwägung erſtickt
werde.   Thierſch, Allgemeine Äſthetik.

486.
Um die Begeiſterung zu läutern, iſt beharr=
licher Fleiß vonnöten. Wie töricht iſt es, zu
glauben, daß das ernſte Studium der Mittel
den Geiſt lähme.   C. M. v. Weber.

487.
Studium hütet dich vor dem Übermut der
                    Naturkraft,
Vor der Schule Manier wahrt dich die ſichre
                    Natur.   W. Menzel.

488.
Manche Lehre wirkt wie ein enthülltes Ge=
heimnis, ein mitgeteiltes Arkanum, und erſpart
viel vergebliche Selbſtverſuche; aber manches
Wort iſt auch eine Weiſſagung, ein Orakel=
ſpruch, deren Sinn man erſt nach vielen Er=
fahrungen begreift.   Kunſtblatt.

489.
Weil er von der Welt ſich abſchloß, nannte
ſie ihn feindſelig, und weil er der Empfindung
aus dem Wege ging, gefühllos. Ach! wer ſich

insight but also that it may become contaminated by its influence and led astray in its naive endeavor; and that enthusiasm excludes thought and would suffocate in the arms of circumspect and deep contemplation.

Thiersch, Allgemeine Aesthetik

486.

In order to refine enthusiasm, persevering diligence is necessary. How foolish to believe that serious study of the means paralyzes the spirit.

C.M. von Weber

487.*

Study protects you from the extravagance of nature's
    forces,
From the mannerism of a school, secure nature
    shields you.

W. Menzel

488.

Some doctrines have the effect of a revealed secret, a shared arcanum, and save many futile personal experiments; yet others are also a prophesy, an oracular statement, which one comprehends only after many experiences.

Kunstblatt

489.

Because he shut himself off from the world, they called him hostile; and because he avoided sentimentality, they called him insensitive. Oh, one who knows himself

hart weiß, der flieht nicht. Gerade das Über=
maß der Empfindung weicht der Empfindung aus.

Grillparzer (Rede an Beethovens Grabe).

490.

Wie? Rellſtab macht es zu arg? — Soll
denn dieſe verdammte deutſche Höflichkeit Jahr=
hunderte fortdauern? Während die literariſchen
Parteien ſich offen gegenüberſtehen und be=
fehden, herrſcht in der Kunſtkritik ein Achſel=
zucken, ein Zurückhalten, das weder begriffen
noch genug getadelt werden kann. Warum die
Talentloſen nicht geradezu zurückweiſen? Warum
die Flachen und Halbgeſunden nicht aus den
Schranken werfen ſamt den Anmaßenden?
Warum nicht Warnungstafeln vor Werken, die
da aufhören, wo die Kritik anfängt? Warum
ſchreiben die Autoren nicht eine eigene Zeitung
gegen die Kritiker und fordern ſie auf, gröber
zu ſein gegen die Werke?

Rob. Schumann (Floreſtan im „Komet", 1833)[1].

491.

Es iſt mir bei dieſer Gelegenheit wieder
recht fühlbar, was eine lebendige Er=
kenntnis auch beim Erfinden viel tut.

Schiller (Goethe=Schillers Briefwechſel).

---

[1] Ein von Schumann geſchriebener Artikel „Leipziger Muſik=
leben" war im Beiblatt des Herloßſohnſchen „Kometen" vom
7. und 14. Dezember 1833 und 12. Januar 1834 erſchienen.
Schumann hat ihn in ſeine „Geſammelten Schriften" nicht auf=
genommen, aber F. Guſtav Janſen fügte ihn der von ihm heraus=
gegebenen und ſehr vermehrten vierten Auflage (1891) ein,
Bd. I, S. 10 ff.

to be hard does not flee. Actually, abundance of feeling avoids sentimentality.

Grillparzer
(Speech at Beethoven's grave)

490.[40]

What? Rellstab is overdoing it? Is this cursed German politeness going to last for centuries? While the literary parties oppose each other and fight openly, music criticism is dominated by a shoulder-shrugging, a reticence which can be neither comprehended nor enough censored. Why not outright reject those who lack talent? Why not kick out the shallow and half-baked together with the presumptuous ones? Why not warning signs on works which stop where criticism begins? Why do authors not write their own journal against the critics and urge them to be harsher against the works?

Rob. Schumann
(Florestan in *Komet* 1833)

491.

On this occasion, I again feel strongly how much live understanding also contributes to invention.

Schiller (Goethe-Schiller Correspondence)

---

[40] Ludwig Rellstab, an influential music critic in Berlin, was defended by Schumann in three essays in the journal *Komet*.

492.

Alle, die mit dem einmal Gelernten fertig
zu sein glaubten, sind klein geblieben; alle, die
immer wieder zu den Urprinzipien zurückkehrten
und Kenntnisse und Fähigkeiten beobachtend,
lernend, übend ausbildeten, sind tüchtig geworden.

Fr. v. Schlegel.

493.

Die Geschichte der Künste wird eine große
Fuge sein, in der die Stimmen der Völker nach
und nach zum Vorschein kommen.   Goethe.

494.

Ich meine, wer fest auf den Füßen ist und
ein scharfes Auge im Kopfe hat, um die rechte
Straße nicht zu verfehlen, darf ohne Gefahr
wohl noch etwas weiter zu gehen sich wagen
als gewöhnlich.   Beethoven (in seinen Studien)[1].

495.

Wüßte nicht, was sie Besseres erfinden
könnten,
Als wenn die Lichter ohne Putzen brennten.

Goethe.

496.

Nur in der Liebe spricht die Wahrheit. Wer
lieblos spricht, urteilt falsch, liebend Irren ist
wahrer als lieblos treffende Wahrheit.

Kunstblatt.

---

[1] Vgl. die Bemerkung im Autorenverzeichnis.

492.[41]

All those who believed they were finished with what they once learned, have remained small; all those who keep returning to the basic principles and, observing knowledge and skills, by practice perfected them, have become efficient.

Fr. von Schlegel

493.

The history of the arts will be a great fugue in which the voices of nations will come to the fore one by one.

Goethe

494.

I think that a man who stands firmly on his feet and has a sharp eye in his head so as not to miss the right road may without danger dare to walk a bit farther than usual.

Beethoven

495.*

I would not know what better they could invent
Than lights which burn without cleaning.

Goethe

496.

Only in love does truth speak. Whoever speaks without love judges falsely. To err while loving is truer than truth reached without love.

Kunstblatt

---

[41] Brahms must have particularly liked this paragraph, for he had earlier entered it in his notebooks; see number 247.

497.

Altes und Bewährtes werde beibehalten, so=
lange man nichts Neues und zuverlässig Besseres
an des Alten Stelle zu setzen hat.

Th. G. v. Hippel.

498.

Jeder Genius muß nur nach dem, was er
selbst will, studiert werden.   Heinse.

499.

Ein Glas sprengt der ihm eigene zu stark
angegebene Ton; so kann auch eines Menschen
Herz, triffst du dessen Ton, ergriffen, bewegt,
zum Mitklingen bis zum Zerspringen gebracht
werden.   C. M. v. Weber.

500.

Zwischen Theorie und Praxis, Regel und
Beispiel, Gesetz und Freiheit bleibt immer ein
unendlicher Bruch übrig, und vielleicht ist eben
dieser Bruch mehr wert als das Ganze. Das
Schöne wäre vielleicht nicht mehr schön, wenn
irgendein Denker das Geheimnis enträtselte.

W. Menzel.

501.

Künstler, wird's im Innern steif,
Das ist nicht erfreulich,
Auch der vagen Züge Schweif
Ist uns ganz abscheulich.
Kommst du aber auf die Spur,
Daß du's nicht getroffen,
Zu der wahren Kunstnatur
Steht der Pfad schon offen.   Goethe.

497.

Something old and tried should be retained as long as one has nothing new and reliably better to put in its place.

Th. G. von Hippel

498.

Every genius must be studied only according to what he himself wants.

Heinse.

499.

A glass breaks when a tone proper to it is sounded too loudly. So also a human heart, hit by the proper tone, can be seized, moved to vibrate until it breaks.

C. M. von Weber

500.

Between theory and practice, rule and example, law and freedom, there always remains an infinite fraction, and perhaps just this fraction is worth more than the whole. Beauty would perhaps no longer be beautiful if some thinker solved the secret.

W. Menzel

501.*

Artist, when the inside stiffens,
This is not pleasant,
And also the rambling of vague pulls
Disgusts us.
But when you track down
Where you have failed,
To true artistic nature
The path has opened.

Goethe

502.

Wohl denen, die des Wissens Gut
Nicht mit dem Herzen zahlen!

Schiller.

[Düsseldorf], Juli 1854. J. B.

503.

Siehe zu, daß dich die Schule zum Leben
führe, daß du immer festen Boden fühlst, daß
sich dein Wissen nicht als trübes Mittel zwischen
deine Kunst und Natur stelle und du nicht etwa
nur lernst, täglich ein größerer Manierist zu
werden.　　　　　　　　　　　　　Kunstblatt.

504.

Es muß sich ein Zunftwesen edlerer Art
bilden, das alles der Kunst Unwürdige ausstößt.

J. Seski.

505.

Glieder erkennt die Menge leicht, aber Geist
nicht; Reize wohl, aber nicht Schönheit.

Jean Paul (Ästhetik).

506.

Für Künstler sind viele glänzende Gesell=
schaften verderblich. Sie fühlen sich erhaben
über die Leutchen, die sie loben und nicht be=
greifen. Das erzeugt eine ironische Stimmung,
welche die musikalische Produktivität schwächt.

August Kahlert.

507.

Der Tondichter soll denken, aber mehr in
Tönen als in Worten.　　　　August Kahlert.

502.

Blessed are they who do not pay with their heart for the possession of knowledge.

Schiller
[Düsseldorf], July 1854, J.B.

503.

See to it that your school lead you to life, that you always feel solid ground, that your knowledge does not put itself like a dim cloud between your art and nature, and that perchance you do not only learn to become a greater mannerist every day.

Kunstblatt

504.

A guild of nobler kind must be formed which expels from art all that is unworthy.

J. Feski

505.

The masses easily recognize parts but not spirit; charm, but not beauty.

Jean Paul (Aesthetik)

506.

Musicians are corrupted by too many brilliant social gatherings. They feel superior to the little people who praise without understanding them. This produces an ironical state of mind which weakens musical productivity.

August Kahlert

507.

The composer should think, but in tones more than in words.

August Kahlert

508.

Die plastische Kunst wählt zur Darstellung den Augenblick der Konsonanz. Die Tonkunst aber darf in derselben nicht stehen bleiben, denn sie bedarf der Bewegung. Sie geht durch die Dissonanzen wie der denkende Geist durch Zweifel zum Wissen.   August Kahlert.

509.

Die Werke der Tonkunst zu beurteilen, ist darum so schwer, weil in keiner Kunst das bloße Material eine so große Gewalt über den Menschen hat, als bei ihr. Ein einziger Ton wirkt oft Wunder. Weil nun die Musik aus diesem Grunde immer etwas Mehrdeutiges an sich hat, so darf es uns nicht befremden, wenn der Unverstand ihr allen Inhalt abspricht.
                    August Kahlert.

510.[1]

Wohl uns, wenn solche Schritte Aufsehn
machen,
Es tut uns Not in einer Zeit wie diese,
Wo alles in der Welt nur kriecht und schleicht.
                    3. Werner.

511.

Ein schwerer Gram ist ein verdorbnes Blut,
Das immer kreisend jegliches entzündet,
Bis man ihm einen Weg nach außen bahnt.
                    Raupach.

---

[1] Brahms hatte hierüber die Namen „Lißt, Berlioz" in Klammern gesetzt, sie aber später mit Bleistift zweimal durchstrichen.

508.

Plastic art chooses for representation the moment of consonance. Music, however, must not remain there, for it requires movement. It passes through the dissonance, like the thinking spirit through doubt to knowledge.

August Kahlert

509.

It is difficult to judge works of music because in no other art does the material alone wield such great power over people. A single tone often produces miracles. Since for that reason music is always open to many interpretations, we should not be surprised when lack of intelligence denies it all contents.

August Kahlert

510.*[42]

Good for us when such steps make a stir,
We need it at a time like the present
Where everything in the world just creeps and
    sneaks.

Z. Werner

511.*

A heavy sorrow is like tainted blood
Which, circulating, infects everything
Until an outlet is prepared for it.

Raupach

---

[42] Above this entry in his notebooks, Brahms had written the names of "Liszt, Berlioz" in parenthesis, but he later crossed them out twice with pencil.

512.

Wem die Natur, die erhabene, aus ihrer
unendlichen Fülle
Mannsinn gab und ein Herz, tatenbegierig und
groß —
O, der fall auf die Knie und danke der Göttin
mit Zittern,
Denn ein gefährlich Geschenk hat sie dem Staube
vertraut.
                                        v. Sonnenberg.

513.

Je mehr sich die Künste um den gemeinen
Sinn bemühen, sich zu ihm herablassen, sich ihm
aufdringen, desto mehr gewöhnt sich dieser, sie
zu ignorieren, zu vernachlässigen, ja endlich zu
verachten.   *Aus dem Kunstblatt.*

514.

Das Vorzüglichste, was uns erhalten ist,
ward nirgends durch den Geschmack des halb-
gebildeten großen Haufens vom Untergange ge-
rettet, sondern durch die Tätigkeit einiger Aus-
erwählter.   *Thibaut (Über Reinheit der Tonkunst).*

515.

Italienische Musikinstrumentation.

Oboi coi Flauti. Clarinetti coi Oboi. Flauti
coi Violini. Fagotti col Basso. Viol 2do col
1mo. Viola col Basso. Voce ad libitum,
Violini colla Parte.   *C. M. v. Weber.*

512.*

To whom lofty nature, in its infinite fullness,
Has given a manly sense and a great heart eager for
action—
O, he ought to kneel down and trembling thank the
goddess,
For she has entrusted to dust a dangerous gift.

von Sonnenberg

513.

The more the arts cater to common taste, the more
they stoop down and thrust themselves upon it, the more
it becomes used to ignore, neglect, and finally disdain
them.

From the *Kunstblatt*

514.

Everything first-rate preserved for us was saved from
decline, not by the taste of the half-educated masses, but
rather by the activities of a few elects.

Thibaut (On Purity of Music)

515.

Italian Orchestration

Oboi coi Flauti. Clarinetti coi Oboi. Flauti coi
Violini. Fagotti col Basso. Viol 2do col 1mo. Viola col
Basso. Voce ad libitum, Violini colla Parte.

C.M. von Weber

516.

Den ferne von meinem Pfad,
Des Herz nur träg' im frostigen Busen bebt,
Dem nur Gefühle matt wie Hausluft
Aus der umnebelten Seele schleichen.

Heydenreich.

517.

Alles verwandelt sich: nichts stirbt. In schöner
Verwandlung wird das Verlorene Gewinn.

Herder.

518.

Übers Vergleichen.

Die Frage: ob man bei Betrachtungen von
Kunstleistungen vergleichen soll oder nicht, möchten
wir folgendermaßen beantworten: Der aus=
gebildete Kenner soll vergleichen; denn ihm
schwebt die Idee vor, er hat den Begriff gefaßt,
was geleistet werden könne und solle; der Lieb=
haber, auf dem Wege zur Bildung begriffen,
fördert sich am besten, wenn er nicht vergleicht,
sondern jedes Verdienst einzeln betrachtet; da=
durch bildet sich Sinn und Gefühl für das All=
gemeinere nach und nach aus. Das Vergleichen
der Unkenner ist eigentlich nur eine Bequemlich=
keit, die sich gern des Urteils überheben möchte.

Goethe.

519.

Die Dilettanten, wenn sie das Möglichste
getan haben, pflegen zu ihrer Entschuldigung
zu sagen, die Arbeit sei noch nicht fertig! Frei=
lich kann sie nie fertig werden, weil sie nie
recht angefangen ward. Der Meister stellt sein

516.*

Keep far away from my path
Whose heart beats only sluggishly in his frozen
bosom,
Whose feelings, languid like stale air,
Creep out of his hazy soul.

Heydenreich

517.

Everything transforms, nothing dies. In beautiful
transformation, the loss becomes gain.

Herder

518.

On Comparing

The question: whether to compare works of art while
contemplating them, we would like to answer as follows:
the highly educated connoisseur should compare; for the
idea hovers before him, he has grasped what could and
should be accomplished; the amateur on the way toward
an education profits most by not comparing but by contemplating each achievement by itself; by so doing he
gradually develops sense and feeling for universal issues.
For the ignorant person, comparison is actually only a con-
venience which comfortably replaces judgment.

Goethe

519.

When dilettantes have done their utmost, they usually say, as an excuse, that the work is not yet finished! Of
course, it can never be finished because it was never properly begun. The master presents his work with a few strokes

Werk mit wenigen Strichen als fertig dar, aus=
geführt oder nicht, schon ist es vollendet. Der
geschickteste Dilettant tappt im Ungewissen, und
wie die Ausführung wächst, kommt die Unsicher=
heit der ersten Anlage immer mehr zum Vor=
schein. Ganz zuletzt entdeckt sich erst das Ver=
fehlte, das nicht auszugleichen ist, und so kann
das Werk freilich nicht fertig werden.

Goethe.

520.

Man kann über nichts urteilen, wovon man
kein Ideal hat, und das entwirft der Verstand
mit der Wahl aus vielem.   W. Heinse.

521.

Ein großer Teil des Publikums hat über=
haupt nur Sinn und Kraft für das Mittelmäßige.
Das aber kann man verlangen, daß die, welche
bloß das Gemeine oder Mittelmäßige verstehen
und lieben, sich des Urteils über eigentliche
geniale Kunstwerke enthalten.

Thibaut (über Reinheit der Tonkunst).

522.
Beethoven.

So staunet an der Pöbel,
Pöbel in Purpur und gehüllt in Schulstaub,
Den Erde höhnenden Gesang
Der Begeisterung.   Fr. v. Stolberg.

as finished, executed or not, it is already completed. The most dextrous dilettante gropes in the dark, and the more he puts into execution, the more evident becomes the uncertainty of the first conception. Only at the very end the irreparable mistakes are discovered and thus, of course, the work cannot ever be finished.

Goethe

520.

One cannot judge anything of which one does not have an ideal, which reason projects by choosing from a multitude.

W. Heinse

521.

A great part of the public has a sense and power only for the mediocre. But we can at least demand that those who understand and like only commonplace and mediocrity should abstain from passing judgment on real art works of genius.

Thibaut (On Purity of Music)

522.*

Beethoven

The rabble, dressed in purple
and covered with school dust,
gapes at the song of enthusiasm
which derides this earth.

Fr. von Stolberg

523.

Man kann wohl satt werden, Musik zu hören, aber nicht zu machen, und jeder Musiker könnte sich wie eine Nachtigall tot schmettern.

Jean Paul.

524.

Geschicklichkeit hat einen ganz besonderen stärkenden Reiz, und es ist wahr, ihr Bewußtsein einen dauerhafteren und deutlicheren Genuß als jenes überfließende Gefühl einer unbegreiflichen, überschwenglichen Herrlichkeit.   Novalis.

525.

Nicht auf den ersten Blick ergründen sollst
     du das Kunstwerk,
Wo es dir dämmernd erscheint, forsche mit fröh=
     lichem Fleiß.

Streckfuß.

526.

Nur das Ganze, mein Freund, wie es lebt und
     im Leben sich spiegelt,
Dies sei dein Ideal, fern von der Formel Ge=
     spenst.   Fr. Schlegel.

527.

Strebt weiter und weiter, doch haltet nur
An der ewig wahren, der alten Natur.

Goethe.

523.

One certainly can become satiated with hearing
music but not with making music, and every musician
could, like a nightingale, warble himself to death.

Jean Paul

524.

Proficiency has a particularly invigorating allure. It
is true, awareness of it gives a more lasting and clearer joy
than that overflowing feeling of an inconceivable, exag-
gerated glory.

Novalis

525.*

Do not at a first glance try to fathom the work of art.
Where it appears to you dim,
There search with pleasure and diligence.

Streckfuss

526.*

Only the whole, my friend, be your ideal as it lives
and is mirrored in life, far from the spectre of a formula.

Fr. Schlegel

527.*

Strive further and further but hold secure
To the eternally true, primal nature.

Goethe

528.

Viel Menſchen ſchleichen matt und träg'
Ins kalte Grab hinein;
Doch fröhlich geht des Sängers Weg
Durch lauter Frühlingsſchein.   Th. Körner.

529.

Die großartige deutſche Muſik iſt das Er=
zeugnis von Männern — eine Muſik der Philo=
ſophie, des Heldenmutes, des Geiſtes, der Phan=
taſie, zu welcher die Kompoſitionen des modernen
Italiens in der Tat weichlich und erkünſtelt er=
ſcheinen.   Bulwer (Maltravers).

530.

Nicht Kunſt und Wiſſenſchaft allein,
Geduld will bei dem Werke ſein.
                              Goethe.

531.

Man muß mehr als ein Werk und viel von
einem Meiſter geſehen haben, ehe man ihn recht
kennen lernt. So geht's auch mit den Menſchen
überhaupt; es iſt nichts eitler und törichter als
die Reiſenden und Hoffſchranzen, die einen wich=
tigen Mann gleich beim erſten Beſuch und Ge=
ſpräch weg haben wollen.   W. Heinſe.

532.

Des Sehers und des Sängers Gaben ſind
Von Gott und heilig; ehrt den Gott in euch;
Fröhnt nicht mit Heiligen dem Weltlichen,
Buhlt mit der Lyra nicht um ſchnöden Lorbeer
Und nicht um ſchnödes Gold.   Chamiſſo.

528.*

Many people feeble and tired creep into their cold grave; but the singer's way leads gaily through pure lustre of spring.

Th. Körner

529.

The magnificent German music is the product of men—a music of philosophy, of heroic courage, of the spirit, of fantasy, compared to which the compositions of modern Italy actually appear feeble and artificial.

Bulwer (Maltravers)

530.*

Not art and knowledge alone,
But also patience must attend the work.

Goethe

531.

One has to see more than one work and very much of one master before one really gets to know him. That's how it goes with people generally; nothing is vain and sillier than the travellers and courtly flatterers who claim to know an important person immediately after the first visit and conversation.

W. Heinse.

532.*

The prophet's and the singer's gifts come from God and are holy; honor the God within you; do not let the holy serve the secular, do not use the lyra to woo base laurel and base gold.

Chamisso

533.

Es schläft das Lied in tiefster Brust
Und träumt sich selber unbewußt
Und will sich nicht gestalten. Chamisso.

534.

Beethoven[1]).

Ein Geist, den die Natur zum Mustergeist
beschloß,
Ist, was er ist, durch sich, wird ohne Regeln groß;
Er geht so kühn, er geht auch ohne Weisung
sicher,
Er schöpfet aus sich selbst, er ist sich Schul' und
Bücher. Lessing.

535.

Jeder Künstler hat Stunden, Tage der Ent=
mutigung, wo er die Schöpfungskraft in sich
erloschen, sein schön'res Leben abgelaufen glaubt.
Raupach.

536.

Der letzte, aber vielleicht bedeutendste Wink,
den man geben kann und schwerlich zu oft, ist
dieser: Freunde, habt nur vorzüglich
wahres, herrliches Genie, dann werdet
ihr euch wundern, wie weit ihr's treibt.
Jean Paul.

537.

Das Verschwinden der geborenen Genies,
welche aus unbewußtem Drange Großes leisten,

---

[1]) „Beethoven" ist natürlich von Brahms hinzugesetzt.

533.*

The song sleeps in the deepest breath.
Unconsciously it dreams itself
and does not want to take shape.

Chamisso

534.*[43]

Beethoven

A genius whom Nature chose for a model spirit
Is, what he is, through his own self, becomes
    great without rules;
His stride is bold, his walk secure without
    instruction,
He creates out of himself, he is to himself
    school and books.

Lessing.

535.

Every artist has hours, days of discouragement,
when he believes that his creative power is extin-
guished and the best part of his life expired.

Raupach

536.

The final but perhaps most significant hint one
can give, and hardly too often, is this one: Friends,
have preferably true, glorious genius, and you will
be amazed how far you will get.

Jean Paul

537.

The disappearance of born geniuses who ac-
complish great things through an unconscious urge,

---

[43] The title "Beethoven" was added by Brahms. Lessing could not
have known of Beethoven.

und das Auftauchen von Talenten, die mit
Bewußtsein und Freiheit nach gleich hohem,
auch noch höherem Ziel streben, ist eine welt=
historische Erscheinung.   Kunstblatt.

538.
(Beethoven, 9te) [1]).

Schaust du zum Himmel empor, sternreich er=
                        scheint er — doch blicke
Schärfer ihn an, und es mehrt stets sich die
                        leuchtende Schar.
                                        Streckfuß.
539.

Das Technische einer Kunst muß eigentlich
in frühern Jahren ordentlich erlernt werden.
Regt sich erst der Geist von innen heraus, so
muß die Sorge für äußere Darstellung beseitigt
sein, und wer das schöne Handwerk kennt, wird
gestehen, daß es gleichsam Dichten hilft; denn
es rührt die Lust und macht den Trieb frei.
                                        Zelter.
540.

Das ist eine von den alten Sünden,
Sie meinen, Rechnen das sei Erfinden.
                                        Goethe.
541.

Erst Empfindung, dann Gedanken,
Erst ins Weite, dann zu Schranken,
Aus dem Wilden hold und mild
Zeigt sich dir das wahre Bild.
                                        Goethe.

------
[1] Von Brahms hinzugesetzt.

and the emergence of talents who with consciousness and freedom strive for equally high, even for higher goals, is a phenomenon in world history.

Kunstblatt

538.*[44]
(Beethoven's 9th)

If you look up at the sky, it seems to abound in
    stars—
But look at it more sharply and the radiant host ever
    increases.

Streckfuss

539.

The technical aspect of an art should really be thoroughly learned at an early age. Later, when the spirit stirs from within, the concern for the outward presentation must have been removed, and one who knows the beautiful trade will admit that this helps, as it were, the poetizing; for it arouses the desire and liberates the drive.

Zelter

540.*

This is one of the old sins,
They think that calculating means inventing.

Goethe

541.*

First feeling, then thought,
First into the distance, then into bounds.
Out of the wilderness, gentle and mild,
The true image appears to you.

Goethe

---

[44] The title "Beethoven, 9th" was added by Brahms in parenthesis.

542.

Ich halte dafür, der Dichter soll seine Kennt=
nisse auf ein weitläufig gewobenes Zeug auf=
reißen, damit der Musiker vollkommen Raum
habe, seine Stickerei mit großer Freiheit und
mit starken oder feinen Fäden, wie es ihm gut
dünkt, auszuführen. Der Operntext soll ein
Karton sein, kein fertiges Bild.   Goethe.

543.

Liebe sei vor allen Dingen
Unser Thema, wann wir singen;
Kann sie gar das Lied durchdringen,
Wird es um so besser klingen.
                    Goethe.

544.

Theorie und Praxis wirken immer auf=
einander. Aus den Werken kann man sehen,
wie es die Menschen meinen, und aus den
Meinungen voraussagen, was sie tun werden.
                    Goethe.

545.

Die meisten jetzigen Sangvögel singen nach
einer Drehorgel als Muster, nicht aus heißem
Bruttrieb, wie die Nachtigall.   Jean Paul.

546.

Wenn Schmerz mit Lust des Sängers Brust
                    durchglüht,
Entspringt aus ihr das farbenreichste Lied:
Wenn Regen in den Glanz der Sonne quillt,
Entsteht des Regenbogens zartes Bild.
                    Just. Kerner.

542.

I am of the opinion that the poet should delineate his ideas on a loosely woven cloth so that the musician will have perfect space to complete his embroidery with great freedom and with thick or thin thread, just as he sees fit. The libretto for an opera should be a sketch, not a finished picture.

Goethe

543.*

Love above all else should be
Our theme when we sing;
If it can permeate our song,
The sound will be all the better.

Goethe

544.

Theory and practice always influence each other. From their works we can see how people think, and from their thoughts predict what they will do.

Goethe

545.

Most singing birds of today sing after the barrel organ as a model, not because of a burning urge in the breast like the nightingale.

Jean Paul

546.*

When pain with passion glow in the singer's breast,
The most colorful song springs from it:
When rain trickles in the splendour of the sun,
The tender image of the rainbow originates.

Just. Kerner

547.

Rührung paßt nur für Frauenzimmer, dem
Manne muß Musik Feuer aus dem Geist schlagen.

Beethoven (Brief an Bettina) [1].

548.

Drum prüfe du nur allzumeist
Ob du Kern oder Schale seist.

Goethe.

549.

Manchen erhabenen Geist zertrümmerten
Stürme des Unglücks,
Schöne Ruinen jedoch ließen sie immer zurück.

v. Brinkmann.

550.

Ekel an der Wiederholung, insofern Wieder=
holung die Idee verstärkt, ist fast ein untrüg=
liches Kennzeichen vom Verfall des Geschmackes
einer Nation.   C. F. D. Schubart.

551.

Die Geschichte der großen Künstler beweist
es, wieviel Schweiß bei ihren Übungen troff,
wieviel unvollkommene Versuche sie im Kamin
aufdampfen ließen, wie tief in der Einsamkeit
verborgen sie Finger, Ohr und Herz übten, bis
sie endlich auftraten und der Welt durch Meister=
werke Beifall abnötigten.   C. F. D. Schubart.

---

[1] Vergl. die Ausführung im Autorenregister.

547.[45]
Sentimental emotion fits only women, music to a man strikes fire from his spirit.

Beethoven (Letter to Bettina)

548.*
Test yourself thoroughly to find out
Whether you are kernel or shell.

Goethe

549.*
Many a lofty spirit was crushed by the storms of
misfortune,
Yet they always leave beautiful ruins behind them.

von Brinckmann

550.
Disgust for repetition, inasmuch as repetition strengthens an idea, is an almost certain sign of the deterioration of a nation's taste.

C.F.D. Schubart

551.
The history of great artists proves how much sweat dripped when they practiced, how many incomplete experiments they turned to steam in the fireplace, how deeply hidden in solitude they practiced fingers, ear, and heart, until they finally stepped forward and elicited the world's applause by their masterworks.

C.F.D. Schubart

---

[45] Krebs rightly calls this entry apocryphal. Bettina von Arnim (cf. Annotated List of Authors) had faked it while corresponding with the composer.

552.

Frankreich goutiert, Deutschland erfindet, Welschland schmückt. Dieses uralte Sprichwort ist noch heute wahr und wirft auf alle musikalischen Schulen Licht.   C. F. D. Schubart.

553.

Aus dem Leben heraus sind der Wege zwei dir geöffnet,
Zum Ideale führt einer, der andre zum Tod.
Siehe, daß du beizeiten noch frei auf dem ersten entspringest,
Ehe die Parze mit Zwang dich auf dem andern entführt.   Schiller.

554.

Das Talent ist freilich nicht erblich; allein es will eine tüchtige physische Unterlage, und da ist es dann keineswegs einerlei, ob jemand von kräftigen und jungen, oder von schwachen und alten Eltern ist gezeugt worden. Merkwürdig ist übrigens, daß sich von allen Talenten das musikalische am frühesten zeigt.
Eckermanns Gespräche mit Goethe.

555.

Das musikalische Talent kann sich wohl am frühesten zeigen, indem die Musik ganz etwas Angeborenes, Inneres ist, das von außen keiner großen Nahrung und keiner aus dem Leben gezogenen Erfahrung bedarf.   Goethe.

552.

France is a gourmet, Germany an inventor, Italy a decorator. This very old proverb is still true today and sheds light on all musical schools.

C.F.D. Schubart

553.*

Two ways are open to you away from life,
One leads to the ideal, the other to death.
See that in good time, still free, you jump off the first
Ere the Parcae carry you off with force on the other.

Schiller

554.

Talent is indeed not hereditary, but it requires a sound physical foundation, and then it is by no means the same whether one is born of strong and young, or weak and old, parents. It is moreover noteworthy that of all talents, the musical shows itself earliest.

Eckermann (Conversations with Goethe)

555.

Musical talent may well show itself earliest, for music is something innate, internal, which needs little nourishment from the outside and no experience drawn from life.

Goethe

556.

. . . Alles erwogen, was gegen ihn zeugen
könnte, ist dieser Leipziger Kantor eine Er=
scheinung Gottes: klar, doch unerklärbar.

Zelter.

557.

Streitende Kräfte besaiten das Herz; ihr
mächtiger Einklang,
Nicht ihr lärmendes Spiel, bildet den männ=
lichen Mut.

v. Brinkmann.

558.

So war's immer, und so wird's bleiben, die
Unmacht hat die Regel für sich, aber die Kraft
den Erfolg.

Schiller.

559.

Auch die mittelmäßigen Sachen mögen in
Ehre bleiben, wenn sie nur nicht ungesund und
verzerrt sind. Der Mensch ist nicht jeden Augen=
blick aufgelegt, die Psalmen oder den Homer zu
lesen.

Thibaut.

560.

Musik ist die Kunst der Liebe,
In der tiefsten Seel' empfangen
Aus entflammendem Verlangen
Mit der Demut heil'gem Triebe.

A. W. v. Schlegel.

556.

Considering everything that could testify against him, this Leipzig cantor is an apparition of God: clear but inexplicable.

Zelter

557.*

Conflicting forces equip the heart with strings; their mighty unison, not their noisy play, creates virile courage.

von Brinckmann

558.

This is the way it's always been, and this is the way it will remain: incompetence has the rules for itself, but force has the success.

Schiller

559.

Even mediocre things may continue to be honored as long as they are not unwholesome and distorted. Man is not always in the mood to read the Psalms or Homer.

Thibaut

560.*

Music is the art of love,
Received in the deepest soul
From a burning desire
With the sacred drive of humility.

A. W. von Schlegel

561.

Doch mir deucht nur ein Dichter, der noch
sänge,
Der seinen Wohllaut noch verströmen müßte
Wo keines Menschen Stimme zu ihm dränge:
Im stillen Meer an unwirtbarer Küste,
Zuhören nur die wilden Felsgehänge.

G. Herwegh.
(Steht in der Neuen Zeitschrift für Musik über einer
Rezension F. Hillerscher Sachen.)

562.

. . . Wenigstens haben die Vögel, die singen,
und die Blumen, die duften, immer einige Ähnlich=
keit miteinander, nicht nur im Gesange und Duft,
sondern auch in der Farbe; sie sind beide mehr
farblos.

Die ersten Singvögel haben zugleich die aller=
einfachsten Farben, als da sind: die Lerche, die
Nachtigall, der Star, die Amsel, der Kanarien=
vogel usw. Die buntesten Vögel sind immer
keine Singvögel: der Pfau, der Papagei, der
Kolibri.

Die duftvollsten Blumen sind immer solche,
die am wenigsten Farbe haben, als da sind:
die Nachtviole, Lilie, Nelke, und zwar duften
die einfarbigen Nelken immer mehr als die
bunten, die Tuberosen, die Rosen, die Hya=
zinthen, wie die bunten wieder weniger als die
einfachen duften.

Wie viele Ähnlichkeit hat nicht eine Nacht=
viole mit einer Nachtigall! Jene ist unter den

561.*
I consider a poet only someone who could continue
to sing,
Who would need to pour out his harmonious sounds
Where no human voice would reach him:
In the silent sea at an inhospitable coast
Only the wild rocky declivities are listening.

G. Herwegh
(Published in the *Neue Zeitschrift für Musik*
above a review of pieces by F. Hiller.)

562.
....At least the birds that sing and the flowers that
are fragrant have always some similarity, not only in song
and fragrance but also in color; both are more colorless.

The first singing birds also have the simplest colors,
they are: the lark, the nightingale, the starling, the thrush,
the canary, etc. The many-colored birds do not sing: the
peacock, the parrot, the colibri.

The most fragrant flowers are always those that have
the least color, they are: the nightviolet, lily, carnation,
the monochrome carnations always more than the many-
colored. On the other hand, the many-colored amaryllis,
roses, hyacinths are less fragrant than the simple.

How much similarity is there between a nightviolet
and a nightingale! The former is among flowers the most

Blumen die duftreichſte, dieſe unter den Vögeln
die tonreichſte; jene duftet, dieſe ſingt nur bei
Nacht; beide haben gänzlichen Mangel an Farbe.

Juſtinus Kerner (Reiſeſchatten).

563.

Bilde, Künſtler! rede nicht!
Nur ein Hauch ſei dein Gedicht.

Goethe.

564.

Was konnte dies anders für eine Wirkung
auf das Gemüt unſeres Künſtlers (Francesco
Francia) haben, als daß ſein lebhafter Geiſt ſich
zu dem edelſten Künſtlerſtolze emporhob und er
an einen himmliſchen Genius in ſeinem Innern
zu glauben anfing. Wo findet man jetzt dieſen
erhabenen Stolz? Vergebens ſucht man ihn
unter den Künſtlern unſerer Zeiten, welche wohl
auf ſich eitel, aber nicht ſtolz auf ihre
Kunſt ſind. Wackenroder, Phantaſien über die Kunſt,
herausgegeben von L. Tieck.

565.

Zur Erlernung jeder (bildenden) Kunſt, ſelbſt
wenn ſie ernſthafte oder trübſelige Dinge ab=
ſchildern ſoll, gehört ein lebendiges und auf=
gewecktes Gemüt; denn es ſoll ja durch all=
mähliche mühſame Arbeit endlich ein voll=
kommenes Werk, zum Wohlgefallen aller Sinne,
hervorgebracht werden, und traurige und in ſich

fragrant, the latter among birds the richest in tones; the former is fragrant, the latter sings only at night. Both completely lack color.

Justinus Kerner (Reiseschatten)

563.*
Create, artist! Don't talk!
Let your poem be just a breath.

Goethe

564.
What other effect could it have had on the mind of our artist (Francesco Francia) than that his lively spirit rose to the noblest artistic pride and that he began to have faith in a heavenly genius inside himself? Where can one now find this pride? One looks in vain among the artists of our time who have vanity for themselves but no pride in their art.

Wackenroder (Phantasien über die Kunst)
edited by L. Tieck

565.
The attainment of each (visual) art, even when it depicts serious or dreary objects, demands a lively and active disposition; for the task is to bring forth, by gradual and painstaking labor, a perfect work pleasing all senses. People sad and locked up in themselves have no impetus

verſchloſſene Gemüter haben keinen Gang, keine
Luſt, keinen Mut und keine Stetigkeit hervor=
zubringen.   Wackenroder.
(Aus einem verzagten A . . . fährt kein fröhlicher S . . .) [1]

566.

(In kurzer Zeit überholte er ſeine Lehrer.)

Ein Beweis, daß die Kunſt ſich eigentlich
nicht lernt und nicht gelehrt wird, ſondern daß
ihr Strom, wenn er nur auf eine kurze Strecke
geführt und gerichtet iſt, unbeherrſcht aus eigener
Seele quillt.   Wackenroder.

567.

Ein Maler (Komponiſt) ſoll ſich allgemein
machen und nicht alle Dinge nach einem einzigen
angewöhnten Handgriff, ſondern ein jedes nach
ſeiner beſonderen Eigentümlichkeit darſtellen; —
und dann, daß man ſich nicht an einen Meiſter
hängen, ſondern ſelbſt frei die Natur in allem
ihren Weſen erforſchen ſolle, indem man ſonſt
ein Enkel, nicht aber ein Sohn der Natur genannt
zu werden verdient.   Wackenroder.

568.

Vergleichung iſt ein gefährlicher Feind des
Genuſſes; auch die höchſte Schönheit der Kunſt

[1] Dieſer von Brahms zitierte Ausſpruch ſtammt bekanntlich
von Luther.

and no perseverance for creation.

Wackenroder

(Out of a faint a..... passes no cheerful f...)[46]

566.

(In a short time he surpassed his teachers.)

A proof that art cannot actually be learned nor taught, but that its stream, when guided and regulated for only a short stretch, springs uncontrollably from the depth of the soul.

Wackenroder

567.

A painter (composer) should make himself universal and present all things not according to one single, accustomed procedure but rather to the distinct characteristics of each.— Then also he should not attach himself to one master but rather free himself to explore nature in all its essence, otherwise he deserves to be called a grandson but not a son of Nature.

Wackenroder

568.

Comparison is a dangerous enemy of enjoyment; even the supreme beauty of art exercises its full power over

---

[46] Luther is the author of this vulgar saying quoted in parenthesis by Brahms.

übt nur dann, wie sie soll, ihre volle Gewalt
an uns aus, wenn unser Auge nicht zugleich
seitwärts auf andere Schönheit blickt. Der
Himmel hat seine Gaben unter die großen
Künstler der Erde so verteilet, daß wir durch=
aus genötigt werden, vor einem jeglichen stille
zu stehen und jeglichem seinen Anteil unserer
Verehrung zu opfern.   Wackenroder.

569.

In dem tobenden und schäumenden Meer
spiegelt sich der Himmel nicht; — der klare
Fluß ist es, worin Bäume und Felsen und die
ziehenden Wolken und alles Gestirn des Firma=
mentes sich wohlgefällig·beschauen.
                                        Wackenroder.
570.

Immerfort höre ich die kindische und leicht=
sinnige Welt klagen, daß Gott nur so wenige
recht große Künstler auf die Erde gesetzt habe;
ungeduldig starrt der gemeine Geist in die Zu=
kunft, ob der Vater der Menschen nicht bald
einmal ein neues Geschlecht von hervorglänzenden
Meistern werde auferstehen lassen. Ich sage
euch aber, es hat die Erde der vortrefflichen
Meister nicht zu wenige getragen; ja es sind
ihrer einige so beschaffen, daß ein sterbliches
Wesen sein ganzes Leben hindurch an einem
einzelnen zu schauen und zu begreifen hat; aber
wahrlich! viel, viel zu wenige sind derer, welche
die Werke dieser (aus edlerem Ton geformten)

us, as it should, only when our eye is not at the same time stealing sidelong glances at another beauty. Heaven has distributed its gifts among the great artists of the earth in such a way that we are compelled to stand still before each and offer each a share of our admiration.

Wackenroder

569.

In the stormy foaming sea, the sky is not mirrored. It is the clear river in which trees and rocks and passing clouds and all the stars of the firmament see themselves pleasantly reflected.

Wackenroder

570.

Continually I hear the childish and frivolous world complain that God has set only so few really great artists on this earth; impatiently the ordinary mind stares into the future to see whether the father of mankind will not soon resurrect a new race of brilliant masters. But surely I tell you, the earth has not carried too few outstanding masters; yes, some of them are so constituted that a mortal being can spend his whole life studying and comprehending one of them; but truly! there are far too few people who are capable of intimately understanding and (what is

Wesen innig zu verstehen und (was dasselbe ist)
inniglich zu verehren imstande sind.
                                        Wackenroder.

571.

Mit Ungeduld fliege ich über den ersten An=
blick hinweg; denn die Überraschung des neuen,
welche manche nach immer abwechselnden Ver=
gnügen haschende Geister wohl zum Haupt=
verdienste der Kunst erklären wollen, hat mir
von jeher ein notwendiges Übel des ersten An=
schauens geschienen. Der echte Genuß erfordert
eine stille und ruhige Fassung des Gemütes und
äußert sich nicht durch Ausrufungen und Zu=
sammenschlagen der Hände, sondern allein durch
innere Bewegungen. Es ist mir ein heiliger
Feiertag, an welchem ich mit Ernst und mit
vorbereitetem Gemüt an die Betrachtung edler
Kunstwerke gehe; ich kehre oft und unaufhörlich
zu ihnen zurück, sie bleiben meinem Sinne fest
eingeprägt, und ich trage sie, so lange ich auf
Erden wandle, in meiner Einbildungskraft, zum
Trost und zur Erweckung meiner Seele, gleich=
sam als geistige Amulete mit mir herum und
werde sie mit ins Grab nehmen. Wackenroder.

572.

Es ist doch eine köstliche Gabe, die der
Himmel uns verliehen hat, zu lieben und zu
verehren; dieses Gefühl schmelzt unser ganzes
Wesen um und bringt das wahre Gold daraus
zutage.   Wackenroder.

the same); ardently revering the works of these beings (shaped from nobler clay).

Wackenroder

571.

Impatiently do I skip over the first viewing, for the surprise of the new (which those who always snatch at continually varying diversion declare to be the chief merit of art) has always appeared to me to be a necessary evil of the first view. Genuine enjoyment requires a quiet and calm composure of the mind and expresses itself not by exclamations and clapping hands but only by inmost movements. It is a sacred holiday for me when I prepare myself seriously to contemplate noble works of art; I return to them often and incessantly. They remain firmly imprinted on my mind, and as long as I wander on earth I carry them with me in my imagination like spiritual amulets for the consolation and revival of my soul, and I will also take them with me to my grave.

Wackenroder

572.

It is a precious gift which heaven has bestowed on us: to love and to adore. This feeling melts our whole being and brings forth its true gold.

Wackenroder

573.

Es ist in der Welt der Künstler gar kein höherer, der Anbetung würdigerer Gegenstand als: — ein ursprünglich Original! — Mit emsigem Fleiße, treuer Nachahmung, klugem Urteil zu arbeiten — ist menschlich; — aber das ganze Wesen der Kunst mit einem ganz neuen Auge zu durchblicken, es gleichsam mit einer ganz neuen Handhabe zu erfassen, i st g ö t t l i ch.

Wackenroder.

574.

... Sind diejenigen vielleicht glücklicher ge= bildet, in denen die Kunst still und heimlich wie ein verhüllter Genius arbeitet und sie in ihrem Handeln auf Erden nicht stört? Und muß der immer Begeisterte seine hohen Phantasien doch auch vielleicht als einen festen Einschlag kühn und stark in dieses irdische Leben einweben, wenn er ein echter Künstler sein will? — Ja, ist diese unbegreifliche Schöpfungskraft nicht etwa überhaupt ganz etwas anderes, und — wie mir jetzt erscheint — etwas noch Wundervolleres, noch Göttlicheres als die Kraft der Phantasie?

Wackenroder.

575.

Was wollen sie, die zaghaften und zweifelnden Vernünftler, die jedes der 100 und 100 Ton= stücke in Worten erklärt verlangen und sich nicht darein finden können, daß nicht jedes eine nenn= bare Bedeutung hat wie ein Gemälde? Streben sie die reichere Sprache nach der ärmeren ab= zumessen und in Worte aufzulösen, was Worte

573.

In the world of artists there is no higher subject worthy of adoration than—a fresh original! To work with diligence, faithful imitation, and intelligent judgment—that is human; but to penetrate the whole essence of art with a totally new eye, to grasp it, as it were, with a totally new handle—that is divine.

Wackenroder

574.

...Are they perhaps more happily formed in whom art is working quietly and secretly like a veiled genius, without disturbing them in their activities on earth? And must the enthusiast, brave and strong, perhaps weave his high fantasies as a firm woof into this worldly life if he wants to be a true artist?—Yes, is this incomprehensible creative force not something totally different and—as it now appears— something more wonderful, more divine, than the force of fantasy?

Wackenroder

575.

What do the timorous and doubting reasoners want when they demand to have each of the 100 and 100 musical compositions explained in words and are not satisfied that not every piece has an enunciable meaning like a painting? Do they strive to measure the richer language by the poorer one and dissolve in words that which scorns

verachtet? Oder haben sie nie ohne Worte
empfunden? Haben sie ihr hohles Herz nur
mit Beschreibungen von Gefühlen ausgefüllt?
Haben sie niemals im Inneren wahrgenommen
das stumme Singen, den vermummten Tanz der
unsichtbaren Geister? oder glauben sie nicht an
die Märchen.   Wackenrober.

576.
Auf Alandern.

Alander, hör' ich, ist auf mich gewaltig wild;
Er spöttelt, lästert, lügt und schilt.
Kennt mich der gute Mann? Er kennt mich
                                  nicht, ich wette.
Doch was? als ob nicht auch sein Bruder an
                                  der Kette
Auf die am heftigsten, die er nicht kennet, billt.
                                  Lessing.

577.
An Einen.

Du schmähst mich hinterrücks? das soll mich
                                  wenig kränken.
Du lobst mich ins Gesicht? das will ich dir ge=
                                  denken!   Lessing.

578.
Der Affe und der Fuchs.

Nenne mir ein so geschicktes Tier, dem ich
nicht nachahmen könnte! so prahlte der Affe
gegen den Fuchs. Der Fuchs aber erwiderte:

169

words? Or have they never felt without words? Have they stuffed their hollow hearts with mere descriptions of sentiments? Have they never perceived inside the silent song, the masked dance of the invisible spirits? Or don't they believe in fairy tales?

Wackenroder

576.*
On Alander

Alander, I hear, is mightily wild toward me;
He mocks, slanders, lies, and scolds.
Does the good man know me? He does not know
        me, I bet.
So what? As if his chained brother not also barks
Most violently at those he does not know.

Lessing

577.*
To Someone

You revile me behind my back? That does not much
        annoy me.
You praise me into my face? I shall remember you
        for it.

Lessing

578.
The Monkey and the Fox

Name an ever so clever animal that I could not imitate! thus the monkey bragged to the fox. But the fox replied:

und du nenne mir ein so geringschätziges Tier,
dem es einfallen könnte, dir nachzuahmen.
Schriftsteller meiner Nation! — — Muß ich
mich noch deutlicher erklären! *Lessing.*

579.

Was soll man zu den Dichtern sagen, die so
gern ihren Flug weit über alle Fassung des
größten Teils ihrer Leser nehmen? Was sonst,
als was die Nachtigall einst zu der Lerche sagte:
„Schwingst du dich, Freundin, nur darum so hoch,
um nicht gehört zu werden?"

Nach Percy von Herder.

580.

Der Rabe bemerkte, daß der Adler ganze
30 Tage über seinen Eiern brütete. Und daher
kommt es ohne Zweifel, sprach er, daß die
Jungen des Adlers so allsehend und stark werden.
Gut! Das will ich auch tun.

Und seitdem brütet der Rabe wirklich ganze
30 Tage über seinen Eiern; aber noch hat er
nichts als elende Raben ausgebrütet.

Nach Percy von Herder.

581.

Singe doch, liebe Nachtigall! rief ein Schäfer
der schweigenden Sängerin an einem lieblichen
Frühlingsabende zu.

Ach, sagte die Nachtigall, die Frösche machen
sich so laut, daß ich alle Lust zum Singen verliere.
Hörst du sie nicht?

And you name an inferior animal who might consider imitating you. Authors of my nation!—Do I have to explain myself more clearly?

Lessing

579.

What can one say to the poets who like to fly far above the comprehension of the majority of their readers? What else than what the nightingale once said to the lark: "Do you wing yourself, dear friend, so high in the sky only in order not to be heard?"

After *Percy* by *Herder*

580.

The raven noticed that the eagle sits full 30 days on his eggs. This is doubtless the reason, he said, that the eaglets become so farsighted and strong. Good! I shall do the same.

And since then, the raven actually sits full 30 days on his eggs; but he has never hatched anything but miserable ravens.

After *Percy* by *Herder*

581.

Please sing, dear nightingale! a shepherd called to the silent singer on a lovely spring evening.

Alas, said the nightingale, the frogs are so loud that I lose all desire to sing.

Don't you hear them?

Ich höre sie freilich, versetzte der Schäfer.
Aber nur dein Schweigen ist schuld, daß ich sie
höre.   Nach Percy von Herder.

582.

Der gelehrte Salden pflegte zu sagen, daß
Volkslieder das treueste Bild der Zeiten und den
wahren Geist des Volkes enthielten, sowie man
an einem in die Luft geworfenen leichten Stroh=
halm eher sehen könne, woher der Wind kommt,
als an einem schweren, großen Stein.
                                         Nach Percy von Herder.

583.
Sonett an Shakespeare.

Du selbst Musik dem Ohr, fliehst vor den
                              Tönen?
Süß kriegt mit Süß nicht, Lust freut sich der Lust.
Liebst du etwas, damit dich's mag verhöhnen?
Drückst du den Schmerz mit Jubel an die Brust?

Stört dich der Einklang wohlgestimmter Saiten,
Die sich zu schöner Harmonie vermählt?
Sie schelten dich nur, weil dein Widerstreiten,
Da du als Einzelner beharrst, sie quält.

Sieh! Eine Saite, als der andern Gatte,
Greift ineinander wechselseitig ein,
Und ist des Manns, des Kinds, der Mutter Schatte,

Und alle singen gleiche Melodein.
Was viele singen, scheint, als säng's nur einer,
Und tönt dir wortlos: Einzeln wirst du Keiner.
                                     Übersetzt von Ortlepp.

I certainly hear them, answered the shepherd. But
it is the fault of your silence that I hear them.

After *Percy* by *Herder*

582

The erudite Salden used to say that folksongs contained the most faithful image of the times and the truest
spirit of the people, just as one can see more easily which
way the wind is blowing by tossing into the air a light
stalk of straw rather than a heavy big stone.

After *Percy* by *Herder*

583.*46

Sonnet VIII

Music to hear, why hear'st thou music sadly?
Sweets with sweets war not, joy delights in joy.
Why lovest thou that which you receivest not gladly,
Or else receivest with pleasure thine annoy?
If the true concord of well tuned sounds,
By unions married, do offend thine ear,
They do but sweetly chide thee, who confounds
In singleness the parts that thou shouldst bear.
Mark how one string, sweet husband to another,
Srikes in each by mutual ordering;
Resembling sire and child and happy mother,
Who, all in one, one pleasing note do sing:
Whose speechless song, being many, seeming one,
Sings this to thee: 'Though single wilt prove none.'

Shakespeare

---

[46] The heading on the German "Sonnet to Shakespeare" is strange. The
German translation is by Ernst Ortlep. The text here printed is the original
by Shakespeare.

584.

„Es hat gefallen, oder es hat nicht gefallen," sagen die Leute. Als ob es nichts Höheres gäbe als den Leuten zu gefallen.

R. Schumann.

585.

Licht senden in die Tiefe des menschlichen Herzens — des Künstlers Beruf!

R. Schumann.

586.

Niemand kann mehr, als er weiß, Niemand weiß mehr als er kann.

R. Schumann.

587.

Wer in der Literatur nicht das Bedeutendste der neuen Erscheinungen kennt, gilt für ungebildet. In der Musik sollten wir auch so weit sein.

R. Schumann.

588.

Worüber die Künstler tage=, monate=, jahrelang nachgedacht haben, das wollen die Dilettanten im Husch weghaben.

R. Schumann.

589.

Das Schwerste ist, den Beifall des Toren zu ertragen, und man kann sich geduldig auspfeifen lassen, während man bei dem Bravo des Unverständigen ihn gerne hinter die Ohren schlagen möchte. Wer das verwinden und hinunterschlucken kann, hat es schon weit in der Selbstverleugnung und Weltklugheit gebracht, und ich gratuliere.

C. M. v. Weber.

584.

"I liked it or I didn't like it," the people say, as if there were nothing higher than to please the people.

R. Schumann

585.

To send light into the depths of the human heart— the artist's vocation!

R. Schumann

586.

No one can do more than he knows. No one knows more than he can do.

R. Schumann

587.

One who in literature does not know the most important new publications is considered uneducated. In music we should also be thus far.

R. Schumann

588.

What artists have pondered for days, months, years, the dilettantes want to get in a hurry.

R. Schumann

589.

The most difficult is to endure the applause of fools, and one can patiently let oneself be hissed off the stage whereas amidst the bravos of morons one would like to box their ears. A man who can overcome and swallow this has already made great progress in self-denial and wordly wisdom, and I congratulate.

C.M. von Weber

590.

Ein Stern ist das auf den Rock genagelte
Patent, alles, was man sagt, mit einer Ver=
beugung beantwortet zu sehen.   Goethe.

591.

Der rohe Mensch ist zufrieden, wenn er nur
etwas vorgehen sieht; der Gebildete will emp=
finden, und Nachdenken ist nur dem ganz Aus=
gebildeten angenehm.   Goethe.

592.

Von welcher Wirkung ist dieser Übergang!
Ja! nun wird die in drei oder vier oder gar
nur in einem Takte bestehende Modulation ge=
nommen und in den geistigen Weingeist gesetzt.
Wodurch sie herbeigeführt, warum sie so und
nicht anders wirken muß, weil sie so gestellt
ist, daran denkt kein Mensch. Es ist so, als
wollte man eine einzelne Nase oder einen glück=
lichen Lichtpunkt aus einem Gemälde schneiden
und einzeln als Rarität zeigen. Die Zusammen=
stellung ist's und nicht die Sache.
                                    C. M. v. Weber.

593.

Der Schulmeister Agesel.

Anerkennung, mein Gönner, braucht jeder=
mann. Der größte Held und der größte Dichter
blieben ohne sie — und zeigte sie sich auch nur
durch wütende Feindseligkeit — gewiß nicht
Held und Dichter. Es ist töricht, wenn kalte

590.
A star is the order nailed to the coat to answer with
an obeisance everything one has said.

Goethe

591.
The crude person is satisfied when he only sees something happening; the educated person wants to feel, and
thinking is agreeable only to the fully cultured one.

Goethe

592.
How effective is this transition! Yes! Let us take this
modulation of three or four bars, or maybe even just one
bar, and put it in the spiritual spirit of wine. What leads
up to it, and why it must have this particular and no other
effect because it is thus placed, no man considers. It is
like cutting out of a painting one nose or one fortunate
point of light and exhibiting them singly as rarities. The
context makes it and not the incident.

C.M. von Weber

593.[48]
The Schoolmaster Agesel
Recognition, my patron, is essential to everybody.
The greatest hero and the greatest poet would without it
certainly not remain hero or poet—even if it is demon-
strated only by furious hostility. It is foolish of cold people

---

[48] Immermann (see Annotatefd List of Authors) had made Münchhausen's
adventures popular in Germany.

Menschen einen in dieser Beziehung Darbenden
auf sein eigenes Bewußtsein verweisen, weil
gerade die besten und tüchtigsten Seelen immer=
dar an sich zweifeln und von anderen eine so
große Meinung haben, daß sie in deren Schätzung
ihr Gewicht finden. Alle Eigenschaften können
durch tote Gleichgültigkeit der Umgebungen zu=
grunde gerichtet werden.

Aus Immermanns Münchhausen. Bd. II.

594.

Oftmals zeichnet der Meister ein Bild durch
wenige Striche,
Was mit unendlichem Wust nie der Geselle
vermag.   Platen.

595.

Noch ungewiß, ob mich der Gott beseele,
Zu seinem Priester ob er mich geweiht,
Malt ich die Bilder meiner Seele
In glücklicher Verborgenheit.   Platen.

596.

Ein Dichter lädt an keinen kargen Tisch,
Er fühlt sich reich und lebt verschwenderisch,
Weil er sich eher jeden Fehl verzeiht,
Nur nicht gedankenlose Nüchternheit.   Platen.

597.

Wer sich der List bediente,
Anstatt der Kraft, erreicht den Zweck wohl auch,
Doch es ermangelte sein Innerstes
Der freien, großen Äußerung.   Platen.

to refer someone starved in this respect to his own consciousness, because precisely the best and worthiest souls always doubt themselves and think very highly of others whose judgment helps them find their own worth. All qualities can be ruined by deadly indifference of the surroundings.

From *Immermann's Münchhausen*. Bd. II

594.*

Often the master draws a picture with a few lines
Which the apprentice can never do
With an infinite clutter.

Platen

595.*

Still uncertain whether I was God-inspired,
Whether he has consecrated me to be his priest,
I painted the image of my soul
In happy seclusion.

Platen

596.*

A poet does not invite to a meager table,
He feels himself rich and lives lavishly,
Because he will rather forgive himself for every defect
Than for thoughtless sobriety.

Platen

597.*

He who would use cunning
Instead of strength may well achieve the aim,
But his innermost would miss
The free, great expression.

Platen

598.

Sernatius:

Der Menſch muß eine feſte Beſtimmung, einen
bleibenden Aufenthalt haben. Er bedarf ein
jährliches Einkommen, damit ihm die Sorgen
nicht über den Kopf wachſen ſollen.

Jdwin (der Minneſänger):

Wie aber, wenn er größer wäre als ſeine
Sorgen und immer größer würde mit ſeinen
Sorgen, wie ſollen ſie ihm über den Kopf
wachſen?   Platen (Treue um Treue.)

599.

An die Muſe.

Anna, das Kind warſt du, nun biſt du Ge=
liebte des Jünglings.
Gattin werde dem Mann, Pflegerin werde dem
Greis.
Noch beſitz ich dich nicht, noch ſtrebe ich, dich zu
beſitzen:
Täuſch' ich mich? Wirſt du mir auch liſpeln
das bindende Ja?
Platen.

600.

Ein jedes Band, das noch ſo leiſe
Die Geiſter aneinanderreiht,
Wirkt fort auf ſeine ſtille Weiſe
Durch unberechenbare Zeit.   Platen.

601.

Das Alter wägt's und mißt es,
Die Jugend ſpricht: So iſt es!   Platen.

598.*

Servatius:

A man must have a firm destiny, a lasting sojourn.
He needs a yearly income to keep his worries from growing over his head.

Idwin (The Minnesinger):

But if he were bigger than his worries and would get
even bigger with his worries, how could they grow over
his head?

Platen (Treue um Treue)

599.*

Anna, you were the child, now you are loved by the
    youth,
Become wife of the man, nurse of the old man.
Still you are not yet mine, still I desire you:
Do I delude myself? Will you lisp to me the binding
    Yes?

Platen

600.*

Every bond that even softly connects the spirits
Has its effect in its quiet way
Through immeasurable time.

Platen

601.*

Old age ponders and measures it,
Youth speaks: This is it!

Platen

602.

Wir sind so an die Eroberung des Inter=
essanten gewöhnt, daß, wenn heutigentags in
unserer aus allem dilettierenden Zeit alle Dramen
wieder aufgeführt werden, es nicht das längst
erstorbene Gefühl für die antike Schicksals=,
Lebens= und Kunstwelt ist, welche die Leute in
das Theater führt, sondern das Interessante,
die Neugier Spannende, zu sehen, wie sich die
Antigone auf den Brettern ausnimmt, wo eben
Raupachs Zeitgeist spielte, oder der Birchpfeiffer
Pfefferrösel ihre Lebkuchen feil bot.

Allg. Zeitg. Nr. 13, 1844.

603.

Den Geschmack kann man nicht am M i t t e l =
g u t bilden, sondern nur am A l l e r v o r z ü g =
l i c h s t e n. Goethe.

604.

Durch unaufhörliches freies Nachdenken muß
man sich begeistern. Hat man gar keine Zeit
zum Überschauen, zum freien Meditieren, zum
ruhigen Durchlaufen und Betrachten in ver=
schiedenen Stimmungen, so schläft selbst die
fruchtbarste Phantasie ein, und die innere Mannig=
faltigkeit hört auf. Für den Dichter ist nichts
nützlicher als eine flüchtige Betrachtung der
vielen Weltgegenstände und ihrer Eigenschaften
sowie der mancherlei Wissenschaften.

Novalis.

602.

We are so much used to take what is interesting that when today, in all regards a dilettantish time, all dramas are again performed, it is not the long-dead feeling for the antique world of fate, life, and art which leads people into the theater but what is interesting, what thrills the curiosity, and to see how Antigone looks on the stage where recently Raupach's up-to-date plays have been performed and the salesgirl barked her gingerbread.

Allg. Zeitg. No. 12, 1844

603.

Taste cannot be formed through middling quality but only through the very best.

Goethe

604.

One has to inspire oneself by continual free thinking. If one does not find time for reviewing, for clear meditating, for quiet traversing and contemplating in various moods, then even the most fertile imagination goes to sleep and the inner diversity ceases to exist. To the poet nothing is more useful than a cursory contemplation of the many affairs of the world and their qualities as also of the various branches of knowledge.

Novalis

605.

Nichts ist dem Geist erreichbarer als das Unendliche.   Novalis.

606.

Nur ein Künstler kann den Sinn des Lebens erraten.   Novalis.

607.

Lebendig sein und Fortschreiten ist fast eines und dasselbe. Was das Leben — des einzelnen oder der Nationen — aufregt, bringt beide vorwärts, beschleunigt die Entwicklung ihrer geistigen Anlagen, ist Stärkung aller tätigen Kräfte und Anlaß zum Erwachen vieler, welche noch schlummern.   R. v. Rotteck.

608.

Aus Wilhelm Meisters Wanderjahren.

Buch I, Kap. 4.

Montan:

„Es ist nichts schrecklicher als ein Lehrer, der nicht mehr weiß, als die Schüler ebenfalls wissen sollen. Wer andere lehren will, kann wohl oft das beste verschweigen, was er weiß, aber er darf nicht halbwissend sein."

Goethe.

609.

Aus Wilhelm Meisters Wanderjahren.

Montan:

„Was der Mensch leisten soll, muß sich als ein zweites Selbst von ihm ablösen, und wie könnte das möglich sein, wäre sein erstes Selbst nicht ganz davon durchdrungen."

605.

Nothing is more within reach of the spirit than the infinite.

Novalis

606.

Only an artist can divine the meaning of life.

Novalis

607.

To be alive and move forward are almost one and the same. What creates life—of an individual or of nations—excites, carries both forward, accelerates the development of their spiritual endowments, gives strength to all active forces, and is the cause of awakening many which are still slumbering.

R. von Rotteck

608.[49]

Montan: "There is nothing more terrible than a teacher who does not know more than the scholars also ought to know. He who wants to teach others may often indeed be silent about about the best he knows, but he must not be half-instructed himself."

Goethe
From *Wilhelm Meister's Years of Travel* I/4

609.

Montan: "Whatever man would achieve must loosen itself from him like a second self; and how could this be possible if his first self were not entirely penetrated by it?

---

[49] The structure and thought of Goethe's novel *Wilhelm Meister's Years of Travel* are complex and challenging. Montan, who figures in numbers 608 to 617, is one of the prominent characters in this work.

Wilhelm Meister:
„Man hat aber doch eine vielseitige Bildung
für vorteilhaft und notwendig gehalten."

Montan:
„Sie kann es auch sein zu ihrer Zeit; Viel=
seitigkeit bereitet eigentlich nur das Element
vor, worin der Einseitige wirken kann, dem
aber jetzt genug Raum gegeben ist. Ja, es ist
jetzt die Zeit der Einseitigkeiten; wohl dem,
der es begreift, für sich und andere in diesem
Sinne wirkt. Bei gewissen Dingen begreift sich's
durchaus und sogleich."   Goethe.

610.

Übe dich zum tüchtigen Violinisten, und sei
versichert, der Kapellmeister wird dir deinen
Platz im Orchester mit Gunst anweisen.

[Goethe, Wilh. Meisters Wanderjahre], Buch I, Kap. 4.

611.

Allem Leben, allem Tun, aller Kunst muß
das Handwerk vorausgehen, welches nur in der
Beschränkung erworben wird. Eines recht wissen
und ausüben gibt höhere Bildung als Halbheit
im Hundertfältigen.

[Goethe, Wilh. Meisters Wanderjahre], Buch I, Kap. 10.

612.

Und so ist Jesus Wandel für den edlen Teil
der Menschheit noch belehrender und fruchtbarer
als sein Tod: denn zu jenen Prüfungen ist
jeder, zu diesem nur wenige berufen.

[Goethe, Wilh. Meisters Wanderjahre], Buch II, Kap. 2.

Wilhelm Meister: "But yet a many-sided education has been held to be advantageous and necessary."

Montan: "It may be so, too, in its proper time. Many-sidedness prepares actually only the element in which the one-sided man can work, who just at this time has room enough given him. Yes, now is the time for the one-sided; good for him who comprehends it, and who works for himself and others in this sense. In certain things it is understood thoroughly and at once."

Goethe
From *Wilhelm Meister's Years of Travel* I/4

610.

Practice till you are an able violinist and be assured that the director will with pleasure assign you a place in the orchestra.

Goethe
From *Wilhelm Meister's Years of Travel* I/4

611.

In all life, all action, all art, craftsmanship comes first, which can only be won by limitation. To know and practice one thing well gives higher education than half-hearted attempts at a hundred.

Goethe
From *Wilhelm Meister's Years of Travel* I/10

612.

And thus the life of Jesus is for the noble part of humanity more instructive and fruitful than his death; for to the one test everyone is called, but to the other only a few.

Goethe
From *Wilhelm Meister's Years of Travel* II/2

613.

Wilhelm Meister:

„Große Gedanken und ein reines Herz, das ist's, was wir uns von Gott erbitten sollten."

[Goethe, Wilh. Meisters Wanderjahre], Buch I, Kap. 10.

614.

Wilhelm Meister:

„Habt ihr eben auch, so wie ihr das Leben dieses göttlichen Mannes als Lehr- und Musterbild aufstellt, sein Leiden, seinen Tod gleichfalls als ein Vorbild erhabener Duldung herausgehoben?"

„Auf alle Fälle, sagte der Älteste, „hieraus machen wir kein Geheimnis; aber wir ziehen einen Schleier über diese Leiden, eben weil wir sie so hoch verehren. Wir halten es für eine verdammungswürdige Frechheit, jenes Martergerüst und den daran leidenden Heiligen dem Anblick der Sonne auszusetzen, die ihr Angesicht verbarg, als eine ruchlose Welt ihr dies Schauspiel aufdrang, mit diesen tiefen Geheimnissen, in welchen die göttliche Tiefe des Leidens verborgen liegt, zu spielen, zu tändeln, zu verzieren und nicht eher zu ruhen, bis das Würdigste gemein und abgeschmackt erscheint.

[Goethe, Wilhelm Meisters Wanderjahre.]

615.

. . . Nach dem Grundsatz, daß man nichts lerne, außer dem Elemente, welches bezwungen werden soll.

[Goethe, Wilh. Meisters Wanderjahre], Buch II, Kap. 9.

613.
Wilhelm Meister: "Great thoughts and a pure heart,
this is what we should beg God to give us."

Goethe

From *Wilhelm Meister's Years of Travel* I/10

614.
Wilhelm Meister: "Have you then, besides represent-
ing the life of this Divine Man as a model of teaching,
also exalted his sufferings, his death, as a model of sublime endurance?"

"By all means," said the elder. "We make no secret
of it, but we draw a veil over these sufferings, just because
we honour them so highly. We hold it for repulsive au-
dacity to expose that scaffold of agony and the Saint suffering on it to the gaze of the sun, which hid its face when
a reckless world obtruded this sight upon it; to play, to
trifle with these deep mysteries in which the divine depth
of suffering lies hidden; to decorate them, and not to rest
until the most worthy seems commonplace and vulgar."

Goethe

From *Wilhelm Meister's Years of Travel*

615.

...According to the axiom that one should not learn
anything except the element which ought to be conquered.

Goethe

From *Wilhelm Meister's Years of Travel* II/9

616.

Lebenstätigkeit und Tüchtigkeit ist mit aus= langendem Unterricht weit verträglicher, als man denkt.

[Goethe, Wilh. Meisters Wanderjahre], Buch II, Kap. 9.

617.

Was uns aber zu strengen Forderungen, zu entscheidenden Gesetzen am meisten berechtigt, ist: daß gerade das Genie, das angeborene Talent sie am ersten begreift, ihnen den willigsten Gehorsam leistet. Nur das Halbvermögen wünschte gern seine beschränkte Besonderheit an die Stelle des unbedingten Ganzen zu setzen und seine falschen Griffe unter Vorwand einer unbezwing= lichen Originalität und Selbständigkeit zu be= schönigen. Das lassen wir aber nicht gelten, sondern hüten unsere Schüler vor allen Miß= tritten, wodurch ein großer Teil des Lebens, ja manchmal das ganze Leben verwirrt und zerpflückt wird.

Mit dem Genie haben wir am liebsten zu tun, denn dieses wird eben von dem guten Geist beseelt, bald zu erkennen, was ihm nutz ist. Es begreift, daß Kunst eben darum Kunst heiße, weil sie nicht Natur ist. Es bequemt sich zum Respekt sogar vor dem, was man konventionell nennen könnte: denn was ist dieses anders, als daß die vorzüglichsten Menschen übereinkommen, das Notwendige, das Unerläßliche für das beste zu halten; und gereicht es nicht überall zum Glück? [Goethe, Wilh. Meisters Wanderjahre.]

616.
Activity and practical ability are far more compatible with efficient instruction than one thinks.

Goethe
From *Wilhelm Meister's Years of Travel* II/9

617. [= 483]
But what mostly justifies our strict demands and definite laws, is that it is precisely genius, the inborn talent, which grasps them first and yields them the most willing obedience. Only mediocrity would fain substitute its limited specialty for the unlimited whole and glorify its wrong ideas under the pretense of an incontrolable originality and independence. This, however, we do not let pass, but we protect our pupils against all false steps, whereby a great part of life, nay, often the whole life becomes confused and broken up.

We love best to deal with genius, for he is specially animated by the good spirit of recognizing quickly what is useful to him. He sees that Art is called Art, precisely because it is not Nature. He accommodates himself to proper respect even for that which might be called conventional, for what else is this but that the best men have agreed to regard the necessary, the inevitable, as the best? And does it not everywhere lead to good fortune?

Goethe
From *Wilhelm Meister's Years of Travel*

618.

Wandert nicht der Maler mit Staffelei und Palette von Gesicht zu Gesicht, und werden seine Kunstgenossen nicht bald da, bald dorthin berufen, weil überall zu bauen und zu bilden ist? Lebhafter jedoch schreitet der Musiker daher, denn er ist es eigentlich, der für ein neues Ohr neue Überraschung, für einen frischen Sinn frisches Erstaunen bereitet.   Simrock.

619.

„Es gibt vortreffliche Menschen," sagte Goethe, „die nichts aus dem Stegreife, nichts obenhin zu tun vermögen, sondern deren Natur es verlangt, ihre jedesmaligen Gegenstände mit Ruhe tief zu durchdringen. Solche Talente machen uns oft ungeduldig, indem man selten von ihnen erlangt, was man augenblicklich wünscht, allein auf diesem Wege wird das Höchste geleistet."
                    Eckermanns Gespräche mit Goethe.

620.

Aus gemessener Rezitation der Worte entsprangen Gesang und Lied, aus dem Lied alle andere Dichtung, aus Gesang durch gesteigerte Abstraktion alle übrige Musik, die nach aufgegebenem Wort geflügelt in solchen Höhen schwimmt, daß ihr kein Gedanke sicher folgen kann.   Jakob Grimm.

618.

Does the painter not wander with easel and palette from face to face, and are his fellow artists not called now here, now there, because everywhere there is something to build and shape? The musician, however, strides in a livelier manner, for it is really he who prepares for a new ear a new surprise, for a fresh mind a fresh amazement.

Simrock

619.

"There are some excellent people," Goethe said, "who are not able to do anything spontaneously or on the spur of the moment, but whose nature demands that they quietly penetrate the subject matter at hand. Such talents often make us impatient, for we seldom receive from them instanteously what we demand, yet in this way occur the highest accomplishments."

Eckermann, Conversations with Goethe

620.

From measured recitation of words sprang up song and verse; from verse, all further poetry; from song, through intensified abstraction, all further music which, abandoning words, floats on wings at such heights that no thought can follow it securely.

Jakob Grimm

621.
Hebbel an Schumann (über Debrois)[1].

Jedenfalls wird er nicht streng genug zu
Arbeiten angehalten werden können, denn alles
Produzieren außerhalb der Formen ist doch im
Grunde eine Schwelgerei und führt zur Ver=
wechslung des allgemeinen Elements mit dem
individuellen Eigentum.

622.
Goethe (Farbenlehre).

Wenn man die Kunst in einem höheren Sinne
betrachtet, so möchte man wünschen, daß nur
Meister sich damit abgäben, daß die Schüler auf
das strengste geprüft würden, daß Liebhaber
sich in einer ehrfurchtsvollen Annäherung glück=
lich fühlten. Denn das Kunstwerk soll aus dem
Genie entspringen, der Künstler soll Gehalt und
Form aus der Tiefe seines eigenen Wesens
hervorrufen, sich gegen den Stoff beherrschend
verhalten und sich der äußeren Einflüsse nur
zu seiner Ausbildung bedienen.

623.
Kleine Freuden laben wie Hausbrot immer
ohne Ekel, große wie Zuckerbrot zeitig mit Ekel.

Jean Paul.

[1] Debrois van Brunk, Komponist und Musikschriftsteller
(1823—1902), hat sich namentlich durch seine „Technische und
ästhetische Analyse des wohltemperierten Klaviers" bekannt
gemacht.

621.[50]
Hebbel to Schumann (about Debrois)
In any case, it will not be possible to hold him severely enough to works, for all production outside of forms is basically a revelry and leads to confusing the general element with individual property.

622.[51]
Goethe (*Theory of Color*)
If one considers art in a higher sense, one would wish that only masters did occupy themselves with it, that students would be most severely tested, and that art lovers felt happy in a respectful approach. For the work of art shall spring from the genius, the artist shall evoke content and form from the depth of his proper being, act dominating toward the subject matter, and employ outside influences only for his development.

Goethe

623.
Small pleasures refresh like the daily bread always without disgust, big ones like cookies eventually with disgust.

Jean Paul

[50] A footnote by Krebs informs us that Debrois van Bruyk (1823-1902) became known as the author of *A Technical and Aesthetic Analysis of The Well-Tempered Clavier.*
[51] Goethe's *Theory of Color* with its sharp criticism of Newton has never ceased to arouse controversy. Modern scientists treat it with increasing respect. Brahms's attention to it late in life is noteworthy.

624.

Beſichtige die Nachbarſchaft deines Lebens uſw.
Halte eine Reſidenzſtadt nur für eine Kollekte
von Dörfern und ein Dorf für die Sackgaſſe in
einer Stadt, den Ruhm für das nachbar=
liche Geſpräch unter der Haustür.

Jean Paul (Quintus Firlein).

625.

Sein Auge war der offne Himmel, den ihr
in tauſend fünfjährigen und nur in zehn fünfzig=
jährigen Augen antrefft.   *Jean Paul.*

626.

Die Menſchen lieben ihre Freuden mehr als
ihr Glück, einen guten Geſellſchafter mehr als
den Wohltäter, Papageien, Schoßhunde und
Affen mehr als nützliche Haustiere.

Jean Paul.

627.

Nichts verengert den Tanzplatz des Witzes
ſo ſehr, als wenn eigene Meinungen und
Wahrheitsliebe darin als feſte, dicke Säulen
ſtehen.   *Jean Paul.*

628.

Der ſchlimmere Menſch hat eine größere
Freude über eine ſich abgerungene gute Tat
als der beſſere.   *Jean Paul.*

629.

Zum Lieben zwei, zum Trinken drei, zum
Singen vier, das lob' ich mir.

624.

Inspect the neighborhood of your life etc. Consider a metropolis only a collection of villages, and a village a dead-end street in a city, and fame as the neighbors' chat at the front door.

Jean Paul (Quintus Fixlein)

625.

His eye was like the open sky, such as you find in a thousand five-year olds, and only in ten fifty-year old eyes.

Jean Paul

626.

People love their pleasures more than their luck; a good companion more than a benefactor; parrots, lap dogs, and monkeys more than useful domestic animals.

Jean Paul

627.

Nothing narrows the dance floor of wit so much as when personal opinions and love of truth stand on it like firm, thick pillars.

Jean Paul

628.

A worse man derives greater pleasure than a better man from a good deed wrung from himself.

Jean Paul

629.*

Two to make love, three to drink, four to sing—that I think is right.

[anon.]

630.

Armut ist die einzige Last, die schwerer wird, je mehrere daran tragen. Jean Paul.

631.

In der Politik tut niemand etwas für den anderen, wenn er nicht zugleich auch sein Interesse dabei findet. Bismarck (Denkschrift von 1857).

632.

Ich glaube, daß es so schwer nicht ist, das Gewähltwerden. Wenn man nur versprechen kann, so kann man auch gewählt werden. Bismarck (Juni 1865).

633.

Die Basis des konstitutionellen Lebensprozesses ist überall der Kompromiß. Bismarck (Januar 1865).

634.

Der Handelnde ist immer gewissenlos; es hat niemand Gewissen als der Betrachtende. Goethe (Sprüche in Prosa).

635.

Ich frage gar nichts danach, ob eine Sache populär ist, ich frage nur danach, ob sie vernünftig oder zweckmäßig ist; die Popularität ist eine vorübergehende Sache. Bismarck (Juni 1882 im Reichstag).

630.
Poverty is the only burden which becomes heavier
the more people bear it.

Jean Paul

631.
In politics no one does anything for others if it does
not at the same time also further his own interest.

Bismarck (Denkschrift, 1851)

632.
I believe it is not so difficult to be elected. If one
only can make promises, then one can also be elected.

Bismarck (June 1865)

633.
The basis of the constitutional life process is always
the compromise.

Bismarck (January 1865)

634.
The man of action is always unscrupulous; nobody
has a conscience except the man who contemplates.

Goethe (Sayings in Prose)

635.
I do not ask whether a thing is popular, I only ask
whether it is reasonable or purposeful; popularity is a passing affair.

Bismarck
(June 1882 in the Reichstag)

636.

Tapferkeit, meine Herren, läßt sich im
einzelnen nicht belohnen; sie ist, Gott sei Dank,
ein Gemeingut deutscher Soldaten.

[Bismarck] 1871 im Reichstag.

637.

Alle Gesetze sind von Alten und Männern
gemacht. Junge und Weiber wollen die Aus=
nahme, Alte die Regel.

Goethe (Sprüche in Prosa).

638.

Die Abschätzung und Tragweite eines mili=
tärischen Sieges in dem Moment, wo er er=
fochten wird, ist eine der schwierigsten Aufgaben
der Politik.   Bismarck (im Reichstag 1866).

639.

Die Jünglinge (Requiem für Mignon).

Wohl verwahrt ist nun der Schatz, das schöne
Gebild der Vergangenheit! Hier im Marmor
ruht es unverzehrt; auch in eurem Herzen lebt
es, wirkt es fort. Schreitet, schreitet ins Leben
zurück! Nehmet den heiligen Ernst mit hinaus!
Denn der Ernst, der heilige, macht allein das
Leben zur Ewigkeit.   Goethe (Wilh. Meister).

640.

„Nach neun ist alles vorbei," sagt der Schau=
spieler.   Bismarck (in einem Brief).

636.

Bravery, gentlemen, cannot be rewarded individually; it is, thank God, the common property of German soldiers.

([Bismarck] 1871 in the Reichstag)

637.

All laws are made by elders and men; youngsters and women want the exception, not the rule.

Goethe (Sprüche in Prosa)

638.

The appraisal and significance of a military victory in the moment it has been achieved is one of the most difficult tasks of politics.

Bismarck (in the Reichstag 1866)

639.

The Youths (Requiem for Mignon)

Securely the treasure is now preserved—the beautiful image of the past! Here in marble it rests free from decay, and it also lives actively in your hearts. Go back, go back into life! Take the holy earnestness along with you! For holy earnestness alone turns life into eternity.

Geothe (Wilhelm Meister)

640.

"After nine everything is gone," says the actor.

Bismarck (in a letter)

641.

Mit andern kann man fich belehren,
Begeistert wird man nur allein.   Goethe.

642.

Quand on désespère de faire une chose
belle, naturelle et simple, on en tente une
bizarre.   Diderot.

643.

Das Standrecht ist ein Rechtsstand, vor dem
kein Recht Stand hält.
                    Kladderadatsch 1849 (S. 79).

644.

(Omnibus hoc vitiumst [cantoribus])
Satira 3 [Lib. I].

Sämtliche Sänger entstellt der Fehler, daß
                    unter den Freuden,
Bittet man, niemals fie den Entschluß fich faßten
                    zu singen,
Ungeheißen jedoch nicht ermüden.
                    Horaz, 3. Satire.

. . . Wie die Musici, wann man fie bittet,
so singen sie nicht, bittet man sie aber nicht, so
können sie nicht aufhören.
                    M. Luther (Tischreden, S. 554).

645.

Doch kennet kein Mensch weder die Liebe
noch den Haß irgendeines, den er vor fich hat.
                    Prediger Salomo IX, 1.

641.*

With others one can learn something,
One becomes enthusiastic only by one's self.

Goethe

642.

If one despairs of making a beautiful, natural, and
simple thing, one attempts something bizarre.

Diderot

643.[52]

Martial law makes a stand which no law can with-
stand.

Kladderadatsch 1849 (p.79)

644.*

(*Omnibus hoc vitiumst [cantoribus]*)
Satira 3 [Lib. 1]
All singers have this fault: if asked to sing among
their friends,
they are never so inclined;
if unasked, they never leave off.

Horace, 3rd Satire

...Like musicians, if asked, they don't sing; but if one
does not ask them, they cannot stop.

M. Luther (Tischreden, p. 554)

645.[53]

No man knoweth either love or hatred by all that is
before them.

Ecclesiastes IX/1

---

[52] A sophisticated triple pun that defies translation.
[53] In his "Four Serious Songs," one of the composer's last compositions,
recognized as his conscious farewell to the world, Brahms used *Ecclesiastes*
for the text of the first two songs. There is something very moving about
the fact that Brahms turned to the same biblical source for his last notebook
entry.

ANNOTATED LIST OF CITED AUTHORS

ALLGEMEINE ZEITUNG 1844, No. 13. A daily Munich
newspaper. 602.

ARNIM, Bettina von(1775-1859). The sister of Klemens
Brentano and wife of Ludwig Achim von Arnim,
editors of the famous romantic folksong collection
Des Knaben Wunderhorn, Bettina lived in a society
totally devoted to literature. Knowing Goethe
personally, she created a sensation three years
after his death by publishing *Goethes Briefwechsel mit
einem Kinde* (Goethe's Correspondence with a
Child), a mixture of real letters and fantastic invention. The quotation is from *Die Günderode,* an
equally fantastic correspondence with her poetic
friend who committed suicide. 217.

AUERBACH, Berthold (1812-1882). Jailed for a few
months because of his political activities in a university fraternity, he later established his reputation as a
writer of *Dorfgeschichten,* artificially naive village
stories sprinkled with philosophical reflection. The
22 volumes of his published works include treatises
on Jewish history and philosophy. 74, 75, 76.

BEETHOVEN, Ludwig van (1770-1827). Krebs comments
that Brahms used *Ludwig van Beethovens Studien im
Generalbass, Kontrapunkt und in der Harmonielehre*
published by Ignaz von Seyfried in 1832, which he

faithfully accepted as authentic in every point. Cf. however the correction by Gustav Nottebohm in *Beethoveniana* 1872, pp. 154 ff. Beethoven's comment in No. 547 is apocryphal and stems from a probably spurious letter of August 1812 by Bettina von Arnim (see above) to Beethoven . 402, 413, 494, 547.

BISMARCK, Otto von (1815-1898). Founder of German empire. His letters, speeches, etc. readily available in print. 631, 632, 633, 635, 638, 640.

BLUM, Robert (1807-1848). Political writer and liberal agitator. Sentenced to death and shot in Vienna during the 1848 Revolution. 176.

BLUMAUER, Aloys (1755-1798). Writer and anticlerical bookdealer in Vienna. 109.

BRINCKMAN, Karl Gustav von (1764-1848). Swedish diplomat and poet. Ambassador to Prussia and then London. 382, 549, 557.

BÜCHNER, Georg (1813-1837). Author of two revolutionary dramas, *Danton's Death* and *Woyzeck* (made into an opera by Alban Berg). Founder of a secret society for Human Rights, he escaped the German police by moving to Zürich where he earned an M.D. and specialized in diseases of the nervous system. 342, 343, 348, 349, 350.

BULWER, Edward (Lord Edward George Lytton) (1805-1873). Writer, famous for *The Last Days of Pompeii* and other historical romances. 529.

BÜRGER, Gottfried August (1747-1794). Professor of philosophy in Göttingen, he caused a stir by the

passion of his ballads and poems but also by his dramatic life which served as the basis for the plots of several 20th-century novels. 114, 173.

BYRON, Lord George Gordon (1788-1824). Much read and admired in Germany. Brahms used passages from *Manfred*, a drama to which Schumann had composed music. 393, 453.

CHAMISSO, Adalbert von (1781-1838). Having left his native France in the wake of the Revolution, he settled in Berlin. He was a co-founder of the *Musenalmanach* in which his first poems appeared. As a professional botanist, he made a scientific journey around the world, but his international fame rests on his story of *Peter Schlemihl* who sold his shadow and on his poetic cycle *Frauenliebe und-leben* set to music by Schumann. 141, 174, 368, 407, 532, 533.

CICERO, Marcus Tullius (106 B.C.-43.B.C.). Roman orator, politician, and author. *De deorum natura* (On the nature of Gods) ranks high among his famous essays. 123.

COLLIN, Heinrich von (1772-1811). Son of a French physician living in Vienna, he was primarily a dramatist mixing French classicism with German romanticism. His patriotic poems written during the Napoleonic oppression(1809) made a significant impact. 406, 448, 449.

DANTE, Alighieri (1265-1321). Brahms cites an entire sonnet from the *Vita nuova* addressed to Beatrice. 84.

DIDEROT, Denis (1713-1784). The famous encyclopedist

whose dialogue *Rameau's Nephew* in Goethe's German translation was widely read in Germany. 642.

DIOGENES (c. 412. B.C.-323 B.C.). Austere Greek philosopher. 221.

DOHL, G.A. Waldemar. Not identifiable in standard sources. 27.

ECKERMANN, Johann Peter (1792-1854). Famous for recording his conversations with the old Goethe which Nietzsche praised as one of the three most beautiful prose works in the German language. 482, 554, 619.

EICHENDORFF, Josef Freiherr von (1788-1857). A distinguished representative of the best German romanticism. His lyrical and nature-bound poems often give the impression of youthful simplicity. His imaginative verses inspired Schubert and Schumann. 132, 172, 275, 276, 277, 367, 391, 404, 408, 411, 438.

FESKI, J. Not identifiable in standard sources. 504.

FREILIGRATH, Ferdinand (1810-1876). His early lyric poetry earned him a pension from the Prussian king which he renounced when his sympathy with liberalism turned him into a revolutionary writer during the 1848 upheavals. Briefly arrested, he lived in exile in London for seventeen years. His *Neue politische und soziale Gedichte* (New Political and Social Poems) show the influence of Victor Hugo. He translated Longfellow's *Hiawatha*. 139.

GEIBEL, Emanuel (1815-1884). A popular and successful writer of dramas as well as poems, he sympathized

with the 1848 revolution but later cheered the creation of the German empire. His opera libretto *Lorelei* was composed in part by Mendelssohn and completed by Max Bruch. 142.

GLUCK, Christoph Willibald (1714-1787). His articulate prefaces to his reform operas are important aesthetic statements. Brahms quotes from the preface to *Alceste*. 387.

GOETHE, Johann Wolfgang (1749-1832). After Jean Paul, the author most frequently quoted by Brahms. In the wide range of sources, one notes Goethe's chal lenging and scientifically complex *Farbenlehre* (Theory of Color). 112, 143, 148, 149, 150, 151, 152, 153, 154, 155, 156, 157, 158, 159, 160, 161, 164, 165, 166, 167, 168, 169, 170, 184, 223, 224, 227, 233, 258, 344, 346, 383, 399, 409, 429, 483, 493, 495, 501, 518, 519, 527, 530, 540, 541, 542, 543, 544, 548, 555, 563, 590, 591, 603, 608, 609, 610, 611, 612, 613, 614, 615, 616, 617, 622, 634, 637, 639, 641.

GRABBE, Christian Dietrich (1801-1836). His dramas, notably the original *Don Juan und Faust*, con tain many ideas and passages worth preserving. 311, 312, 313, 314, 315.

GRILLPARZER, Franz (1791-1872). A civil servant in the Austrian empire, he wrote many poetic, historic, and classical plays which have gained a secure place in the active theatrical repertory. He tried unsuccessfully to write an opera libretto for Beethoven. His speech at Beethoven's grave attests to his musical sensitivity. 82, 83, 489.

GRIMM, Hermann (1828-1901). Art historian and author whom the young Brahms had met through Clara Schumann. 470.

GRIMM, Jacob (1785-1863). His many volumes on German language, grammar, history, and myth laid the foundation for modern philological research. Among his collections of linguistic sources, the *Kinder-und Hausmärchen* have forever associated his name with Fairy Tales. 620.

GRÜN, Anastasius (1806-1876). Member of an old Austrian aristocratic family, he extolled in his writings — epics, poems, essays — political and personal liberty with such articulate enthusiasm that they were banned in Austria. 403.

GRYPHIUS, Andreas. (1616-1664). The miseries of the Thirty Years' War accompanied and colored his life and work. While his poetry has a tone of religious resignation, his tragedies and comedies attack basic social issues with often severe irony. All his writings attest to his superior intelligence and education. He was probably the earliest German dramatist to be influenced by Shakespeare. 178, 179.

HALLER, Albrecht von. (1708-1777). Swiss physician whose idyllic poem "Die Alpen" (The Alps) has preerved his memory more vividly than his numerous scientific publications. 178, 179

HAMMER-PURGSTALL, Joseph (1774-1856). Austrian orientalist who translated and published many Arabic and Persian authors. 105

HEBBEL, Friedrich (1813-1863). Author of many passion-

ate tragedies, psychologically daring to the point of extravagance. His autobiography is a moving document. 254. 621.

HEINSE, Wilhelm (1749-1803). Editor, librarian, and art critic, his writings made an impact on German romanticism. Four years spent in Italy helped shape his thoughts and taste. 133, 498, 520, 531.

HERBART, Johann Friedrich (1776-1841). His early meeting with Pestalozzi confirmed his convictions as an educator. He soon widened to establish himself, in the spirit of Kant, as one of Germany's leading metaphysicians and philosophers. His difficult treatises touch on many fields including music. 425.

HERDER, Johann Gottfried (1744-1803). His wide-ranging interests, articulate thoughts, and voluminous writings gave a distinguished mark to the entire intellectual life in Germany of his period. He was a philosopher, poet, historian, theologian, philologist, anthropologist, translator, evolutionist, educator, critic of art and literature, collector of ethnic myths and songs, and a personal friend of Diderot, Goethe, Schiller, Jean Paul, et al. 8, 9, 10, 11, 12, 251, 517.

HERWEGH, Georg (1817-1875). Revolutionary poet who earned his living as a writer. Fled to Switzerland in 1842 after writing an offensive letter to the Prussian king. Leading a rebellious band of workers during the 1848 upheavals, he saved his life by escaping again to Switzerland. His poems, though censored and confiscated in Germany, were widely read. 385, 410, 561.

HEYDENREICH, Karl Heinrich (1764-1801). Philosophy professor in Leipzig, best known for his *System der Aesthetik* and his concern with art education for the young. 516.

HIPPEL, Theodor Gottlieb von. (1741-1796). Strongly influenced by Laurence Sterne, he wrote novels full of philosophical digressions containing also lyrical and satirical observations. An essay on feminism, *Frauenfrage,* is also noteworthy. 175, 497.

HOFFMANN, E.T.A. (1776-1822). In his internationally famous tales, he created the prototype of the romantic musician, the Kapellmeister Johannes Kreisler. Schumann's *Kreisleriana* is inspired by him. Hoffmann, a professionally trained composer with one viable opera, *Undine,* to his credit, expressed many excellent thoughts about music and musicians in his own or Kreisler's voice. He was one of the earliest articulate admirers of Bach and Beethoven. 7, 341.

HOFFMANN, Friedrich (1804-1881).Philosopher and author. 128.

HÖLDERLIN, Johann Christian Friedrich (1770-1843). Suffering acutely from the present, he transposed Greek classicism to (in his words) the "barbaric" German soil. The dithyrambic language of his poems, prose, and dramas is singularly beautiful and often impenetrable. A sensitive critic compared it to "black roses." Hölderlin spent the last four decades of his life in harmless insanity, occasionally punctuated by poetic outbursts. 401.

HORACE, Quintus Horatius Flaccus (65-B B.C.) One of the few Roman poets of antiquity who has remained

popular today. The Satire quoted must have pleased the old Brahms by its enduring modernity. 644.

HORN, Franz (1781-1837).

HUMBOLDT, Alexander von. 1769-1859). Internationally famous, even during his lifetime, for his significant and basic contribution to the natural sciences. His extensive travels to many parts of the world enabled him to gather first-hand observations which provided a solid foundation for his theoretic writings. 278, 279.

IMMERMANN, Karl Leberecht (1796-1840). A Prussian civil servant, whose reform and management of the Düsseldorf theater made it famous. The poetic imagination of his dramas and novels show an increasing trend toward realism, with satirical attacks against commercialism. 351, 400, 593.

JACOBI, Johann Georg (1740-1814). University professor of philosophy and literature, he wrote many attractive lyrical poems. He was also the publisher and editor of a literary journal to which Goethe, Jean Paul, Herder, and other first-rate writers contributed. 220, 392.

JEAN PAUL (Friedrich Richter) (1763-1825). By far the author most frequently quoted by Brahms. Goethe wrote: "No German writer has come closer to the oriental poets....than Jean Paul...The works of this friend reveal a reasonable, observant, insightful, knowledgeable, mature, and withal benevolent devout sense. A so gifted spirit, cheerful and bold, looks in a kind of oriental manner at the world around him, creates the rarest connections, binds

antagonisms, but so that a secret ethical thread runs through it, leading the whole to a secure unity....One feels comfortable near this sympathetic man, his sentiments touch us. He stimulates our imagination, flatters our shortcomings, and strengthens our virtues." Jean Paul is a master of the German language. His virtuoso juggling and inventing of words, phrases, and structures — critical, humorous — demand respectful attention from German readers while defying a representative translation. Hence he is barely known outside German-speaking countries. His collected works fill 64 volumes. 2, 3, 5, 6, 13, 14, 15, 16, 17, 18, 21, 67, 68, 69, 70, 90, 91, 92, 93, 94, 95, 96, 97, 98, 99, 100, 101, 113, 138, 145, 146, 162, 163, 215, 222, 245, 255, 263, 264, 268, 269, 270, 271, 272, 273, 274, 288, 289, 290, 291, 292, 293, 294, 295, 297, 298, 302, 303, 304, 305, 306, 307, 308, 309, 310, 323, 324, 325, 326, 327, 328, 329, 330, 331, 337, 338, 339, 340, 354, 355, 356, 357, 358, 359, 360, 361, 362, 363, 364, 370, 371, 372, 373, 374, 375, 376, 377, 378, 379, 380, 384, 439, 454, 455, 456, 457, 458, 459, 460, 462, 463, 473, 477, 478, 479, 505, 523, 536, 545, 622, 623, 624, 625, 626, 627 628, 630.

JOACHIM, Josef (1831-1907). Highly respected as the most "musical" and thoughtful violin virtuoso of the century. Close friend of Brahms whose music he sponsored. He copied a few entries into a notebook Brahms had lent him, identifying his contributions by his motto f.a.e., "Frei aber einsam" (Free but alone). 225, 226, 228, 230, 231, 234, 235, 236, 237, 238, 239, 240, 241, 242, 243, 244, 250.

KAHLERT, Karl August (1807-1864). Novelist, poet, and music critic. His *Blätter aus der Brieftasche eines Musikers* (Leaves from the Portfolio of a Musician; 1832), are notweorthy. 507, 508, 509.

KERNER, Justinus (1786-1862). A practicing physician who leaned toward mesmerism, magnetism, and spiritualism. His writings similarly blend fantasy, science, and superstition, but the lyrical folksy tone of his poems made him very popular. 171, 206, 546, 562.

KINKEL, Gottfried (1815-1882). Wrote poems, verse tales, and one opera libretto. Fighting in the 1848 revolution, he was captured and sentenced to life imprisonment but escaped to England and the United States where he lectured and taught. He spent the last sixteen years of his life as professor of archeology and art history in Zürich. 134, 135, 136, 137.

KLADDERADATSCH Berlin weekly founded in 1848. Its sharp political satires made it very popular but also vulnerable to persecutions. It maintained itself by a certain nationalistic attitude. 643.

KLEIST, Ewald von. (1715-1759). His career as an army officer (killed in battle during the Seven Years' War) did not affect the charming tone and tasteful sentiment of his poetry. His chief work *Frühling* (Spring), a long poem in hexameters describing the beauties of nature, harks back to Thomson's *Seasons* (immortalized by Haydn's composition). 104.

KLEIST, Heinrich von. (1777-1811). His stories and dramas deal with extraordinary ethical and psychological

conflicts. The passion with which he treats them is balanced by his crystal-clear, controlled language. His insights are keen. Injustice and tyranny could drive him into a rage, an emoton he was able to discipline in his writings but which landed him for six months in a Napoleonic jail. He died by shooting himself. 103.

KLOPSTOCK, Gottlieb Friedrich (1724-1803). His best-known work, influenced by Milton's *Paradise Lost,* is the *Der Messias,* twenty cantos in hexameters. Genuinely poetic and religious, he considered his career a mission. When the French republic sent him a diploma of honorary citizenship, he returned it in protest against the oppression of liberty in France. He wrote many religious and secular odes in which he poured German feelings into classical Greek forms. 26, 177, 418.

KNABEN WUNDERHORN, DES (1805). A huge collection of old German folksongs edited by the poets Achim von Arnim and Clemens Brentano who happily mixed some of their own efforts into "The Boy's Cornucopia." 447.

KÖRNER, Theodor (1791-1813). By the time he was barely twenty years old, he had published a volume of poems and written opera librettos, comedies, and tragedies. He volunteered for the army to fight against Napoleon and was killed in a battle at the age of twenty-two. After his death, his father published patriotic and political warsongs under the title *Leier und Schwert* (Lyre und Sword) which have kept Körner's name alive. 528.

KULMANN, Elisabeth (1808-1825). Precocious Russian-German girl whose poetry caught Schumann's attention long after her early death. 252, 369.

LAUBE, Heinrich (1806-1884). In his early years, his revolutionary sympathies brought him into frequent conflict with the police, leading to the confiscation of his writings, exile from Saxony, and several jail terms. He is remembered as a very successful theater manager in Vienna and Leipzig. His collected writings (dramas, comedies, books and essays) were published in 29 volumes. 484.

LESSING, Gotthold Ephraim (1729-1781). He was recognized by his(sometimes argumentative) contemporaries and by his devoted followers as the early intellectual teacher and leader in art, poetry, drama, religion, and philosophy. Universal tolerance was high on his mind. He used Aristotle to turn the German theater from the influence of France to Shakespeare. Besides books and essays he wrote plays (which continue to appear on the stage inside and outside Germany) as models realizing his theories. "We lose much in him," Goethe said after Lessing died. 71, 182, 196, 197, 198, 199, 200, 201, 202, 203, 214, 280, 281, 282, 283, 412. 451, 534, 576, 577, 578.

LICHTENBERG, Georg Christoph (1742-1799). An eminent physicist at the University of Göttingen, he is admired to this day not only for his keen intelligence and wide knowledge but also for his mastery, clear and elegant, of the German language. He published a wealth of essays, observations, aphorisms,

etc. on a multitude of issues. His sarcastic wit mercilessly attacked false values wherever he saw them. 19, 204, 205, 207.

LUTHER, Martin (1483-1546). The great reformer was a good musician. He played the flute, composed hymns, and introduced community singing into the service. Many of his comments about music have been preserved. 87, 398, 644.

MACAULAY, Thomas B. (1800-1859). English historian and politician. His major work, *The History of England* in four volumes, gained a vast circulation in England and the United States as soon as it appeared. Brahms quotes from the German edition, one of the earliest translations into almost all European languages. 253.

MAHLMANN, August (1771-1826). His folksy poems and stories were popular with several generations of readers. 102.

MENDELSSOHN, Moses (1729-1786). A poor boy from a Polish ghetto to Berlin, he gained by his philosophic writings and noble character the respect and personal friendship of Lessing and the admiration of Kant.The composer Felix Mendelssohn was his grandson. 72, 73.

MENZEL'S KUNSTBLATT (1836). The casual identification by Brahms was corrected by the scholarly Krebs. Since 1806, there existed a *Morgenblatt für gebildete Stände* (Morning Paper for Educated People). In 1836, it had two supplements, the *Kunst-Blatt* (Art) and the *Literatur-Blatt* (Literature) which Dr.

Wolfgang Menzel edited and from which Brahms quoted. 430, 431, 432, 433, 434, 435, 436, 437, 487, 488, 496, 500, 503, 513, 537.

NEUKOMM, Sigismund (1778-1858). An all-around musician, famous as much for his improvisations on the organ as for his writings. He studied with Haydn and gained his personal friendship. Widely traveled, he knew and was respected by Grétry, Cherubini, Mendelssohn, Moscheles, Talleyrand, et al. 129.

NOVALIS (Friedrich v. Hardenberg) (1772-1801). Poet and philosopher, classicist and forerunner, scientist and metaphysician, secular and religious, in verse and prose, all of it in luminous language written within the last five years of his brief life — Novalis is in a class by himself. The blue flower which the hero of one of his two novels sets out to find became the emblem of the entire German romantic movement. 1, 29, 30, 31, 32, 33, 34, 35, 36, 37, 38, 39, 40, 41, 42, 43, 44, 45, 46, 47, 48, 49, 50, 51, 52, 53, 54, 55, 56, 57, 58, 59, 60, 61, 62, 63, 64, 65, 66, 126, 332, 333, 365, 464, 465, 466, 467, 468, 469, 474, 524, 604, 605, 606.

ORTLEP, Ernst (1800-1864). Poet and author, in 1834 and 1835 Schumann's collaborator at the *Neue Zeitschrift für Musik*, 583.

PERCY, Thomas (1729-1811). Published *Reliques of Ancient English Poetry*, based on an old manuscript collection of English and Scottish ballads. Here quoted from Herder (see above) who like Scott and many romantic authors was strongly influenced by it. 579. 580, 581, 582.

PESTALOZZI, Johann Heinrich (1746-1827). His educational reforms, startling when first articulated and acted out by him, have gained universal respect and exerted their influence to this day. 124.

PLATEN, August (1796-1835). His aristocratic background, boundless ambition, and technical mastery of classical poetic forms did not suffice, as his high intelligence informed him, to make him justifiably famous. His unhappy love for poetry accounts for the melancholic tone of his verse. He spent the last decade of his short life in Italy. 594, 595, 596, 597, 598, 599, 600, 601.

POPE, Alexander (1688-1744). The prominence of English politics and society in his writings, which moreover sparkle with linguistic idiosyncracies, have considerably limited his German readership. 108.

RAUPACH, Ernst Benjamin Salomon (1784-1852). A playwright, today forgotten, who produced mainly dramas but also some comedies. 260, 261, 511, 535.

RICHTER, Adrian Ludwig (1803-1884). Painter and draftsman whose illustrations of folk books made him popular. One year after his death, his son published his *Autobiography*, which Brahms read. 185.

ROLLETT, Hermann (1819-1904). Because of his patriotic poems, he was exiled from his native Austria during the 1848 revolution but permitted to return after six years. 366, 440.

ROTTECK, von. (K.W. Rodecker). (1775-1840). University professor of history whose radical, liberal, and widely

read publications were repeatedly censored. 607.

RÜCKERT, Friedrich (1788-1866). He was a true poet and moral teacher, a combination made possible by his pantheism. He wrote over seven thousand poems. Sensitive to both sound and thought, he was attracted by ancient and eastern wisdom, translating or transforming into his own poetry texts from Chinese, Arabic, Hebrew, Indian, Latin, Sanskrit, Coptic, and more. Gustav Mahler set Rückert to music. 265, 381, 389, 397, 405, 426, 427, 44???, 442, 443, 444, 445, 446.

SAINT-PIERRE, Bernardin de (1737-1814). Dismissed as a young man from the French army for insubordination, he scored a big success with his gaudy novel *Paul et Virginie*. Strongly influenced by Rousseau, he preached the return to nature. 20, 22, 23.

SALLET, Friedrich von. (1812-1843). His satirical novel about military life was the cause of his being cashiered from the army. Somewhat influenced by Hegel, he articulates in his poems a liberal and individualist morality. 125, 320, 321, 450, 471, 472.

SALOMON: ECCLESIASTES. A Book in the Old Testament. 645.

SCHEFER, Leopold (1784-1862). A poet who also composed songs, symphonies etc. 106. 107.

SCHERENBERG, Christian Friedrich (1798-1881). His patriotic poem "Waterloo" made him famous. Wrote many realistic battle poems, a few lyrical ones. 300, 301, 302, 461.

SCHILLER, Friedrich (1759-1805). Historian, philosopher, poet, dramatist—throughout his life and work, his concern for freedom is paramount. He remains one of the most popular authors in German literature. 88, 89, 131, 144, 147, 183, 186, 187, 188, 189, 190, 191, 192, 193, 194, 232, 248, 259, 262, 428, 491, 502, 553, 558.

SCHLEGEL, Friedrich von.(1772-1829). Writer, critic, and classical scholar. Converting in midlife to Roman Catholicism, together with his wife Dorothea, the daughter of Moses Mendelssohn (*see* above), he became increasingly opposed to his earlier romantic vision of freedom. 247, 394, 395, 492, 526, 560.

SCHUBART, Christian Friedrich (1739-1791). Music director at the court of Württemberg. For critical attacks on the social system, he was first dismissed from his job and later sentenced to ten years in jail. His *Ideen zur Aesthetik der Tonkunst* (Ideas on the Aesthetics of Music), published posthumously, has proven very influential. Also wrote poems. 550, 551, 552.

SCHUMANN, Robert (1810-1856). Brahms remained forever grateful to Schumann who had discovered and launched him in his career. For his Notebooks, he copied from Schumann's *Gesammelte Schriften über Musik und Musiker* (Collected Writings on Music and Musicians) which Clara Schumann had given him as a present in 1854. 490, 584, 585, 586, 587, 588.

SEUME, Johann Gottlieb (1763-1810). He walked from Germany to Sicily, dedicating the resulting brilliant

observations to the cobbler who had made his shoes. As a youngster, he was caught and sold by the Hessian ruler to the British who sent him to North America in their fight against the "rebels." Repeated escapes and captures sharpened his independent mind, articulated in his critical collection of *Apocryphen.* 110, 208, 209, 210, 211.

SHAKESPEARE, William (1564-1616). Often translated into German, particularly well in the nineteenth century, he has fully penetrated German culture. 4, 249, 347, 352, 353, 416, 417.

SIMROCK, Karl Joseph (1802-1876). Translated medieval German epics. Lost his civil-service job for writing a poem about the July 1830 revolution. 618.

SOLGER, Karl W. F. (1780-1819). Philosopher and professor in Berlin, his writings on aesthetics and art influenced many romantic authors. His metaphysical realism made him define art as a revelation by God. 218.

SONNENBERG, Franz A. Freiherr von(1779-1805). Widely traveled, he studied law in Jena (where he died falling out of a window). He wrote poems and a long epic *Das Weltende* (The End of the World). 512.

SOPHOCLES (496 B.C. - 409 B.C.). The great Attic dramatist figured strongly in the German romantic movement. 28, 219.

STIFTER, Adalbert (1806-1868). Devoted to education and his art rather than to public success, he wrote pure and noble stories and novels which only long after his death gained for him the deserved reputation as a rare and superior narrator. 452.

STOLBERG, Friedrich Leopold Graf zu (1750-1819). Poet, translator of Homer and Plato, friend of Goethe, and an active member of the famous Göttingen Dichterbund (Poetic League). His conversion to Catholicism became a cause célèbre. 522.

STRAUSS, David Friedrich (1808-1874). His rationalistic and critical book *Leben Jesu* (Life of Jesus), which George Eliot translated, cost him his positions in Berlin and Zürich. 213.

STRECKFUSS, Adolf (1823-1895). Author of novels, stories, and histories. He participated in the March 1848 revolution and was tried for his treason because of his book on the French revolution, but was ultimately acquitted. Krebs, in his list of authors, confused him with an earlier writer of the same name (1778-1844). 140, 525. 538.

SWIFT, Jonathan (1667-1745). The Irish satirist was widely translated and popular. 118, 119, 120, 121, 122.

TASSO, Torquato (1544-1595). Famous for his epic *Gerusalemme liberata* (Jerusalem delivered). Brahms copied the German translation of his sonnets. 85, 86.

THIBAUT, Anton Friedrich (1774-1840). German professor of law in Heidelberg, where he also directed a chorus, but best remembered for his book *Über Reinheit der Tonkunst* (Purity in Musical Art,1825), which Brahms treasured. 390, 414, 514, 521, 559.

THIERSCH, Friedrich (1784-1860). Professor in Munich, he published *Allgemeine Aesthetik in akademischen Lehrvorträgen* (General Aesthetics in Academic Lectures). 485.

TIECK, Johann Ludwig (1773-1853). Thirty-two volumes of his collected works certify to his prolific authorship of poems, stories, novels, essays, critiques, stage plays, translations, etc. During his lifetime, he was occasionally held up as the equivalent of Goethe. His Shakespeare translation jointly with A.W. Schlegel is a superior accomplishment. Yet his stature appears tarnished by his yielding to the temptation of overdone mannered literary experiments. The title of one of his comedies is *Anti-Faust*; that of a five-act "historic play," *Die verkehrte Welt* (The Reversed World.) 116, 117, 334, 335, 475, 476, 481.

TIEDGE, Christoph Adolph (1752-1841). Not identified in standard sources. 256, 257.

UHLAND, Ludwig (1787-1862). Poet, patriot, and politician, his ballads bolstered German nationalism in the Napoleonic period. 195, 316, 317, 318, 319.

VOSS, Johann Heinrich (1751-1826). Philologist and poet, he translated a host of classical authors (Homer, Hesiod, Vergil, etc.). In his successful idyllic poem *Luise*, he applied his style of classical poetry to modern German sentiment. His interests turned him into a polemist against romanticism. 266, 267.

WACKENRODER, Wilhelm Heinrich (1773-1798). He wrote sensitively about the relation of medieval art and literature to religion. His awareness of a musician's conflict with the hard realities of life set the tone for German romanticism. 564, 565, 566, 567, 568, 569. 570, 571, 572, 573, 574, 575.

WAGNER, Richard (1813-1883). Brahms liked opera but never wrote one. Wagner's ideas fascinated him. 212.

WAIBLINGER, Wilhelm Friedrich (1804-1830). Spending much of his life in Italy, he wrote passionate lyrics, dull dramas, and, late in life, satirical antiromantic stories. His huge production barely supported his independence. 77, 78, 79, 80, 81.

WEBER, Carl Maria von (1786-1826). Best known for securely establishing opera in German and the concomitant role of the Kapellmeister, he left scattered writings published posthumously. 130, 486, 499, 515, 589, 592.

WERNER, Zacharias (1768-1823). After converting to Catholicism, he became a fashionable preacher in Vienna where he died. His sermons remained available in print. 388, 396, 510.

WERNICKE, Christian (1665-1725). His *Epigrammata* printed in 1701 covered a multitude of topics: physics, law, women, clergy, etc. Reprinted in 1909 — did Brahms own the original edition? 181.

YOUNG, Edward (1683-1765). His *Night Thoughts* were widely read by many generations outside his native England. 24, 25.

ZEDLITZ, Jospeph Chr. Freiherr von (1790-1862). Writer and teacher in Vienna where he collaborated with Metternich. Among his ballads, "Nächtliche Heerschau" (Army Review by Night) dealt with Napoleon. He translated Byron's *Childe Harold's Pilgrimage*. 419, 420, 421, 422, 423, 424.

ZELTER, Karl Friedrich (1758-1832). For almost a half century, dominated the music life in Berlin. Mendelssohn's teacher, Goethe's intimate friend. 539, 556.

ZIMMERMANN, Johann (1728-1795). A physician by profession, he published four volumes of widely read essays, among which "Vom Nationalstolz" (On National Pride) investigated both the advantages and shortcomings of nationalism. 111, 246.